PUBLIC SERVICE
RAILWAY

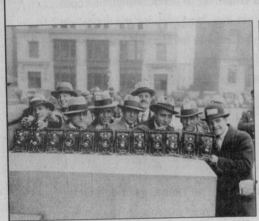

Photographers await verdict at Ruth Snyder murder trial, 1927
The New York Times Photo Archives

Riverside Drive Viaduct, 1928
The New York Times Photo Archives

Construction workers lunching on
© Bettmann / Corbis

Printed and sold by
Harold E. Cox
80 Virginia Terrace
Forty Fort PA 18704

INTRODUCTION

The system built and operated by the Bergen County Traction Company between 1895 and 1900 was the nucleus from which a new and bigger street railway system developed. The new system was the New Jersey and Hudson River Railway and Ferry Company, a long name that was quickly condensed into Hudson River Line.

The Hudson River Line system was extended into Tenafly, Paterson and Newark for a total system mileage of 48.44 miles within Bergen County in 1910. The Hudson River Line replaced the small single-truck cars inherited from its predecessor companies with large, fast double-truck cars. The Hudson River Line improved track conditions to achieve high speed schedules over its routes.

Until 1910, the Hudson River Line was the only remaining large street railway system in the Public Service Corporation of New Jersey territory that had not been merged into the Corporation's railway system. In July 1910, the merger took place and the Hudson River Line's corporate existence ceased after ten years of being one of the most efficient and modern trolley systems in the eastern United States.

While the Hudson River Line was the base upon which Public Service's Bergen Division was built, other electric railway lines served Bergen County, all of which eventually came under control of Public Service Corporation. In addition, the Hudson River ferries were an essential part of the transportation history of Bergen County until after World War II. Their story has also been included in this account.

From the first time I saw a red Public Service Hudson River line trolley car in Hackensack stop on Mercer Street by the Susquehanna depot, its bi-fold platform doors open, its pneumatic step fold down, and passengers board the car, intrigue captured my pre-adolescent mind. My languishing curiosity was invogorated when I met Edward T. Francis in 1958. Together we collaborated to produce material suitable for publication: Ed with his huge photograph and car data collec-tion and my research into newspapers, periodicals, books and archives. Harold Cox revised data on the early rolling stock of the lines concerned, drawing on the archives of New Jersey Transit. We feel that this is the most comprehensive presentation to be published about Bergen County's (New Jersey) electric street railway systems. We hope as you read and study the illustrations you will agree too.

Collaborator Edward T. Francis has observed the decline of street railways for the past 60 years. After college he was first employed by Public Service Electric & Gas Company in electric generating stations and worked with old-timers who had been employed by New Jersey & Hudson Railway & Ferry Company at Edgewater Generating Station and the Riverside and Fort Lee Ferry Company. He was on hand to ride the last trip of the Palisades line and the Hudson River line on the last night of service.

Bernard H. Sennstrom
Pennsville NJ
25 November 1994

CONTENTS

MAPS

CAR PLANS

ROSTERS

1

BERGEN COUNTY TRACTION CO.

Bergen County was established by the General Assembly of East Jersey on 7 March 1683. It remained unchanged until the western section was organized as Passaic County on 7 February 1837. Three years later on 22 February 1840, the southern areas were taken to create Hudson County.

Although directly across the Hudson River from Manhattan, access to Bergen County was hampered not only by the mile-wide river, but also by the 225 million year old barrier called the Palisades, so named in Colonial times because of its resemblance to a stockade or palisade. The Palisades crest in the Fort Lee area is some 200 or more feet almost vertically above the river's mean level. and presented early transportation entrepreneurs with the challenge of scaling the steep cliffs from the steamboat landings.

The relationship between the tidal waters and the low rolling ridges influenced the pattern of early European settlement in northern New Jersey. The region from Newark to Hackensack, accessible around the Palisades through Newark Bay and the Hackensack and Passaic rivers, became the center of settlement for both the Dutch and English. Most of Bergen County lies in what is geologically called the Triassic Piedmont which contains fertile soils and low ridges of Brunswick red shale and some Stockton brownstone. The area contains the Hackensack and Overpeck meadowlands, a former swampy area once teeming with birds, muskrats and other wildlife prior to the arrival of real estate developers.

Thus, the history of Bergen County trolleys begins at the Hudson River shoreline. During the nineteenth century sailboats and steamboats were already

plying the river to such landings in present-day Bergen County as Fort Lee, Pleasant Valley and Shadyside. Before the American Revolution, Peter Bourdette operated a ferry across the Hudson River to the first natural break in the Palisades south of the New York State boundary. George Washington's army built two fortifications above Burdett's (Anglicized form of Bourdette) landing in 1776. In August 1776 the rear redoubt was named Fort Lee and the forward fortified position retained the name Fort Constitution. It was the ferry landings in this area which became the starting point for early street railway ventures.

EARLY RAILWAY VENTURES

Bergen County was the site of numerous railroad projects during the 19th century, including horse and steam proposals, many threatening the transportation monopoly of the Bergen Turnpike which ran between Hoboken and the village of Hackensack. Two abortive efforts to build horse railroads were made by the Bergen Turnpike Co. itself and are discussed in chapter 6. The following ventures are known:

Paterson & Fort Lee RR Co.

On 8 March 1832, Messrs. Daniel Richards, John Voorhis, John Degroot, James H. Brinkerhoff and Abraham Westervelt were granted a charter for the Paterson & Fort Lee Railroad Co. It proposed to connect Paterson Township and Fort Lee with a horse railway.

In Paterson Township the route began at the junction of Main and Market streets, proceeded eastward and crossed the Passaic River into Bergen County

upon or adjacent to the Hackensack & Paterson Turnpike Co. bridge. The turnpike's consent was required. It would then proceed east to the village of Hackensack, cross the Hackensack River, and continue to the Hudson River at Fort Lee, terminating not further than fifty feet from the high water mark. Fares were set at six cents per mile per ton of freight or per passenger.

The incorporators were also granted a charter on 15 March 1832 for the Fort Lee and New York Steamboat Co. to connect the line with Manhattan. No further activity has been found.

Northern R R of New Jersey

The first railway to successfully penetrate the Bergen Turnpike's territory was the Northern RR of New Jersey. It was chartered on 9 February 1854, commenced construction in 1858 and opened between Jersey City and Sparkill on 28 May 1859. It parallelled the toll road between New Durham and Ridgefield, a distance of four miles. In 1859 railroad stations in that area were Hackensack Junction (Ridgefield), English Neighborhood (Fairview), Allertons (Babbitt area of North Bergen Township) and New Durham. Trains between Jersey City and Hackensack Junction required 35 minutes to cover the distance, whereas horse-drawn stages between Hoboken and Hackensack Junction required about one hour and 15 minutes.

Hackensack & New York R R

A second intruder into Bergen County was the Hackensack & New York RR Co. It was chartered on 14 March 1856, commenced construction in 1859 and opened between the junction with the New York and Erie Ry. mainline near Rutherford and Essex Street, Hackensack, on 21 January 1861. Trains between Jersey City and Essex Street required 45 minutes, whereas stages between Hoboken and Hackensack required about two hours and ten minutes to traverse the Bergen Turnpike.

In 1869 the Hackensack and New York Extension RR began surveying a northward route through the Hackensack and Pascack valleys to the state line. In the same year the Lodi Branch RR surveyed west from a junction with the H&NY near Williams Avenue in Hasbrouck Heights to the Rennie Print Works in Lodi.

Bergen Turnpike Co. (1857)

The Bergen Turnpike Co. was a toll road between Hoboken and the village of Hackensack in New Barbadoes Township. It was granted a charter on 30 November 1802, but it wasn't until 1857 that it considered operating rail cars. On 15 March 1858 the company's charter was amended to permit operation of a horse or mule railway, but forbade use of steam locomotives. For further details, see chapter 6.

Westfield & Hackensack Horse Railroad Co.

No less than twenty Bergen County men organized the Westfield & Hackensack Horse RR Co. including five Westervelts, three Demarests, two Bogerts and two Terhunes. The railroad was chartered on 22 March 1860. It was authorized to commence at the Fort Lee (Leonia) depot of the Northern RR of New Jersey (opened on 28 May 1859) and proceed through Hackensack Township over an unspecified route, terminating at some point on Passaic St. in Hackensack village. The area between the Hackensack River and Overpeck Creek may have been called Westfield since the portion of Queen Anne Road north of Fort Lee Road was once named Westfield Avenue. The company was permitted to build and operate one or more branches in Hackensack. The Bergen County Traction Co.'s Hackensack extension of 1899 would closely parallel the proposed route.

The Westfield & Hackensack was reorganized in 1866 and the new organization decided to change the name, route

and motive power. On 14 March 1867, the state granted a charter amendment changing the name to the Cherry Hill RR Co.; allowing a route change to commence from some point at or within one-half mile of Cherry Hill (North Hackensack section of River Edge Borough), and proceeding east to some point on the Northern RR of New Jersey south of Leonia station; and allowing the use of steam locomotives. A further amendment, permitting an extension through Hohokus Township to a point on the New York State line east of the Franklin Turnpike, was granted on 17 March 1870, but the line was never built.

Paterson & Rochdale Horse Railroad Co.

Five men from Saddle River Township were granted a charter for the Paterson & Rochdale Horse RR Co. on 21 March 1866. It was authorized to build a railroad from some point in or near the City of Paterson to Saddle River Township. On 14 March 1871 the State extended the life of the charter, but the line was not built.

Englewood Horse Railway Co.

The Englewood Horse Ry Co. was chartered on 6 April 1866 to build and operate a horse railway in the Alpine region on the Palisades crest in eastern Bergen County. The railway was authorized to begin at some point near Coytesville in Hackensack Township and to run northerly through Englewood Heights and Tenafly on the Palisades crest to the New York State line. On 29 February 1872, the State amended the charter, changing the name to Palisades RR Co., and granted approval for an extension south from Coytesville to the Hudson County boundary. The company was later absorbed into the North Hudson County Ry. Co. (1893) and the southward extension eventually became Public Service Ry.'s Palisade car line (1903-1938) to the Weehawken Ferry Terminal. This route is covered in chapter 7.

New Jersey Midland Ry. Co.

Perhaps the greatest competitive threat to the Bergen Turnpike was the Hoboken, Ridgefield & Paterson RR Co., chartered on 15 March 1866. The railroad was

authorized to construct and operate from a suitable point in Hoboken, at or within one mile north of the Hoboken ferry, over a route south of the village of Hackensack to some point in Paterson city. Originally the railroad was not permitted to run within 2 1/2 miles of the court house in Hackensack. This restriction was lifted on 27 March 1868.

On 17 March 1870, the Hoboken, Ridgefield & Paterson consolidated with three western New Jersey railroads to form the New Jersey Midland Ry. Co. Construction through Hackensack commenced in January 1871. The railroad was opened between Paterson and Hackensack on 10 January 1872, to the Northern RR at Granton on 6 March 1872 and to the New Jersey RR and Transportation Co. at Marion, Jersey City, in November 1872. New Jersey Midland passenger trains began running from the Jersey City terminal on 2 December 1872. The New Jersey Midland and five other railroads were combined to form the New York, Susquehanna and Western RR Co. on 10 June 1881.

Hackensack & Englewood Horse Railway Co.

The prospects for a horse railway in central Bergen County brightened when the Hackensack and Englewood Horse Ry. Co. was chartered on 26 March 1872. The company was authorized to connect with the railroad stations in the Hackensack Commission and to terminate in Englewood village. It could construct, maintain and operate a horse railway on any highway, public road and street between the two named places. One incorporator, Thomas W. Demarest, was an incorporator of the Northern RR of New Jersey in 1854. Another, State Senator Cornelius Lydecker, was one of the owners of the Palisades Mountain House (1860-1884). The financial panic of 1873 probably caused this venture to fail.

Bergen Turnpike Co. (1875)

The Bergen Turnpike was granted another charter amendment on 25 February 1875 authorizing a horse railway in Hackensack Commission. Construction was not started until 1894 and then without consents and franchises. Work began in New Barbadoes Township, but was

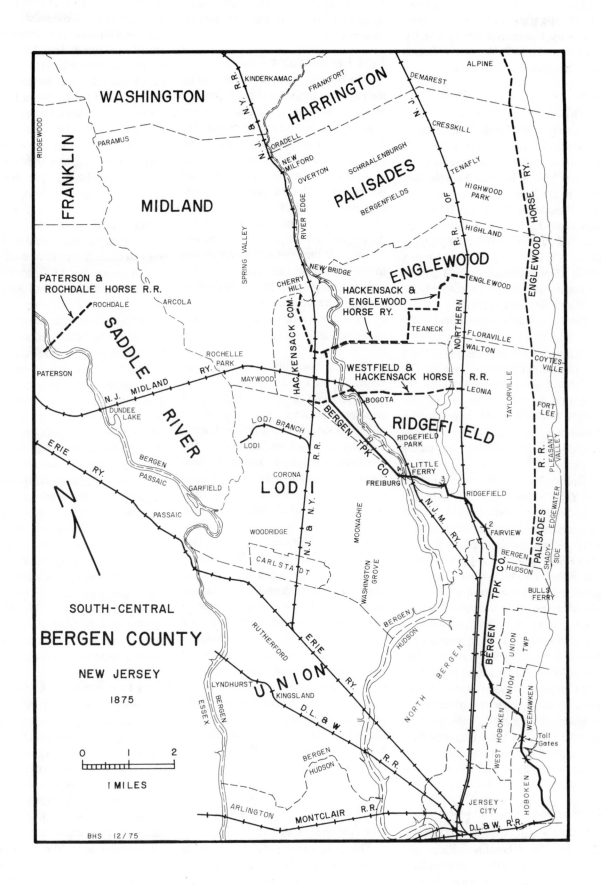

WASHINGTON

HARRINGTON

RIDGEWOOD

FRANKLIN

MIDLAND

PALISADES

KINDERKAMAC

FRANKFORT

ALPINE

DEMAREST

CRESSKILL

PARAMUS

N. J. & N. Y. R. R.

ORADELL

NEW MILFORD

OVERTON

SCHRAALENBURGH

BERGENFIELDS

TENAFLY

HIGHWOOD PARK

HIGHLAND

SPRING VALLEY

RIVER EDGE

NEW BRIDGE

PATERSON & ROCHDALE HORSE R.R.

ROCHDALE

ARCOLA

CHERRY HILL

HACKENSACK COM.

ENGLEWOOD

HACKENSACK & ENGLEWOOD HORSE RY.

ENGLEWOOD

TEANECK

NORTHERN

FLORAVILLE

WALTON

COYTES- VILLE

ENGLEWOOD HORSE RY.

OF

R. R.

PATERSON

SADDLE

ROCHELLE PARK

MAYWOOD

N. J. MIDLAND RY.

WESTFIELD & HACKENSACK HORSE R. R.

LEONIA

TAYLORVILLE

FORT LEE

DUNDEE LAKE

RIVER

LODI BRANCH

LODI

BERGEN-TPK CO.

BOGOTA

RIDGEFIELD

ERIE RY.

BERGEN

PASSAIC

GARFIELD

CORONA

RIDGEFIELD PARK

RIDGEFIELD

PALISADES R. R.

PLEASANT VALLEY

N

PASSAIC

LODI

N. J. & N. Y. R. R.

MOONACHIE

LITTLE FERRY

FREIBURG

3

EDGEWATER SHADY- SIDE

SOUTH-CENTRAL

WOODRIDGE

WASHINGTON GROVE

N. J. M. RY.

2

FAIRVIEW

BERGEN HUDSON

BERGEN COUNTY

CARLSTADT

RUTHERFORD

BERGEN HUDSON

BERGEN TPK CO.

UNION TWP

NEW JERSEY

1875

NORTH BERGEN

UNION

BULLS FERRY

LYNDHURST

UNION

ESSEX

BERGEN

KINGSLAND

D. L. & W.

WEST HOBOKEN

WEEHAWKEN

Toll Gates

0   1   2

I MILES

BERGEN HUDSON

R. R.

HOBOKEN

ARLINGTON

MONTCLAIR R. R.

JERSEY CITY

D. L. & W. R. R.

BHS 12/75

quickly stopped by municipal authorities. The company was absorbed into the Jersey City, Hoboken & Paterson St. Ry. in 1900 which built the trolley line in 1903. See chapter 6 for details.

New York, West Shore & Buffalo Railway Co.

As early as 1862 plans were made for a steam railroad north from Jersey City along the west shore of the Hudson River. The New York & Fort Lee RR was chartered in 1862 and leased by the New York, West Shore & Chicago RR Co. on 5 January 1872. Subsequently the Ridgefield Park RR Co. (1867), Jersey City & Albany RR (in N. J., 1873) and Jersey City & Albany Railway (in N. Y., 1879) companies surveyed routes to Albany, N. Y. through Bergen County.

The last-named company had rights for a line from Weehawken to Fort Montgomery, N.Y. and was merged on 5 May 1881 with the North River Ry. Co. which had been organized in 1880 in the interest of the New York Ontario and Western Ry. Co. to build a line from Fort Montgomery to Albany with a branch to Middletown, the combined line taking the name of the New York, West Shore and Buffalo Ry. Co. By agreement with the NYO&W, the line from Weehawken to Middletown was built by the NYO&W and was paid for with $10,000,000 in first mortgage 5 percent bonds and $2,367,000 in NYWS&B stock. The 4225-foot bore through the palisades at Weehawken was completed in 1881 and the first passenger train ran through to Newburgh, New York on 4 June 1883. The NYWS&B was sold at foreclosure to J. P. Morgan and reorganized as the West Shore RR on 5 December 1885. It was leased to the New York Central and Hudson River RR on 1 January 1886, a separate agreement being made giving the NYO&W trackage rights from Weehawken to Cornwall, New York until 2079. The West Shore RR was the last steam railroad to penetrate Bergen County.

SCALING THE PALISADES

In 1884 within a stretch of 1000 feet at the Hudson River shoreline in Ridgefield Township there were three ferry landings which accomodated steamboats to New York City. It is this small area beneath the towering Palisades bluff in the vicinity of Fort Lee where this historical review begins.

Fort Lee Elevator Co.

The first serious plans for ascending the Palisades in the vicinity of Fort Lee was in 1884 when a funicular inclined plane wagon elevator was proposed. The Fort Lee Elevator Co. was chartered on 16 June 1884 for fifty years for "the transportation of goods, merchandise and passengers and for that purpose to build, construct, maintain, lease, use, and operate an elevator or elevators for carrying passengers and freight at Fort Lee and elsewhere in the State of New Jersey and to lease, own, use and occupy such real and personal property as may be deemed necessary or convenient for the operation of such elevator or elevators." It was capitalized at $50,000, divided into 500 shares.

The first stockholders' meeting convened at Fort Lee on 28 July 1884 at which Thomas C. Doremus of Manhattan was elected president; Vanderbilt Spader of Far Rockaway, treasurer; and Peter J. Hoffman of Brooklyn, secretary. The plans confirmed at this meeting showed the elevator ascending the Palisades from the Orchard St. ferry landing. Two ferry lines were landing at Orchard St. in 1884: The "Peoples" Ferry Co. to Spring St., Manhattan and Edward H. Coffin's Fort Lee Ferry Co. to 130th St., Manhattan.

Time passed without action and company funds were exhausted. A principal stockholder, J. Vanderbilt Spader of Brooklyn, was named trustee and on 1 August 1888 he sold a $10,000 mortgage using a few parcels of real estate owned by the company for collateral. The elevator was never constructed mainly because of engineering difficulties. In June 1889 its holdings were sold to J. Fletcher Burdett, Jr. of Fort Lee and John H. Mannix who later became Bergen County Commissioner of Deeds. The charter was voided during 1893.

Hackensack, Leonia & Fort Lee Railway Co.

During the summer of 1890, J. Fletcher Burdett, Jr. and a group of New York investors began subscribing capital stock for a railway. They opened an office in Buchheister's Hotel at Fort Lee and put up a sign during September 1890 indicating it was the headquarters for the Hackensack, Leonia & Fort Lee Ry. They planned to operate a cable railway from the Orchard St. ferry landing to the Leonia depot of the Northern RR of New Jersey and an electric railway from there to Hackensack. Two major obstacles were obtaining consents from more than half of the abutting property owners along the route and obtaining permission to lay track on the county bridge spanning Overpeck Creek on the Fort Lee and Hackensack Road. Burdett said a certificate of incorporation would not be sought until all obstacles were cleared away.

By November 1890 stock subscriptions attained the goal of $20,000. A survey of the proposed route commenced on 10 November. The surveyor laid out a route for the cable railway from the Orchard St. ferry landing via Park St. and through the Watkins Park estate. It then ascended the Palisades through the Dead Bridge Brook ravine to Palisade Ave., proceeded north to Main St., Fort Lee, then west to the Leonia depot. A franchise for the railway had been secured from Ridgefield Township. There was considerable opposition especially from the owners of the Watkins Park estate. An anticipated result of the cable railway was the loss of business by the hackmen who made a fair living by taking travelers from the ferry landings up the hill in their stages and carriages. Construction of a cable railway proved to be too costly and cable technology was fast falling into obsolescence because of the success of electric railways. The combined difficulties caused the enterprise to fail.

Fort Lee Railway Company

During the winter of 1892 a proposal was made for an electric railway which would begin at the Orchard St. ferry landing, ascend the Palisades via Bulls Ferry (River) Road to Main St., Fort Lee, and continue west to Hackensack. J. Fletcher Burdett, Jr. was one of the original incorporators. The railway filed for a certificate of incorporation on 9 March 1892 and received the certificate on 14 March.

At the first stockholders' meeting, on 22 July 1892, Alven Beveridge of Manhattan was elected president; and Edward

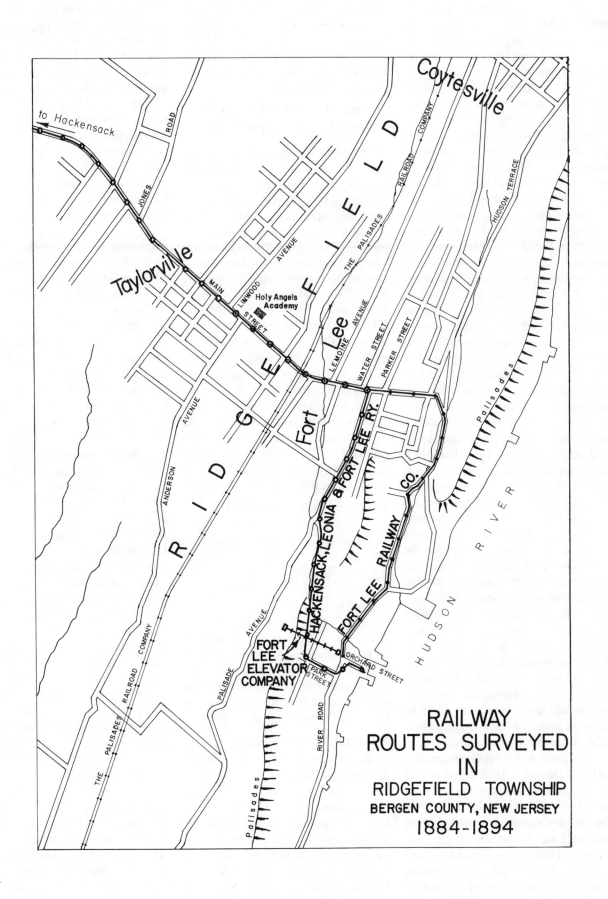

to Hackensack

Coytesville

JONES ROAD

TAYLORVILLE

LINWOOD AVENUE

MAIN STREET

Holy Angels Academy

RIDGEFIELD

Fort Lee

THE PALISADES

RAILROAD COMPANY

HUDSON TERRACE

LEMOINE AVENUE

WATER STREET

PARKER STREET

ANDERSON AVENUE

THE PALISADES RAILROAD COMPANY

Palisades

HACKENSACK, LEONIA & FORT LEE RY.

FORT LEE RAILWAY CO.

Palisades

HUDSON RIVER

FORT LEE ELEVATOR COMPANY

PALISADE AVENUE

RIVER ROAD

PARK STREET

ORCHARD STREET

Palisades

RAILWAY
ROUTES SURVEYED
IN
RIDGEFIELD TOWNSHIP
BERGEN COUNTY, NEW JERSEY
1884-1894

W. Lawson of Fort Lee, secretary and treasurer. Anthony O'Brien, an incorporator, was also principal owner of the Fort Lee Park and Steamboat Co. which had been ferrying passengers between Fort Lee and Manhattan since 1878. Lawson and Beveridge were also directors and officers of the Riverside and Fort Lee Ferry Co. The railway directors voted on 30 July 1892 to obtain a construction mortgage. A $100,000 mortgage was secured from the Title Guarantee & Trust Co. of New York City on 1 August.

Ridgefield Township granted a franchise on 16 April 1892 for 3,960 feet of railway on Bulls Ferry (River) Road from a point 300 feet below School No. 2 by the Van Gelder residence to the intersection of Hudson Terrace and Main St. in Fort Lee. An franchise to extend the railway 4,500 feet on Main St. to Linwood Ave. was granted by the township committee on 8 February 1893. A parcel of land for the power house on the Fort Lee side of a lime kiln was purchased from the Dempsey estate during November 1892.

At the annual stockholders' meeting in March 1893, Joseph M. Gazzam of Philadelphia was elected president; Alven Beveridge of Manhattan, vice president; Edward W. Lawson of Fort Lee, treasurer; and James N. Jameson, secretary.

On 15 May 1893 construction commenced at Orchard St. on Bulls Ferry Road. It was hoped to complete the railway by July. Construction progressed rapidly and as the work advanced, the laborers, having considerable back wages due them, made frequent demands for their salaries. Money was not forthcoming so the laborers quit working during the second week of July, when the railway had been completed to the foot of Dosher's Hill. The company's tool shed was burned down consuming all of its contents including tools and supplies. Construction never resumed.

The Fort Lee Ry. applied for receivership in December 1893. David A. Pell of Hackensack was appointed receiver on 9 April 1894. On 1 November 1894 the company's assets, consisting of about one-half mile of completed single-track railway on Bulls Ferry (River) Road, and a supply of poles, ties and fish plates, were sold to Guy Dempsey, a native of the Pleasant Valley area of Ridgefield

Township, representing William H. Clark of Philadelphia, for $103.00. Control of traction companies scaling the Palisades at Fort Lee now passed into the hands of Philadelphians who would retain this control for sixteen years.

THE BERGEN COUNTY TRACTION COMPANY

During 1894 a group of Philadelphians — Jacob E. Ridgeway, Joseph M. Gazzam, Charles S. Hinchman, Charles J. Colladay, R.M. Hartley and William H. Clark, together with Leon Abbett, Jr. of Hoboken — formed a new railway enterprise to surmount the Palisades at Fort Lee and reach the hinterlands of Bergen County. The Bergen County Traction Co., received its certificate of incorporation on 15 December 1894. It was authorized $500,000 in capital stock and commenced activities with $35,000 in cash. Ridgeway was elected president; Clark, vice president; William N. Barrows, treasurer and secretary; and Edward W. Lawson, general manager. Edward W. Lawson was concurrently general manager of the Riverside and Fort Lee Ferry Co. The company's office was located in Undercliff Borough with the postal address being Foot of West 130th St., New York.

Highland Improvement Co.

Bergen County Traction's management incorporated the Highland Improvement Co., on 16 February 1895 and the certificate of incorporation was received two days later. The objective was to acquire, sell, lease real and personal property in New Jersey. The life of its charter was fifty years. The property at the foot of Dempsey Ave. between River Road and the Hudson River in Undercliff was purchased by the company and title was transferred to the Riverside and Fort Lee Ferry Co. on 1 November 1895.

National Trolley Company

During January 1895 the National Trolley Co. was reported to have filed articles of incorporation. Former State Assemblyman Delos E. Culver of Jersey City was named president. About 25 years previously Culver was the contractor who built the New York, Ontario and Western Ry. (New York & Oswego Midland RR) through Liberty, New York and suffered severe pecuniary difficul-

ties during the financial panic of 1873. The company was to operate under the charter of the New Jersey and New York Bridge Co. and planned electric street railways between Fort Lee, Englewood and Hackensack, apparently as a direct challenge to the Bergen County Traction Co. Culver was involved in a similar scheme in Rutherford in 1894 when it was reported that he had organized a street railway company to block the plans of the Union Traction Co. to connect Newark and Hackensack. Neither proposal was successful.

Building the Railway

The BCT purchased the Riverside and Fort Lee Ferry Co. in 1895. That company is discussed in chapter 5.

Bergen County Traction employed two firms to construct its railway: William Hunter for ferry terminal buildings and track and Ford & Bacon for power and car house buildings and machinery, car equipment and overhead line. Surveyors mapped 35 miles of routes in eastern Bergen County during early 1895 and petitions were filed for franchises in Ridgefield Township and Undercliff and Leonia boroughs. Ridgefield granted a franchise on 26 February 1895 and Leonia on 10 January 1896.

Construction commenced on 20 June 1895 at Pleasant Valley with a force of 150 men although the company's annual report stated 8 June as the date of initial construction. Plans showed the terminus at the new Pleasant Valley ferry landing. The railway was to climb the Palisades on a cliffside shelf with a switchback halfway up the ascent. On the Palisade plateau the route followed Palisade Ave. to Main St., Fort Lee. Construction progressed rapidly to the top of the Palisades, then difficulties arose with the Ridgefield Township Committee. The dispute was heard in the Court of Chancery and on 24 August 1895 it was ruled that the traction company must have the township committee's consent for the track location. The track was, therefore, laid at the side of Palisade Ave. and Main St. as the committee wanted, and not in the center as the traction company planned. Palisade Ave. was too crooked to follow on one side and it was necessary for the tracks to cross the avenue several

View of the Bergen County Traction power station, car house and the upper end of New York City from the switchback. *Street Railway Journal,* June 1896.

times before reaching Fort Lee. This area of the Palisades plateau was heavily wooded and until that time was as wild and desolate as some of the mountainous districts fifty miles further north. The contractor, Kearns & Egan, resumed laying track on 3 September 1895 and predicted completion of the railway to Getche's Hotel in Fort Lee by 1 November 1895.

During the week of 26 August 1895, a surveyor was at work for Ridgefield Township locating the center line of Main St. through Fort Lee. The street was originally 49 feet 6 inches wide but east of Palisade Ave it was discovered that some property owners had encroached on the street by as much as eight feet. The surveyor's map was used to determine the curb line and by 16 September, Kearns & Egan was laying track on the south side of Main St. through Fort Lee towards Leonia. There the franchise required the track to be laid on the south side of Central Ave. except for a distance of 400 feet east of Broad Ave. where the track curved to the center of the avenue.

The Englewood Township committee held a special meeting on 31 March 1896 at Spindler's Hotel to act upon the company's petition for a franchise through Nordhoff. The committee granted approval on 13 April.

While construction was progressing through Ridgefield, work on the power house, car barn, ferry buildings and slips was underway at Undercliff. The contract for the double ferry slip was let to Mr. Evans of Philadelphia, who had, in 1892, erected the NYS&W RR's coal dock and shipping pier at Undercliff. The power house and car house contract was reported as being awarded to a Mr. McPherson of Paterson although the *Street Railway Journal* reported the work was awarded to J.W. Ferguson. The power house was located at the northwest corner of Dempsey Ave. and River Road. The car house was located up the hill at the north side of Dempsey Ave.

The power house was equipped with two belt-driven General Electric 500-Volt DC, 200-kw generators; two E. P. Allis 20-inch by 42-inch, 80 rpm Corliss steam engines; and four Heine safety water tube boilers totaling 450 boiler horse power. The steam engine flywheels each weighed 16 tons and were about 17 feet in diameter. The drive belt was 24 inches wide and the distance between the generator and flywheel shaft centers was about 40 feet. The machinery was painted a dark royal blue with gold striping and lettering. The smoke stack, fabricated from steel plates, was self supporting like a chimney and was 6 feet 6 inches in diameter and 140 feet high. The two 200-kw generators were placed into service for the first time on 27 March 1896.

The ferry house was a wooden build-ing containing the most modern improvements. The interior was finished in hardwood. To the north of the ferry slip were the company offices. In front of these was a large hall for accomodation of trolley parties. To the south of the slip were the ticket offices and waiting room. The ferry house contained one slip. On the north side there was a coal wharf for refueling the ferries and for the power house fuel supply and ash disposal.

The car house measured 65 feet by 104 feet and contained four storage tracks. The exterior, identical in finish to the power house, was of hard-burned brick set in red mortar with Pennsylvania bluestone coping, water table and trimmings. The roof was of slate with steel trusses. It was planned to use the building for night car storage and for light repairs. The main car house was to be at the western terminal of the line.

At this time those responsible for operations were: Edward W. Lawson of Fort Lee, general manager; J. C. B. Spatz of Reading, Pennsylvania, railway superintendent; and J. B. Anderson, engineer in charge of plant. Anderson was previously assistant engineer of the Fourteenth

St. power house of the North Hudson County Ry.

The Monmouth County Route

Bergen County Traction filed an application on 15 October 1895 for a 5-mile trolley line along the Jersey seashore in Wall Township, Monmouth County. The map showed a railway passing through what are today's boroughs of Belmar, South Belmar, Spring Lake and Sea Girt. For most of its length the route parallelled the New York & Long Branch RR to the east at distances varying between 500 and 1000 feet. The purpose of the application is unknown. The line was never constructed.

The Railway is Opened

"The loud clanging of a trolley gong was heard for the first time through the woods on top of the Palisades on Saturday morning." Thus a newspaper reported the opening of service on 11 April 1896 between the ferry terminal and the top of the Leonia hill, about 3.75 miles. The first test trip left the Pleasant Valley power house at 11:45 a.m. and reached the Leonia terminus in fifteen minutes. On board were W.H. Clark, W.N. Barrows, J.R. Hunt, E.W. Lawson, H.K. Stevens and George Spangler. The car was operated by Superintendent J. C. B. Spatz and Conductor Harry Darbeck.

On Sunday, 12 April 1896 the railway was opened to the public from 10 a.m. until 6 p.m. No fare was charged and on each trip the cars were loaded to capacity. Residents of Englewood, Leonia, Undercliff, Coytesville and other neighboring villages all availed themselves of the opportunity. For picturesqueness and magnificent scenery, the trolley line had no equal among suburban lines in the vicinity of New York City. Between Fort Lee and the point where the line started its descent through the cut in the Palisades bluff, the tracks were laid mostly at the side of Palisade Ave.and through this two-mile distance it did not pass a house.

The line officially opened on 20 April. Cars ran every 20 minutes from 5 a.m. until 12:20 a.m. The fare from the ferry to Leonia heights was five cents. With the opening of the railway, Riverside and Fort Lee ferries commenced landing alternately between the Orchard St. and Pleasant Valley landings every half hour.

Motorman U. S. Grant Owens, who operated one of the first cars, was interviewed by *Public Service News* in 1927 and gave the following recollection:

"The headlights on the cars burned oil and you could see only about ten feet ahead. The cars had hand brakes too, and believe me, you had to do some grinding. You knew you had done a days work when your relief took his place. We quite often blew out a fuse when going up the Leonia hill and then we would borrow a hair-pin from a lady passenger, or even a safety pin, to act as a fuse until we reached the ferry. The road bed was single-tracked. We would pass on turnouts, throw the blocks by hand and, if not careful, sometimes they would throw you."

A contemporary issue of *Street Railway Journal* described the Bergen County Traction line thusly: "Starting at the ferry house on River Road and up to the level of the car house there is an eight per cent grade and from this point to the top of the Palisades, except at the level of the switchback, the grade is an average 6 1/2 per cent for 3700 feet, a total vertical rise of about 240 feet.

"This portion of the railway consists of two side hill rock cuts with retaining walls, joined by a switchback at the middle of the hill. The upper and lower approaches are loops, necessitating an embankment for the lower one and a cut for the upper... The special safety turnout at the switchback on the Palisades side hill cut... includes a stretch of track at twenty per cent grade with a bumper at the end of the upper track."

The railway track was all 60-pound standard T rail with a minimum radius of sixty feet except at the car house where the curves were on forty-five feet radii. Track was stone ballasted throughout; 5-inch x 7-inch x 7-foot white oak ties were used, spaced at twelve per thirty-foot section of rail.

The Englewood Extension

On 4 July 1896 the first BCT trolley operated into Englewood Township, the railway being completed as far as the Phelps property on Grand Ave. The line was completed on Dean St. to Englewood Ave. in Englewood City and officially opened on 11 July. One of the new open cars was decorated with red, white and blue incandescent lamps to form stars on the front and rear dashboards and long strings of lamps were strung along the roof, the artistry being the work of Superintendent J. C. B. Spatz. The car left the ferry terminal at 8:30 p.m. with the special trip celebrating the Englewood extension. The car was in charge of Superintendent Spatz and Conductor Harry Darbeck, and carried company officers and guests. The trip took 35 minutes from the ferry to Englewood Ave. At Fort Lee people lined Main St. and as the car passed it was cheered to the echo. At Leonia, residents clebrated by decorating their houses with Japanese lanterns and waving American flags. At Englewood, the car was greeted by about 500 men, women and children. Members of the Englewood Council and a number of prominent citizens were taken aboard the car for the return trip to Pleasant Valley where the guests were shown through the power plant by the company officials.

The track descending the hill through Leonia Borough from the heights at Fort Lee was laid on the south side of Central Ave. to Broad Ave. on a grade varying between 8 and 10 per cent for a distance of 1500 feet. From Leonia into Englewood City, the track was in the center of the streets.

The extension north beyond Englewood Ave. was delayed for more than a year by opposition from citizens and the Northern RR of New Jersey. The traction company wanted to cross the railroad at grade on Palisade Ave. and proceed to Tenafly via Tenafly Road. The Englewood council had granted a franchise to cross the Northern RR at Englewood Ave. and then reach Palisade Ave. via Van Brunt St. Some residents submitted a petition stating, "We, the undersigned residents protest against the granting of the application of the trolley for a change of route so as to run on Palisade Avenue west from Dean St. instead of entering Palisade Avenue via Van Brunt St., according to the existing ordinance... Palisade Ave.between Dean St. and the track of the Northern RR is the busiest and most crowded part of any city street. It is used, not only for business, but by those passing to and from the railroad station and the Post Office. It would be a grave

Two views of the switchback on the Palisades. *Street Railway Journal.*

menace to the safety of vehicles and their occupants were the trolley allowed to invade that part of Palisade Ave., thus creating a 'dead man's curve' at the corner of Dean St. . ." The petition was signed by 90 men and 16 women and was read to the Englewood Council by E. B. Convers on 15 June 1897. The Northern RR at that time scheduled 22 weekday and 10 Sunday passenger trains between Englewood and New York City. The Erie RR, owner of the Northern RR, refused to grant a grade crossing. This meant that trolley passengers would have to transfer by walking across the railroad.

According to BCT Vice President W.H. Clark, "A break at the Northern RR. . .would increase expenses greatly, necessitating another car house, and other things." Clark's reply to the "dead man's curve" argument was: "The trolley had been held up, so to speak, on Dean St., by not being able to get the necessary consents, for nearly a year. That difficulty

was now disposed of. They had come on private property most of the way from the city line to the present terminus, and had done so in deference to the wishes of the people who did not want the cars on public streets. The reason the trolley wants to come up Dean St. to Palisade Avenue, and thence go west on the avenue is simply a business one. The "dead man's curve" was simply absurd. The cars have to slow down in making a sharp turn, else they would go off the track."

The Englewood Council finally granted a franchise over one block on Dean St. between Englewood and Palisade avenues after 13 months of discussions. BCT had succeeded in obtaining the last consent signature necessary for the extension on 17 May 1897.

The Pleasures of the Superintendent of the Traction Co.

The 7 August 1897 issue of the *Englewood Press* printed the following

human interest article about the Bergen County Traction Co.: "The Pleasures of The Superintendent of The Traction Co."

"The general public imagine that the life of a superintendent of a railway company is a pleasant and healthful occupation. It may have been in the years of our ancestors, but each succeeding generation brings with it its quota of what is generally termed "kickers."

"To those who are still of the opinion that the position is a sinecure, we would advise a visit to the office of Superintendent Lawson of the Bergen County Traction Co. and that they remain there for half a day and listen to the many absurd complaints which are made.

"A few days ago while a representative of the *Press* was in the Superintendent's office, a stylishly dressed gentleman came in and inquired of Mr. Lawson if the Superintendent was in. "I am the Superintendent," replied Mr. Lawson. "Well, I have a complaint to

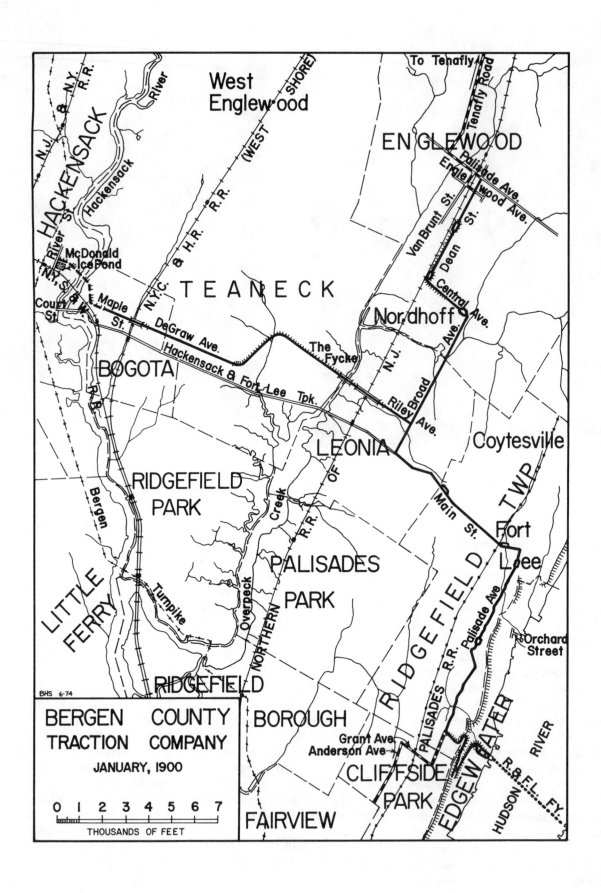

West
Englewood

HACKENSACK

N.J. & N.Y. R.R.

River

(WEST SHORE)

N.Y.C. & H.R. R.R.

To Tenafly

Tenafly Road

ENGLEWOOD

Palisade Ave.

Englewood Ave.

River St.

Hackensack

McDonald
Ice Pond

N.Y.S. & W.

T E A N E C K

Van Brunt St.

Dean St.

Central Ave.

County St.

E. Maple St.

DeGraw Ave.

N.Y.C.

Nordhoff

Hackensack & Fort Lee Tpk.

The Fycke

N.J.

Broad Ave.

BOGOTA

N.J. R.R.

Riley Ave.

Coytesville

LEONIA

TWP.

RIDGEFIELD
PARK

Creek

N.J. R.R.

Main St.

Fort
Lee

Bergen

PALISADES
PARK

RIDGEFIELD

Orchard
Street

LITTLE
FERRY

Turnpike

Overpeck

NORTHERN

PALISADES R.R.

Palisade Ave.

RIVER

BHS 6-74

RIDGEFIELD
BOROUGH

Grant Ave.
Anderson Ave.

EDGEWATER

R.B.F.L. FY.

HUDSON RIVER

CLIFFSIDE
PARK

FAIRVIEW

BERGEN COUNTY
TRACTION COMPANY

JANUARY, 1900

0 1 2 3 4 5 6 7
THOUSANDS OF FEET

Climbing the Palisades. *Street Railway Journal,* June 1896.

make," said the gentleman. "That's what I'm here for," replied Mr. Lawson, "What is it?" "A few days ago I left two shirt-waists," said the man, "with the young lady in charge of the laundry stand in the ferry house, to be done up and only got one in return." "That's very unfortunate," said the Superintendent in a sympathethic voice, "but what have I to do with that?" "Well, if you are Superintendent you should only rent your stands to responsible people," retorted the man angrily, as he backed his way out of the office, giving the door an extra hard bang.

"This gentleman, or rather kicker had no more than left the office when it was again opened, and a man with a red face and hair standing on end, entered holding in his hand a hat which was badly damaged. The Superintendent turned to the reporter, giving him a wink, in an under-tone said, "another." "Donnerwetter!" exclaimed the man, "mein huht," at the same time proferring the Superintendent his damaged head gear. Mr. Lawson looked at the man inquiringly, and came to the conclusion that he must have had his hat broken on the car. "Zwei dollar," screamed the man. The Superintendent picked up the hat and examined it mi-

nutely, turning it over. He finally re-turned it to the German, at the same time saying: "You can get such a hat at Bloomingdale's for $1.98." "Gott in himmel, sie tragen die selven," ejacu-lated the man as he darted through the door. "These are all perfectly harmless," said Mr. Lawson, after the door had been closed, "but it is anything other than pleasant to sit here and have to listen to their senseless complaints."

As the reporter was about to leave. the door opened and a good-looking man entered and addressed the Superinten-dent, demanding to know why the lights are put out in the cars on the switchback. "I am a respectable married man," said the complainant, "and I object to being left in a public car in the dark." Mr. Lawson explained why the car was left in darkness for a few seconds on the switch-back, and the gentleman bowed politely and went out.

Thus it can be seen that the life of a railway Superintendent is not altogether an enjoyable one."

Improvement Plans — 1897

In March 1897 BCT announced that it was considering construction of an in-

clined plane on the face of the Palisades, just north of the existing trolley ascent, for the accomodation of bicycles, but it was not built. To handle bicycle traffic from the ferry, a novel scheme was developed for transporting bicyles up the bluff. Jacob Baker of Fort Lee appeared at the foot of the hill near Churney's Hotel on 1 August 1897 with a wagon which he had constructed to carry bi-cycles. The running gear was similar to that ordinarily used on light delivery wagons, but instead of the box, a bicycle rack large enough to hold ten bicycles was substituted. It was an odd-looking vehicle and attracted the eyes of passers-by. It was no easy task to push a bicycle up the hill and many wheelmen patron-ized Baker's wagon. The fare for carry-ing a bicycle to the top of the Palisades was ten cents. A rig belonging to Under-cliff Councilman George Nelson was fitted out in a similar manner.

At the July 1897 BCT director's meeting, approval was given to build a double track from the ferry to the first turnout on Palisade Ave. in order to

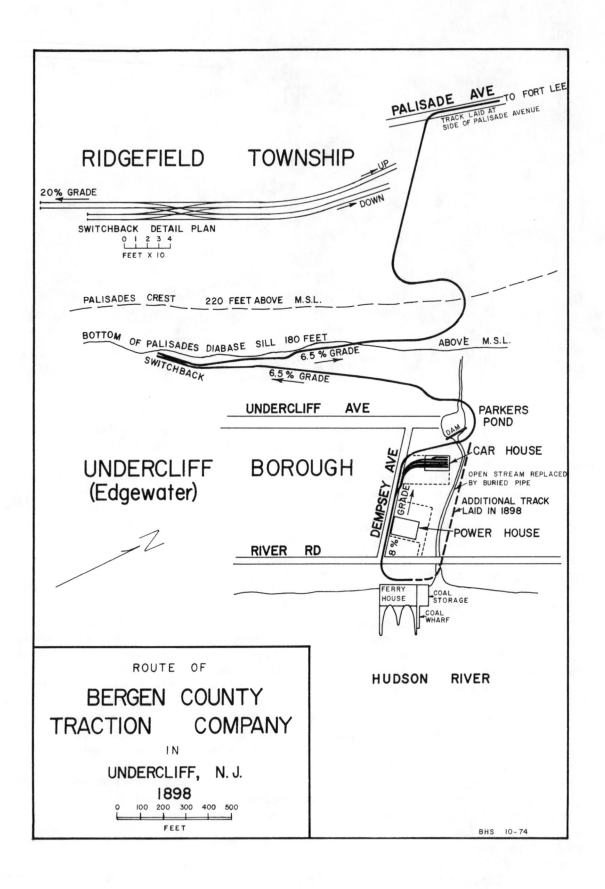

PALISADE AVE   TO FORT LEE
TRACK LAID AT
SIDE OF PALISADE AVENUE

RIDGEFIELD TOWNSHIP

UP

20% GRADE

DOWN

SWITCHBACK DETAIL PLAN

0 1 2 3 4
FEET X 10

PALISADES CREST   220 FEET ABOVE M.S.L.

BOTTOM OF PALISADES DIABASE SILL 180 FEET   ABOVE M.S.L.

SWITCHBACK   6.5 % GRADE

6.5 % GRADE

UNDERCLIFF AVE

PARKERS POND

DAM

CAR HOUSE

UNDERCLIFF BOROUGH
(Edgewater)

OPEN STREAM REPLACED
BY BURIED PIPE

ADDITIONAL TRACK
LAID IN 1898

POWER HOUSE

DEMPSEY AVE

GRADE

8 %

RIVER RD

N

FERRY
HOUSE

COAL
STORAGE

COAL
WHARF

HUDSON RIVER

ROUTE OF

BERGEN COUNTY
TRACTION COMPANY

IN

UNDERCLIFF, N.J.

1898

0 100 200 300 400 500
FEET

BHS 10-74

eliminate the delays at the switchback. Elimination of the switchback also would avoid leaving cars in darkness at night while the trolley poles were changed. A surveyor was put to work during early August to map the route. Undercliff Borough granted permission for a second track from the ferry terminal to Parker's Pond. The track was laid north of the power house and car house properties and formed a loop with the old track. Cars descended to the ferry terminal on the old track and ascended the incline on the new. Parker's Pond was located at the bottom of a glen formed by a stream which leaped in waterfalls two hundred feet down the face of the Palisades. The pond was formed by a dam which impounded 20,000 gallons of water for use of the steam boilers in the BCT power house.

By 1897 passenger traffic had increased greatly although the largest community on the system, Englewood City, had a population of only 6,000. The area served was being settled by commuters using the trolleys to reach the ferry to Manhattan. During the summer of 1897 BCT was doing a large business in pleasure riding. Aided by its strong financial position, the traction company began planning an extension to Hackensack which would branch from the Englewood line at Leonia.

The Hackensack Extension

During autumn 1897, BCT was engaged in securing consents for the extension from property owners along the Fort Lee and Hackensack Road. The line was to enter Hackensack via the Court St. bridge. The company applied for franchises in Teaneck Township on 6 January 1898 and in Bogota Borough on 12 January. The Bergen County Freeholders stipulated that costs of the improvements to the road and bridges on the route must be borne by Bergen County Traction. The requirements were deemed too costly and the traction company decided in early March 1898 to build as much of the extension as possible on private right-of-way. The revised route called for the line to run via Riley (Hillside) Ave. from Broad Ave. to Grand Ave. in Leonia, then west across the undeveloped Overpeck tidal marsh to Teaneck Township and over the Teaneck ridge on DeGraw Ave. into Bogota. The distance from Leonia junction to the terminus at Bogota was 15,400 feet. Leonia granted a franchise on Riley Ave. on 22 April 1898.

Car 5, built by St. Louis in 1896 in front of the Bergen County traction car house. *Street Railway Journal,* June 1896.

Ford, Bacon & Davis were retained as engineers, F. R. Long & Co. was contracted for the bridges and trestles, and Mayor A. E. Neumann of Cliffside Park for grading and track construction. Ground was broken on 2 August 1898 at Leonia. A number of expensive structures were necessary, including a 1150-foot steel viaduct with a 70-foot plate girder span over the Northern RR, a timber trestle 580 feet long with a 70-foot plate girder draw bridge spanning Overpeck Creek, and a 500-foot steel viaduct with a 70-foot plate girder span over the West Shore RR. Plans called for a single-track line with four turnouts.

Entry into Hackensack was to be on a 150-foot drawbridge across the Hackensack River and thence to a terminus at River St. on the McDonald ice pond property north of the NYS&W RR. The Erie RR, which owned a tract of land north of the Susquehanna RR along the river front, granted the traction company a right-of-way. At Bogota the New York Central & Hudson River RR granted per-

17

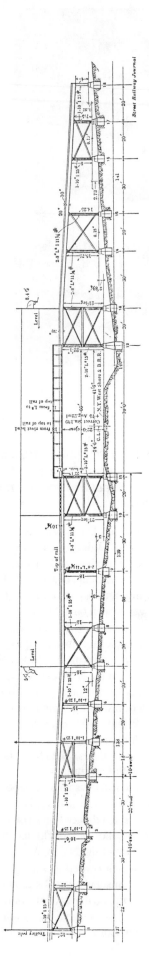

mission to bridge over its West Shore RR line on 23 September 1898.

By the end of September 1898 there were more than 200 men and 75 carts at work. The force was divided into four groups: one at Riley Avenue, Leonia; the second on a strip of land in the Overpeck tidal marsh known as the Fyke; and in Teaneck a third on the De Graw property and the fourth on the Foster property. A wooden building called Hotel de Hemlock with sleeping accomodations for 250 men was erected in a small wood in the center of the tidal marsh west of Overpeck Creek. A store was attached for the men to buy their necessities.

Construction west of Grand Ave., Leonia, required a 21-foot high, 260-foot long fill to connect with the trestle across the Overpeck marsh. Before constructing the trestle, the traction company obtained estimates for a wooden trestle and found the cost to be somewhat less than for steel. Steel was selected, however, because of its durability and to avoid the danger of fire as the marsh grass tended to catch fire in the autumn. The east section was 680 feet long, with a 70-foot plate girder span above the Northern RR, and a 400-foot trestle descending on a five percent grade to the west.

The 70-foot draw bridge across Overpeck Creek consisted of two plate girders each five feet in height and clearing the mean water level by 5 1/2 feet. The center pier was 13 feet in diameter and built of dimension stone, rock faced on the outside. It rested on three layers of 8-inch by 12-inch timber cribbing and twenty-five 12-inch diameter spruce piles. The circular track supporting the swing structure above the draw was 11 feet 6 inches in diameter. The draw bridge was opened manually since very few vessels passed through the creek and bridge openings were not expected more than once in a year or two. The main feed wires were carried overhead 55 feet above mean water level. The wooden pile trestles approaching the draw bridge were 191 feet long on the east side and 167 feet long on the west side and the pile bents were made in two parts to permit renewal of the upper part.

West of the trestle, a 1,000-foot fill was built through the Fyke supported by piles and timber cribbing to prevent its sinking into the marsh. At Teaneck, an 80-foot wide street, curbed with bluestone, was built through the De Graw and Foster estates.

The trestle in Bogota over the West Shore RR was identical to the Northern RR trestle in Leonia. The Bogota steel viaduct was 500 feet long and the span over the railroad consisted of two 70-foot long plate girders. The trestle at the west end descended on an 8.4 per cent grade onto Main St., Bogota. All of the structures on the Hackensack Extension were designed to carry a moving load consisting of two 23-ton double-truck cars. The plate girders for the West Shore span were set into place on 15 January 1899 and for the Northern RR span on 22 January 1899.

It was hoped that the extension would be opened before Christmas 1898. Because of bad winter weather and difficulties in getting steel, the opening was postponed until Lincoln's birthday 1899.

Hackensack Extension Opens

The first car operated a test trip over the Hackensack Extension on 21 February 1899, leaving the ferry terminal at 1:30 p.m. Because of a large snowdrift in a cut east of the West Shore RR, the car did not enter Bogota. On 22 February 1899 the extension formally opened, the first car — St. Louis-built closed car 1 — leaving the ferry at 12:10 p.m. with Assistant Superintendent J. C. B. Spatz at the controller. Vice President W. H. Clark relieved Spatz as motorman when the car reached the new line at Leonia Junction. The car took 50 minutes to reach Bogota, including the time spent for stops to allow inspection of the work and to take aboard invited guests. These included Mayor Casey of Undercliff, John Minners, R. J. Woods, C. Terhune, Judge Bogart, William Bennett, William DeGraw, Samuel Moore, F. C. Thomas and 91-year old George C. Demarest of Teaneck, one of the original incorporators of the Northern RR in 1854 and the Westfield & Hackensack RR in 1860. Demarest was the most honored guest and was presented with the first spike driven on the line, which had been drawn for the purpose and afterward was fashioned into a unique shoebuttoner by a one-armed blacksmith. When the car reached Bogota it was greeted by an enthusiastic crowd, many

Duplex car 11 on the West Shore trestle. *Street Railway Journal.*

of whom were taken aboard, filling the car to capacity, for a trip to Leonia Junction and return. After the second trip the car took the invited guests to the Fyke for a collation aboard the car.

The Extension was placed in regular operation on 27 February 1899 although the first advertised schedule was dated 1 March. Cars left Menzo Davis' store in Bogota at 10 and 40 minutes past the hour and shuttled to Leonia Junction. Here passengers transferred to Englewood cars for either Englewood or the New York ferry. The fare was five cents between Bogota and Leonia Junction and ten cents from there to Englewood or the ferry. One car was used, normally the "barrel" Duplex car No. 11, purchased in 1897.

The continuation of the Hackensack Extension into Hackensack Commission was beset with delays from the War Department over the design for the Hackensack River drawbridge and from the State of New Jersey regarding the fee for riparian rights. In the meantime, passengers desiring to reach Hackensack from Bogota could transfer to a stage operated by Jacob Dunn. BCT paid Dunn eight dollars per day for the use of his stage

which met each trolley, covering about 75 miles per day with three teams of horses and two men to do the work. The stage operated via Main St., Hackensack, to the Court St. bridge, across the river into Bogota to River Road and then north to the trolley terminus on Main St.

The Cliffside Park Route

On 5 December 1898, Bergen County Traction filed a petition in Cliffside Park for a new route running south via Palisade Ave., west on Grant Ave., then south on Anderson Ave., crossing Edgewater Ave., to the Fairview boundary line. The company withdrew the petition on 5 June 1899 although the franchise had been granted by the borough. The company had to complete its railway into Hackensack and could not undertake additional expenditures at the time.

Wire Thieves

Bergen County Traction was harassed by wire thieves in 1899 and attempts at catching them failed. The thieves would cut down about 50 feet of trolley wire in one place, then proceed about a quarter-mile away and remove another section,

foiling the police. On the night of 19 November 1899, thieves made off with 2000 feet of copper wire near Fort Lee and additional wire the next night. On the third night, two company employees hid in the wood beside the track and waited. About 2 a.m. three men emerged from a clump of bushes and proceeded to the trolley track. One was about to climb a pole when the two railway men pounced on them. A struggle ensued and one thief drew a revolver and fired at a railway man but missed. One railway man drew a revolver, fired at the retreating thief and also missed. One thief was nabbed and placed in the County Jail.

An attempt was made on the night of 14 December 1899 to derail and wreck an eastbound Hackensack Extension car. The 10:40 p.m. car out of Bogota was bound for Leonia when in the wooded section of the Overpeck marsh called the Fyke, the motorman found stones and timbers piled high upon the track. The crew alighted and began to remove the obstruction, when shots were fired from the woods. The crew quickly returned to the trolley car, turned off the current and shrouded the car in darkness. One shot passed

Duplex car 11 was one of two cars of that type built by Jackson & Sharp. Builder's photo taken in 1897.

through a car window and narrowly missed the lone passenger. The highwaymen departed and the crew removed the obstruction and continued to Leonia Junction. The incident was reported to the conductor on the Englewood car who telephoned the Englewood police and the traction company's office in Edgewater. Several employees armed with Winchester rifles scoured the neighboring country for several miles, but could find no trace of the highwaymen, believed to be those who had been stealing trolley wire. The employees who caught the one thief in Fort Lee usually operated the car that was held up and it was supposed the thieves were seeking revenge for the arrest of their companion.

Extension into Hackensack Commission

Bergen County Traction pursued the extension into Hackensack Commission during early 1899 despite the unresolved problems with the War Department and the State of New Jersey. The company possessed a right-of-way across the Erie RR property by the river in the Commission, and in March 1899 purchased the McDonald ice pond property, adjacent to the north side of the NYS&W RR on River St., for a terminal. The New Jersey State Riparian Commissioners had fixed a price of $800 for the lease of waterfront property at the drawbridge. W.N. Barrows, treasurer and secretary of BCT, appeared before the commissioners and succeeded in reducing the rent to $500.

During this time Bergen County Traction was being consolidated into the New Jersey & Hudson River Ry. and Ferry Co. The consolidation caused no interruptions to the improvements in progress.

The company submitted no less than seven plans to the U.S. War Department for the proposed Hackensack River drawbridge. The War Department required the draw to be a minimum of 60 feet wide, whereas company plans showed a 50-foot draw. The company eventually complied and the War Department ap-

proved the location and plans during January 1900. A contract was given to F. R. Long & Co. during February to construct the drawbridge under the supervision of Ford, Bacon & Davis. Construction was started in March and completed in June 1900.

The *Street Railway Journal* described the new drawbridge: The approaches were wooden trestles, the west side being 915 feet long and the east side being 285 feet long. The trestle bents were set on 15-foot centers. The chords for the two steel trusses on the bridge were fabricated from two 9-inch channels joined by riveted lattices. The trusses were 22 feet high and 158 feet 8 inches long. The drawbridge swung on a masonry center pier 22 feet in diameter and rested on three layers of 8-inch x 12-inch hemlock timber cribbing atop 49 twelve-inch diameter spruce piles. The bridge was designed for a double-track railway, but initially only one track was laid. The railway track used 60-pound per yard ASCE standard "T" rails. The track centers were 11 feet 1 1/2 inches apart which allowed two 9-foot 6-inch wide cars to pass on each track. The bridge was designed to support two 30-ton trolley cars on each track at the same time. The drawbridge could be opened and closed either manually or electrically. Electric operation was accomplished through a 500-volt D.C., GE 800 motor which delivered 27 horsepower and permitted opening or closing the bridge in 1 1/2 minutes. According to the *Street Railway Journal*, the drawbridge was one of the largest, if not the largest, drawbridge in the United States used exclusively for electric street railway service at the time. The safety devices installed on the bridge approaches were a cluster of five green lamps 800 feet from each end of the drawbridge and a cluster of four red lamps 150 feet from each end. Power for the lamps was controlled by the bridge tender to indicate the position of the drawbridge — open or closed. Trolley cars were allowed to run over the bridge at full speed.

Collisions

Collisions between cars were not uncommon, especially on single-track lines, and Bergen County Traction was not exempt. Its first newsworthy collision occurred on Sunday afternoon, 19 July 1896. It happened on Leonia hill about 3 p.m. and was caused by car 2 leaving the turnout at the top of the hill ahead of time and colliding with car 8 on the middle of the hill. The dashboard of No. 2 was considerably damaged, but no one was injured. The motorman of car 2 was fired at the scene.

On 3 March 1897 car 6 left the ferry at 6 a.m. bound for Englewood with six male passengers. A heavy fog prevented motorman A. K. Bliss from seeing more than a few feet ahead. When the car was about 200 yards south of turnout No. 2 on Palisade Ave., Bliss saw car 3 from Englewood with fifteen passengers on board bearing down on him. The next instant the cars collided. The cries of frightened passengers mingled with the groans of the injured could be heard for a long distance. Dr. Maximilian Wyler of Fort Lee was summoned and the most seriously injured were transported to the Englewood Hospital aboard a second car from Englewood. A wrecker crew from the car house quickly arrived and in about 1 1/2 hours the debris was removed and

service restored. The front platforms and vestibules of both cars were demolished.

The collision reached the court and is described in 62 NJ Law 410. It was thought that possibly the block signals had been tampered with and the court reviewed the block signal system used by Bergen County Traction. "To prevent delays, as well as accidents, the company is using the Ramsey block signal. This system . . . consists of boxes placed about five feet high on poles at the side of the track on which the trolley wires are run. In the boxes are two compartments, in each of which are lamps, and at the bottom of the box are handles which when properly turned control the lights by making a closed circuit between the box at one turnout with the box at the next, which two boxes are connected with the feedwires of the trolley road. In practical operation, when a car comes to a turnout or siding, it either remains on the siding or goes according to the signal displayed, a red light meaning to remain and a dark signal or no light indicating a clear track and to go ahead; and it is the duty of each conductor in passing a siding to turn the handles and thus set the signals for both the car behind and the one approaching not to enter the block."

Ridgefield & Teaneck Ry. Co.

The Ridgefield and Teaneck Ry. Co. was incorporated at Trenton on 16 February 1900. It was authorized to issue up to $500,000 in capital stock and had $250,000 in cash to commence business. The company's Board of Directors and Officers were Armitage Matthews of Manhattan, president: George E. Spencer, secretary; and James C. Young of Jersey City. The office was located at 55 Montgomery St., Jersey City. The railway filed a map at Trenton on 23 February 1900 showing two

routes in Bergen County. Route One began at Winant Ave. in Ridgefield Park and ran northward on Teaneck Road and Schraalenburgh Road through Ridgefield Park, Teaneck, West Englewood, Bergenfield, Dumont, Haworth and Closter, then turned east on Durie Ave. to High St., and south to the Northern RR depot. Route Two began in Ridgefield Park at Teaneck Road and ran west on Winant Ave., then north on Main St. and Queen Anne Road through Bogota, Teaneck and West Englewood to the intersection of Tryon Ave. and Teaneck Road. The line was never constructed and existed as a corporation for only twelve days. On 23 February 1900 an agreement was signed consolidating the Ridgefield & Teaneck Ry. with the Bergen County Traction Co., Riverside and Fort Lee Ferry Co. and Highland Improvement Co. to form the New Jersey & Hudson River Ry. and Ferry Co. The new company received its certificate of incorporation on 27 February 1900.

Bergen County Traction Company.
TIME-TABLE
ON AND AFTER MARCH 1st, 1899.

Leave Ferry for Englew'd and Bogota.		L've Englew'd for Bogota and Ferry.		Leave Bogota for Englew'd and Ferry.	
A. M.	P. M.	A. M.	P. M.	A. M.	P. M.
4 25	2 80	5 05	3 15	5 10	8 40
4 85	8 00	5 15	8 45	5 40	4 10
5 15	8 80	5 45	4 15	6 10	4 40
5 40	4 00	6 15	4 45	6 40	5 10
6 00	4 80	6 45	5 15	7 10	5 40
6 80	5 00	7 15	5 45	7 40	6 10
7 00	5 80	7 45	6 15	8 10	6 40
7 80	6 00	8 15	6 45	8 40	7 10
8 00	6 80	8 45	7 15	9 10	7 40
8 80	7 00	9 15	7 45	9 40	8 10
9 00	7 80	9 45	8 15	10 10	8 40
9 80	8 00	10 15	8 45	10 40	9 10
10 00	8 80	10 45	9 15	11 10	9 40
10 80	9 00	11 15	9 45	11 40	10 10
11 00	9 80	11 45	10 15	P. M.	10 40
11 80	10 00	P. M.	10 45	12 10	11 10
12 00	10 80	12 15	11 15	12 40	11 40
P. M.	11 00	12 45	11 45	1 10	A. M.
12 80	11 80	1 15	A. M.	1 40	12 10
1 00	12 00	1 45	12 15	2 10	12 40
1 80	A. M.	2 15	12 45	2 50	1 05
2 00	12 40	2 42	1 10	3 10	....

All cars leaving Ferry connect at Leonia for Bogota.
All cars leaving Englewood connect at Leonia for Bogota, except the 1.10 A.M. First car Sundays, 6.15 A.M.
All cars leaving Bogota connect with Ferry up to and including the 11.10 P.M. First car Sundays, 6.10 A.M.

E. W. LAWSON, Supt.

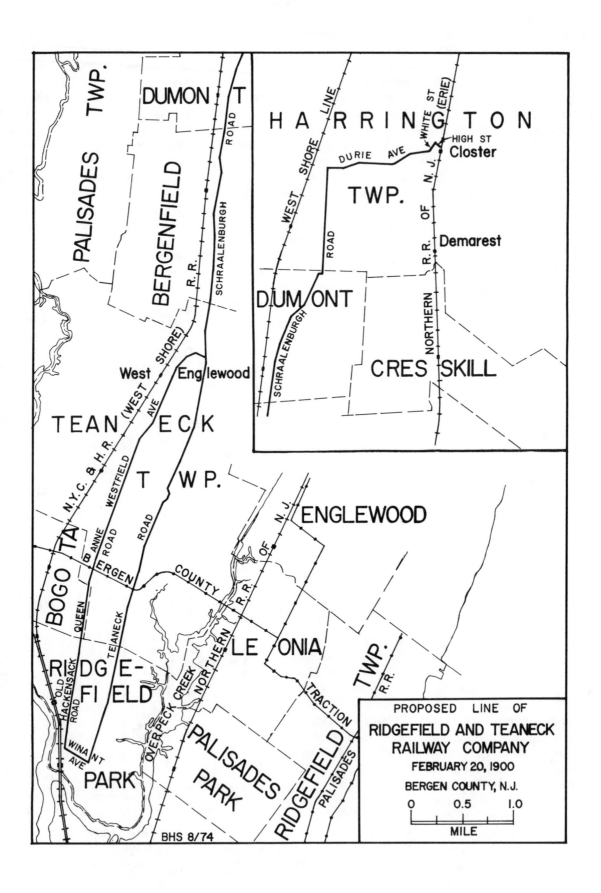

PALISADES TWP.

DUMON T

PALISADES TWP.

BERGENFIELD

SCHRAALENBURGH ROAD

R.R.

HARRINGTON

WEST SHORE LINE

DURIE AVE

WHITE ST

N. J.

HIGH ST

(ERIE)

Closter

TWP.

R.R. OF N. J.

Demarest

DUMONT

SCHRAALENBURGH ROAD

NORTHERN

CRES SKILL

West

Englewood

TEAN ECK

(WEST SHORE)

AVE

N.Y.C. & H.R.

WESTFIELD ROAD

T WP.

N. J.

ENGLEWOOD

R. R.

OF

ROAD

BERGEN

JEANNE ROAD

BOGOTA

QUEEN

TEANECK ROAD

COUNTY

R. R.

OVERPECK CREEK

NORTHERN

LE ONIA

TWP.

R.R.

RIDGE-FIELD

OLD HACKENSACK ROAD

TRACTION

WINANT AVE

PARK

PALISADES PARK

RIDGEFIELD

PALISADES

BHS 8/74

PROPOSED LINE OF

RIDGEFIELD AND TEANECK
RAILWAY COMPANY

FEBRUARY 20, 1900

BERGEN COUNTY, N.J.

0   0.5   1.0

MILE

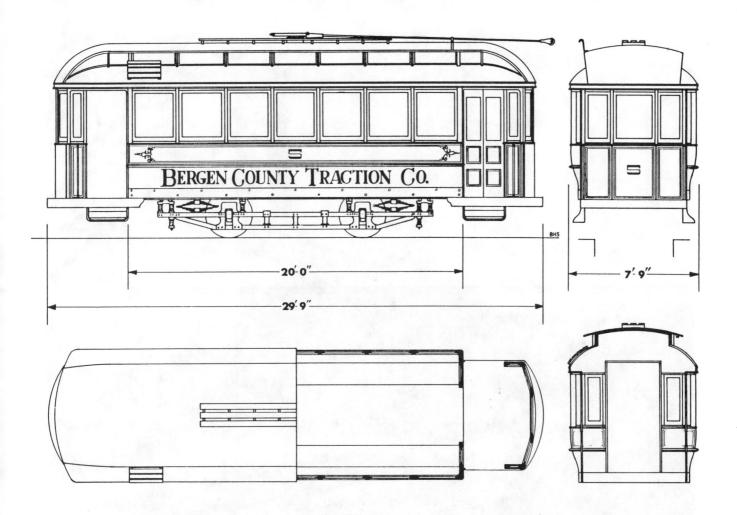

BERGEN COUNTY TRACTION COMPANY — EQUIPMENT ROSTER

Nos.	Type	Builder / SN	Shipped	Trucks	Motors	Roof	Notes
1-6	20-foot closed	St Louis	20 Dec 95	Peckham 6D	2-GE1000	Railroad	A
7-10	9-bench open	Jackson & Sharp 863-866	27 Jun 96	Peckham 6EX	2-GE1200	Deck	
11	duplex	Jackson & Sharp 1030	6 Sep 97	Peckham 6D	2-GE1200	Deck	B

A. These cars had enclosed vestibuled platforms, seven windows on each side, and spring rattan longitudinal seats. Interiors were finished in light mahogany with solid brass fittings and 10 sixteen-candlepower incandescent lights. Each car was mounted on a Peckham No. 6-D extra-long truck having an eight-foot long wheelbase that reduced the oscillations common to single-truck cars. The color scheme was carmine red with light cream trim at the window posts and lower side panel.

B. This car resembled a barrel because of its curved sides and was built under Duplex Car Co. patents. The side panels raised into the roof like a roll-top desk cover, opening the car for summer service. There were sixteen cross seats with throw over backs, seating 32, and a center aisle. Passengers boarded and alighted from the platforms.

All Bergen County closed cars were passed on to the New Jersey and Hudson River Railway and Ferry Co. They were renumbered 14 to 19, apparently not in order. Cars 18 and 19 and were assigned to the Hudson River Traction's Arlington shuttle line in 1904. Cars 14 to 17 were withdrawn from service, then restored to the roster by Public Service Railway as sand cars 5515-5518. The disposition of cars 7 through 11 is unknown.

The Edgewater Power House. This photograph was made on 8 February 1916 and was probably taken as part of the evaluation of Public Service Railway properties conducted during that period.

EDGEWATER POWER HOUSE — 1896-1900

Generating Units: 1896 Two 200 kW, 500 v D.C, belt-driven General Electric generators.

1900 One 500 kW, 500 v D.C./ 375 v A.C. belt-driven GE double-current generator.

Steam Engines: 1896 Two E.P. Allis 300 hp Corliss steam engines, 80 rpm. Flywheels each weighed 32,000 lbs.

1900 One Hamilton Corliss 750 hp cross-compound steam engine.

Steam Boilers: 1896 Four Heine Safety Boiler Co. water tube boilers totalling 450 boiler hp at 150 psig.

1900 Two Heine Safety Boiler Co. water tube boilers totalling 500 boiler hp at 150 psig.

Storage Battery: 1898 Manufactured by Electric Storage Battery Co. and consisting of 258 cells with a capacity of 300 amperes used for smoothing out short-term overloads on generators.

RAILWAY POWER DISTRIBUTION

Four 500 v. D.C. feeders: No. 1 Fed trolley wire from ferry terminal to switchback and to top of Palisades.

No. 2 From top of Palisades to bottom of Leonia hill.

No. 3 From bottom of Leonia hill to Englewood.

No. 4 From bottom of Leonia hill to Englewood and later to the Hackensack Extension.

HUDSON RIVER LINE

New Jersey & Hudson River Ry. & Ferry Co.

The system built and operated by Bergen County Traction between 1895 and 1900 was the nucleus from which a new and bigger street railway, the New Jersey and Hudson River Ry. and Ferry Co., developed. The NJ&HR was extended into Tenafly, Paterson and Newark for a total system mileage in 1910 of 48.44 miles within Bergen County. It replaced the single-truck cars inherited from its predecessor companies with large, fast double-truck cars and improved track conditions to achieve high speed schedules. By 1910, the Hudson River Line was the only remaining large street railway system in Public Service Corporation's service territory that had not been merged into the Public Service Ry. In July 1910 the merger took place and the NJ&HR's corporate existence ceased after ten years of being one of the most efficient and modern trolley systems in the eastern United States.

The NJ&HR is Organized

During January 1900 engineering consultants Ford, Bacon & Davis of New York City and A. Merritt Taylor, president of the Philadelphia & West Chester Traction Co., jointly secured a majority interest in Bergen County Traction. On 23 February 1900 an agreement was made consolidating the Ridgefield & Teaneck Ry. with Bergen County Traction. From this merger a new organization was formed for the purpose of consolidating Bergen County Traction, the Riverside and Fort Lee Ferry Co., and the Highland Improvement Co. The New Jersey and Hudson River Ry. and Ferry Co., applied for a certificate of incorporation on 23 February 1900 which was granted by the state on 27 February.

A. Merritt Taylor was president of the new company; William H. Clark of Philadelphia, first vice president; Frank R. Ford of Manhattan, second vice president and general manager; William N. Barrows, secretary and treasurer: F. W. Bacon, general superintendent of the railway; and Edward W. Lawson, ferry superintendent. Bacon was previously Superintendent of Traffic for the New Orleans & Carrollton RR Co. of Louisiana, another Ford, Bacon & Davis enterprise. Because of NJ&HR's long name, the public quickly accepted the shortened name "Hudson River Line" especially since the company's new cars were lettered "Hudson River" on their sides.

Improvements Continue

The improvements started by Bergen County Traction were continued. A new turnout in the Fyke to permit additional rush hour service; the double-track, started in May, 1899, between Palisade Ave. and the ferry terminal; and the Hackensack Extension were all completed. The initial improvements planned by the new company were construction of a new ferry slip at 130th St., Manhattan and development of a first-class amusement park on the Palisade plateau. The company ordered ten open and five closed cars from the American Car Co. of St. Louis.

During April 1900, work was started on replacing the switchback on the Palisades with a horseshoe curve. The Palisades were blasted away leaving a perpendicular rock face wall over 50 feet high. The rubble was used for building a shelf about 130 feet wide, sufficient for a double-track loop of 45-foot inside radius. There was a retaining wall 55 feet high and 70 feet wide with massive

1901

New Jersey & Hudson River Railway and Ferry Co.
· · TIME TABLE · ·
On and after July 6th, 1900.

L've 130th St. for Engle'd & Hackensack.		Leave Engle-w'd for Hack-ens'k & Ferry		L've Hacken-sa'k for Engle-wood & Fr'y	
A. M.	P. M.	A. M.	P. M.	A. M.	P. M.
5 50	4 20	5 20	3 45	5 20	3 43
6 15	4 50	5 50	4 15	5 48	4 13
6 45	5 20	6 16	4 45	6 15	4 43
7 15	5 50	6 50	5 15	5 48	5 13
7 45	6 20	7 22	5 45	7 20	5 43
8 15	6 50	7 50	6 15	7 48	6 16
8 45	7 20	8 18	6 45	8 16	6 43
9 15	7 50	8 45	7 17	8 43	7 15
9 45	8 20	9 15	7 45	9 13	7 43
10 15	8 50	9 45	8 15	9 43	8 13
10 45	9 20	10 15	8 45	10 13	8 43
11 15	9 50	10 45	9 15	10 43	9 13
11 45	10 20	11 15	9 45	11 13	9 43
P. M.	10 50	11 45	10 15	11 43	10 13
12 15	11 20	P. M.	10 45	P. M.	10 43
12 45	11 50	12 15	11 15	12 13	11 16
1 15	12 30	12 47	11 45	12 45	11 43
1 45		1 15	A. M.	1 13	A. M.
2 15		1 45	12 15	1 43	12 13
2 45		2 15	12 45	2 13	12 43
3 15		2 45		2 43	1 16
3 45		3 15		3 13	

Last boat leaves Edgewater, N. J., 12:15 a. m., midnight.
Boats are run on Saturdays and Holidays under 15 minutes headway.
Cars leaving Hackensack at 11:43 and Englewood at 11:45 p. m. connect with ferry for New York.

Two views of the horseshoe curve on the Palisades at Edgewater. The top view, taken 7 September 1906, shows the landscaping in the loop of the curve. The lettering at the edge of the flower bed says "Hudson River."

The lower picture, taken in 1909, shows open car 60 to the left, bound for Englewood, and car 66 on the right, heading for Paterson. Both cars were part of an order built for the New Jersey and Hudson River by the American Car Co. in 1900.

buttresses. The curve was completed at 3 a.m. on 19 February 1901. Construction was done mainly at night so that normal daytime traffic was not hampered.

Originally, there was a gap in the wire at each end of the Overpeck Creek draw to allow opening for vessels. The gap required the cars to slow down to prevent the pole from coming off the wire. The wire was made continuous in May 1900, which prevented opening the bridge but allowed trolleys to operate at normal speed.

The stage coaches between Bogota and Hackensack stopped running at noon on 19 April 1900 when Jacob Dunn, the proprietor, was refused an increase in pay by the NJ&HR.

Construction of the Hackensack River drawbridge began in March 1900 and was completed in June. The first car over the new structure — one of the new open cars gaily decorated for the occasion — left the Edgewater ferry terminal at 4:30 p.m. on Thursday, 21 June 1900. At Hackensack, it was greeted by President Clarendon of the Hackensack Improvement Commission, other Hackensack officials and several county officers. Over

100 guests from Hackensack, Englewood, Leonia and surrounding communities boarded the cars and were brought to the Fyke where a large table with refreshments was set up in the woods and speeches were made proclaiming the new extension. Hackensack at this time had more than 10,000 inhabitants and was the largest community on the Hudson River line. Regular service began on Saturday, 23 June 1900 with through cars between Hackensack and the ferry terminal. The Hackensack terminus was located on the former McDonald Ice Pond property on River St. adjacent to the north side of the Susquehanna (NYS&W) RR.

The Palisades Commuters' Association held a mass meeting at Fort Lee on 21 June 1900 to continue agitating against the high fares charged by the Palisade RR. Through the efforts of this association, the Hudson River management considered an extension north from Fort Lee about three miles to the end of Palisade Ave. in Englewood Township, but the project was never pursued.

The Hudson River management completed all of the projects planned by Bergen County Traction management

A view of the Hackensack River drawbridge, looking west, taken in 1909. Open car 13 is signed for New York Ferry. The picture was taken before the installation of the second track on the drawbridge, which was completed in June 1901.

except a second car house at the western terminus of the system. Instead, the new management decided to consolidate car maintenance facilities at the Edgewater headquarters. On 31 August 1900, ground was broken for the second car house adjoining the east wall of the old building. An old walnut tree, planted in 1720, was felled to make room. The new car house was designed to hold twelve large cars and four small cars, whereas the old car house accomodated eight small cars. It was completed in November 1900.

On 15 October 1900, more than a year after the first franchise request, the Hudson River line filed a second petition with the Cliffside Park Borough Council. This was for a new route running south over Palisade Ave. to Claremont Ave., then west over private property to Fairview

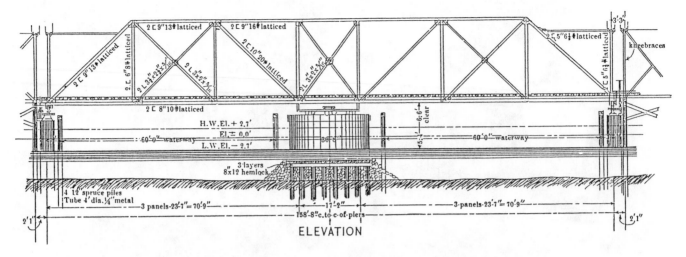

Side elevation of the Hackensack River Bridge.

and a connection with the proposed Bergen Turnpike Co. line from Hoboken. The franchise was granted on 3 December, but the line was never built.

A second track was laid across River Road at the north end of the Edgewater ferry terminal on 27 February 1901. Borough authorities sent a force of men to tear out the track which the borough council declared to be illegal. When the street commissioner's force started to rip up the rails, a lineman employed by the railway threw a coil of wire across the overhead trolley wire and connected the ends to the disputed rails. Four laborers who were sawing at the rails were hurled several feet by the current. The lineman was arrested and after the wires were disconnected, the track was removed.

During June 1901 the Hudson River line began double tracking the Hackensack Extension, adding a second track except over the Overpeck marsh trestle and the Overpeck Creek drawbridge. Also during June, F.R. Long & Co. was contracted to construct the single-track truss bridge over the NJ&NY RR on the extension through Hackensack. In Leonia a franchise was granted on 16 September 1901 permitting relocation of the railway's track onto a cutoff via Pine Terrace between Woodridge Place and Central Ave. The track intersecting Broad Ave. at Central Ave. was abandoned.

The Park on The Palisades

During early 1901 the Hudson River line developed a landscaped park on the Palisades. The area had long been a favorite outing spot for rambles and picnics for New Yorkers interested enough to climb the rough Palisades ascent. After completion of the electric railway from the ferry to the top of the Palisades, trolley excursions became frequent. The demand for a place devoted to the necessities and pleasures of recreation seekers soon brought about the new park. In six months the wild untouched landscape underwent a change that transformed it into a public park of studied, though informal design. Thousands of shrubs, vines and flowers were planted and nature's awakening call completed the picture in green and color in 1901. It was named *The Park on The Palisades* and contained 80 acres, fifteen being at the base of the Palisades in Pleasant Valley. The entrance was on River Road north of the ferry terminal. A winding walk up the hill passed through the River Grove picnic grounds, formerly called Glen Echo, in Pleasant Valley and continued on a zig-zag path up the bluff. The walk, cut out from the side of the cliff, extended to the top of the Palisades where it passed under the trolley tracks through a stone tunnel. At the top, paths fanned out in various directions, one to the Palisades' Groves picnic grounds and another to the Esplanade which was famous for its numerous seats and view of the Hudson River. William Hunter, previously consulting engineer for construction of Bergen County Traction's ferry buildings and track, was made park superintendent.

The Hudson River line operated special cars between the ferry terminal and the park entrance where they termi-nated on a loop that had unloading and loading platforms, the latter being roofed over to form a 60' x 90' shelter. Special park cars from other points on the Hudson River line also used the park loop.

A newspaper reported on 10 September 1905 that Thompson & Dundy, the owners of Luna Park at Coney Island and the Hippodrome in New York City, had leased 14 acres of land from the Hudson River line in Cliffside Park. The land was known as Grantwood Park and the lessees planned to spend $250,000 for development as an amusement park. Construction was to begin in February 1906 and the park was to be fully operational by Memorial Day.

The Park on The Palisades property which had been acquired by the Northern New Jersey Land Co. was sold to the West Manhattan Realty Co. on 15 October 1907. Forty of the acres were to be divided into 20-foot building lots in 1908 on which cheap cold-water tenements would be erected. Instead, a gang of mechanics started work on 18 May 1908 to transform the area into the famous Palisades Amusement Park.

The Paterson Extension

The Hudson River line, continuing its advance westward across Bergen County, applied to the Hackensack Commission on 8 December 1900 for an extension from the McDonald ice pond via River St. to Mercer St., double track on Mercer St. to Main St., and single track to the Gamewell property on State St., then continuing westward over private right-of-way parallel to the Susquehanna

Car 69 was built by Stephenson for the Jersey City Hoboken & Paterson in 1902 as car 10 and was renumbered and sold to the NJ&HR in 1904. The view is believed to have been taken in Paterson.

(NYS&W) RR. It crossed over the NJ&NY RR on a bridge, then ran north over First St. to Passaic St. The track passed under the NYS&W RR at River St. and First St. On 30 January 1901, the application was amended to request double track for its entire length within the Hackensack Commission and an extension west to the Maywood boundary via Pleasant Ave. The Commission granted the franchise on 29 April 1901. The NJ&HR was required to use grooved girder rails on paved streets, to pave Mercer St. curb-to-curb, and to use standard "T" rails on macadamized streets.

The route was surveyed during the middle of 1901 and consents secured from property owners in Maywood, Arcola and Saddle River Township. The company planned to lay its tracks on private right-of-way for most of the distance and would become the shortest and most direct trolley line between Paterson and New York City. With two large urban centers at each end of the Hudson River line, the company felt assured of financial success.

In June 1901 construction commenced westward through Hackensack on River St. One of the first projects was to raise and lengthen the NYS&W RR bridge spanning River St. to enable the trolleys to pass under the railroad. Track construction was completed on Mercer St. and the Gamewell property to Union St. during October. The first car to run beyond the River St. terminal was line car 10 busily stringing the overhead trolley wire on 25 October 1901. The car was labeled "special," and was a special attraction to spectators gathered along the line. Regular service to Union St. began the same day. Cars began regular service from Edgewater to Summit Ave., Hackensack on 9 November 1901. The line was completed to Maywood Ave., Maywood on 24 December. A special car opened the line on Christmas Day and the regular schedule commenced on 26 December between Maywood and Edgewater. Extra morning cars were run to connect with the Susquehanna commuter trains at Hackensack.

During April, 1902, the Jersey City, Hoboken & Paterson St. Ry. Co. and the NJ&HR entered into an agreement for a track connection in Saddle River Township east of the Passaic River. The JCH&P agreed to extend its Broadway tracks eastward from 33rd St. to the Passaic River, to construct a single-track trestle across the river north of the Broadway highway bridge and to construct about 200 feet of track in Saddle River Township to connect with the Hudson River line. The connection was called Passaic River Junction.

On 14 April 1902, the Hudson River line commenced construction west of Maywood Ave., Maywood, with 250 men grading and laying 90-lb. rail towards Paterson. Some obstacles still remained to be cleared; the first being permission to enter Paterson and the second being a

A view of the Edgewater Terminal in 1911. The small signs on the terminal porch posts advertise Bell telephone service. The sign on the post in the center of the picture announces that the next car is destined for Fort Lee.

crossing of the Erie RR's Bergen County RR at Warren Point in Saddle River Township. The first obstacle was removed on 8 July 1902 when the Paterson Board of Aldermen, by a vote of 16 to 6, over Mayor Hinchliffe's veto, passed the ordinances authorizing the JCH&P extension on Broadway from East 33rd St. to the Passaic River. The second obstacle was more difficult to clear. The Erie RR refused to allow a grade crossing of the Bergen County RR. On 1 December 1902, the NJ&HR agreed to construct an underpass below the railroad on Broad-

way at Warren Point with a 60-foot-wide street. Construction was delayed because the Saddle River Township Committee wanted a 110-foot-wide street. As the track construction progressed westward, the Maywood terminus was relocated four blocks west to Spring Valley Road, regular service beginning on 28 November 1902. This was later established as a fare zone boundary.

The Paterson extension officially opened on 31 March 1903 when two special cars filled with guests made the first trip between Edgewater and Paterson. The cars were met at Passaic River Junction by JCH&P officials and ran into downtown Paterson with JCH&P Superintendent Warren Hall at the controls of the first car. Scheduled service began on 1 April. The route in Paterson initially was west on Broadway, south on Main St., east on Park Ave. and north on East 33rd St. to Broadway for the return to

Edgewater. This route was slow and circuitous and cars were rerouted straight down Broadway to downtown Paterson where they looped around the Broadway terminal property to Van Houten St., then to Main St. and back to Broadway. Transfers were issued to all local car lines to points within Paterson. JCH&P crews operated NJ&HR cars in Paterson and as far as Passaic River Junction. In order to speed up service and maintain schedule time, the railway painted a white ring on certain poles to designate car stops. The four miles between Maywood and Warren Point was scheduled to be covered in six minutes, an average speed of 40 mph.

The NJ&HR management was obliged to operate its lighter open and single-truck closed cars for two weeks in October 1902 because a generator broke down at the Edgewater power house. This reduced the power demand and permitted the remaining generators to supply suffi-

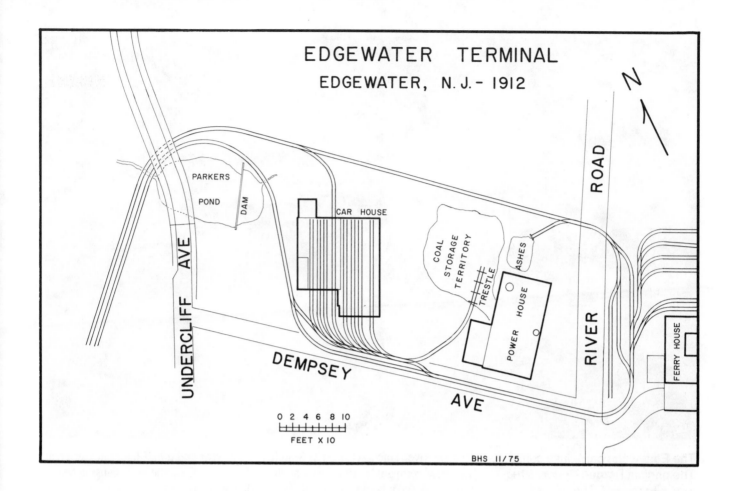

EDGEWATER TERMINAL
EDGEWATER, N.J. - 1912

PARKERS POND

DAM

CAR HOUSE

COAL STORAGE TERRITORY

TRESTLE

ASHES

POWER HOUSE

UNDERCLIFF AVE

DEMPSEY AVE

RIVER ROAD

FERRY HOUSE

0 2 4 6 8 10
FEET X 10

BHS 11/75

cient power for normal schedules. The failure prompted the railway to order an additional generator for 1903 delivery.

An electric substation at Arcola in Midland Township, completed March, 1903, fed 500-volt D.C. power to the Paterson extension overhead from a 600-kw rotary converter. Public Service Electric and Gas Co. retired the Arcola Substation in 1958.

Englewood Line Extensions

In Englewood the NJ&HR continued its efforts to extend north on Dean St. toward Tenafly from the Palisade Ave. terminus where it had been halted since 1897. On 6 February 1900 the Englewood City Council had passed an ordinance authorizing Bergen County Traction to construct west over Palisade Ave., but the ordinance was not accepted by the company within the 60 days allotted time. Early in 1901 the NJ&HR requested permission to extend the Englewood line to Demarest Ave. and the Northern RR via Dean St., but Messrs. Murray Olyphant and John Beattie opposed the request on the grounds that the Hudson River line

would not reveal its plans for further extensions on Demarest Ave. The railway had planned to proceed west through Waldo Place, but this was opposed during March 1902 by St. Cecelia's R.C. Church because the church planned a school at that location. The NJ&HR even discussed tunneling under the Northern RR at Slocum Ave. to avoid a grade crossing, then proceeding to Tenafly via Tenafly Road. The Englewood Council finally agreed during August 1902 to authorize an extension north to the Tenafly boundary line on Dean St. Credit for the agreement was given to Englewood's "Trolley Tim" Rafferty who agitated for the extension at council meetings.

Construction on Dean St. began during July 1903. The extension was completed to Chestnut St. during February 1904 and express service, in addition to local service, was started between Chestnut St. and the Edgewater ferry terminal on 1 March. Three express cars ran each weekday morning, operating as locals between Chestnut St. and Leonia Junction, then as non-stop expresses to the Edgewater ferry. Residents of the

Highwood section of Englewood, desirous of having access to trolleys, presented a petition to the City Council on 6 September 1904, requesting a further extension from Chestnut St. to the north city limits, a distance of one mile.

Nyack, New York, Plans

NJ&HR Vice President F. R. Ford appeared before the Nyack (New York) Board of Trustees on 19 May 1902 to apply for a franchise for a trolley line on Broadway and Cedar Hill Ave. It was the intention of the Rockland RR to start in Upper Nyack and run through Nyack, South Nyack, and Piermont to connect with the West Shore RR at Tappan. The project remained dormant until 23 May 1910 when Vice President Miller of the Rockland RR appeared before the Nyack Trustees. Miller said that within thirty days construction would start at the corner of Broadway and Main St. He boasted that he would have the line completed to Tenafly, New Jersey during the summer of 1910, but there were several matters remaining to be cleared up with the New York State PUC. It was

31

The Edgewater car house complex. The original Bergen County structure is to the left. The new barn at the right was completed in November 1900. From left to right the cars are 20 (renumbered 65 in 1903), 18 (63), 16 (61), and 23, all built by American Car Company in 1900. The picture was taken between November 1900 and the spring of 1903.

reported that Ford, Bacon & Davis had purchased the one-fifth interest of Gibson T. Williams and that the engineering firm would be the construction manager for the Rockland RR. Mr. Clark of the National Bank of New York also joined the company at this time. The Rockland project never progressed beyond the talking stage and further interest disappeared after the sale of the NJ&HR to the Public Service Corporation in 1910.

Hudson River Traction Co.

In 1902, the NJ&HR set up a new organization to extend to Newark through Rutherford via the financially-ailing Newark & Hackensack Traction Co. Messrs. Samuel B. Lawrence, Henry C. Everdell and George B. Hanford received a certificate of incorporation for the

Hudson River Traction Co. on 21 March. The new company's office was at the Edgewater ferry house. Frank R. Ford was vice president and William N. Barrows was secretary. A two-mile-long track connection via Summit Ave., Hackensack between the Newark & Hackensack Traction Co. at Lodi Road, Hasbrouck Heights, and the Hudson River line at First St., Hackensack, was completed on 30 July 1903. However, service did not commence until 7 December. The Newark and Hackensack route is covered in chapter 3.

The 1903 Passaic River Flood

Paterson, a city of 105,171 inhabitants in 1900, experienced two calamities shortly after the turn of the century in which a fire and two floods devastated the city's low-lying business section. The influx of immigrants caused serious shortages in housing, jobs and recreational facilities. To further aggravate the misery of Paterson's citizens, the February 1902 fire swept away the heart of the business section, raging with unsubdued fury for two days. In less than a month's time the greatest flood ever known to the Passaic valley came upon the city, cresting on 2 March, and hundreds of the poor were again driven from their homes.

A year and a half later another great flood inundated the area, causing heavy damage. The Passaic River basin had been the recurrent victim of storm run-off flooding as far back as 1810, but nothing ever equalled the deluge of October 1903 when 35,000 acres were inundated to depths of 10 to 15 feet. The 1903 flood was about 40 per cent greater than the 1902 flood. The peak discharge over the Great Falls at Paterson was measured at 34,000 cubic feet per second! On 10 October the raging waters washed out the JCH&P's wooden trestle used by the Hudson River line cars to enter Paterson. The Broadway highway bridge was also washed away, leaving no means of crossing the Passaic River at this location. The Freeholders of Bergen and Passaic counties authorized the NJ&HR to construct a temporary foot bridge on 13 October. The bridge extended from the abutment of the washed out highway bridge on the Bergen County shoreline to the easterly end of what remained of the bridge near the Paterson shoreline. It was six feet wide and 130 feet long and was opened to the public on 20 October.

While the pedestrian bridge was in use, the Public Service Corporation, owners of the JCH&P St. Ry., contracted F.R. Long & Co. to construct a new

32

wooden trestle across the Passaic River a short distance north of the original (March 1903) bridge. There was a public protest when it became apparent that the railways were preparing to replace the original structure with another of similar construction and the Citizens' Association of Paterson hoped to block the project. By working 100 men all day on 22 November 1903, the railways outwitted their opponents and avoided service of an injunction. The Hudson River trolleys began using the new bridge, described as poorly constructed, on 8 December. A more substantial single-track trestle was placed into service on 17 January 1904. This served the Hudson River line until 1931 when the tracks were relocated to the new State Highway 4 bridge.

Route Extensions and Connections — 1904-05

By 1903 it was common to refer to the Paterson route as the Hudson River line, the Englewood route as the Englewood line, and the Newark route as the Hackensack line despite the fact that all NJ&HR cars were lettered "Hudson River" on their sides.

Hudson River Traction announced in January 1904 that it would build a connection between the Hackensack line near Hasbrouck Heights and the Public Service Corporation's Saddle River Traction route at Lodi. This was completed on 10 May 1904 and opened for service on 16 May. The connection enabled Public Service to operate its Main St. line from Hackensack's NYS&W RR depot through Lodi, Garfield, Passaic, Clifton and Paterson to the Broadway Terminal. The Lodi route is covered in chapter 8.

During January 1905 a plan was revealed to extend the Hudson River Line from Arcola northward along the east side of Paramus Road to Franklin Ave. at Ridgewood. The route, which was never built, was entirely within Midland Township, an area eventually subdivided into Paramus and Rochelle Park boroughs.

Car 49 (Stephenson, 1906) outbound on the Hudson River line at the Edgewood ferry terminus. In addition to the Public Service-type wood Hudson River sign on the roof end, there is a Hunter roll sign in the lower half of the left front window which reads "Leonia, Hackensack, Paterson." Car 26 (American, 1900) is at the left alongside the ferry building.

The Morsemere Extension

The Hudson River line petitioned several municipalities in eastern Bergen County for a new route via Morsemere through Leonia, Palisades Park and Ridgefield Township during 1902. In August 1902 petitions were filed in Palisades Park and Leonia boroughs for a double-track railway on Broad Ave. During January, 1903 a petition was filed in Ridgefield Township for a double-track railway to extend west from Palisade

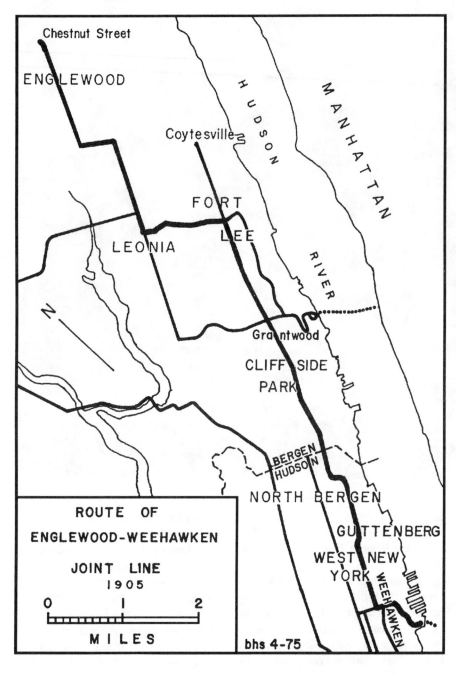

Chestnut Street

ENGLEWOOD

HUDSON

MANHATTAN

Coytesville

FORT

LEE

LEONIA

RIVER

N

Grantwood

CLIFFSIDE
PARK

BERGEN
HUDSON

NORTH BERGEN

GUTTENBERG

WEST NEW
YORK

WEEHAWKEN

ROUTE OF

ENGLEWOOD-WEEHAWKEN

JOINT LINE
1905

0   1   2

MILES

bhs 4-75

Englewood-Weehawken Joint Line

Fort Lee granted permission to construct a turnout on Main St. east of Public Service's Palisade Line crossing and a connection between the Hudson River line Main St. track and the Palisade line private right-of-way track on 6 April 1904. The switch was completed in the third week of August, 1904, permitting eastbound Hudson River cars to turn right onto the Palisade Line and continue south.

A new "rapid transit" scheme connecting Englewood directly to the West Shore RR's Weehawken ferry terminal commenced service on 4 August 1905. The route, named the "Englewood-Weehawken Joint Line," was operated jointly by Public Service Corporation of New Jersey and the NJ&HR. Cars started at Chestnut St., Englewood and proceeded to Main St., Fort Lee where they switched to the Public Service Palisade Line and continued to the Weehawken terminal. Free transfers to Hoboken and Jersey City cars were provided at Union Hill. Public Service supplied the cars for the joint line and intended to use single-end cars but the Englewood City Council refused permission to build a "Y" for turning the single-end cars on property Public Service had purchased at Chestnut St. for a future electric substation. Therefore, the cars assigned to the line were low-numbered 1900-series, double-end, semi-convertibles built by J.G. Brill in 1903. The cars were transferred from Public Service's Main St. Line in the Passaic Division and on the eve of the opening of the new route several chrome yellow 1900s were stored overnight at the Edgewater car house. The Joint Line was not a paying one and the "pie wagons," which the yellow cars were called, carried few passengers. Service was discontinued on 14 October 1905.

Service and Safety Improvements — 1905-1908

A collision on 11 September 1905 at Fort Lee where the old route through Fort Lee switched off onto Palisade Ave. from the new Morsemere route caused a grand jury investigation into NJ&HR operations. Two cars left the Edgewater ferry terminal shortly after midnight. Car 29,

Ave. at Grantwood over a private right-of-way to Broad Ave. at Morsemere. Leonia granted a franchise on 4 March 1903 requiring the company to have at least a single-track line in operation within twelve months. In February 1905 the franchise was amended extending the time for completion to 1 September 1905.

Construction began on 16 January 1905. Rumors circulated that the old route via Main St., Fort Lee would be discontinued upon opening of the Morsemere route. Service began on 25 May 1905 when Hudson River officials rode over the route in a special car. Commencing 27 May, Englewood cars were rerouted over the Morsemere route reducing the scheduled time between Leonia and the ferry terminal by 15 minutes. The Hudson River line cars continued using the old route via Main St., Fort Lee. Hackensack Line cars from Newark commenced through service via Hackensack to the Edgewater ferry terminal on 11 July 1905, one day after completion of the double-track between Hackensack and Leonia. The Hackensack Line cars also used Main St. in Fort Lee.

bound for Fort Lee, was first up the Palisade followed by No. 57 bound for Englewood. After the Fort Lee car switched onto Palisade Ave., it was the conductor's duty to reset the switch for the Morsemere route to give the Englewood car a clear track. The conductor on the Fort Lee car failed to reset the switch and while he was setting a signal, the Englewood car crashed into the rear of the Fort Lee car. A male passenger standing on the Fort Lee car's rear platform with his wife and son was killed. The Bergen County Grand Jury presented its findings to the railway company and all NJ&HR cars were required to display lighted red marker lamps at each end on both sides at night effective 18 October 1905.

A shuttle car commenced operating between Leonia Junction and Palisade Ave., Englewood on 9 November 1905. Former Bergen County single-truck closed car 3 was assigned to the run. The shuttle was timed to meet the cars arriving from Hackensack at Leonia Junction so that passengers could reach Englewood without a long wait for the Englewood cars.

A new air whistle for the NJ&HR cars was tested during January 1906. Quoting a newspaper account of the tests: "the old

signal, which sounded like the last cry of a 'lost soul' may give way to a deep basso profoundo squawk which is not unpleasant and resembles the groan of a dying hen tossed to one side by the electric vehicle. The trolley people have placed several of the whistles on their cars and the difference between the ear-splitting shrieks of the old kind and the gentle buzz of the new is marked. . ."

The NJ&HR also installed electric clocks on buildings adjacent to principal stopping points on its lines. The first location was the window of Robert Livingston's stationery store at the corner of Dean St. and Englewood Ave., Englewood. A second was placed at the NYS&W RR's Hackensack depot on the side facing Mercer St.

On 11 June 1906, Paterson (Hudson River Line) and Newark (Hackensack Line) cars were rerouted to operate via the Morsemere route; the Englewood-Leonia shuttle was discontinued; and the Fort Lee Line, was started between the Edgewater ferry and Englewood via Main St., Fort Lee, on a half-hour headway between 7:42 a.m. and 7:12 p.m. Paterson and Newark cars operated as locals over the Morsemere route while Englewood cars operated as expresses. On 2 July 1906 weekday evening rush-hour

The Jersey City, Hoboken & Paterson purchased two open and two closed cars identical to the New Jersey & Hudson River cars as their share of the rolling stock needed to operate the joint line to Paterson. As is shown in the picture of 55 or 56 above, the ownership was shown on the right end of the car sill or, in the case of the closed cars, on the platform sill just below the entrance door.

express service between Edgewater and Maywood began with first car leaving the ferry terminal at 4:25 p.m. The cars made limited stops along the Morsemere route and the running time was cut to 25 minutes between the ferry terminal and Hackensack for an average speed of 20 mph. Starting on 8 October 1906 Englewood-bound cars on the Fort Lee Line waited at Leonia Junction for any passengers transferring from the eastbound cars from Hackensack.

A story concerning trouble between the Public Service Ry. and the NJ&HR gained wide circulation in Paterson on 13 March 1907. It was reported that because of the trouble, the big red cars of the Hudson River Line had been taken from

that route and placed on the Broadway and Park Ave. lines in local service as a retaliatory measure by Public Service. It was also reported that small "dinky-dink" Public Service cars replaced the big red cars on the Hudson River Line. The truth was that some of the big red cars were not running on the Hudson River Line because of a heavy snow storm and these cars were not fitted with snow guards or snow plows, as they were called by the trolley men. Few of the red cars owned by the NJ&HR entered Paterson after the snow storm and two of the red cars, Nos. 32 and 33, were owned by the JCH&P and were not fitted with snow plows. Consequently, they were unfit for deep snow in the rural areas. A third car, Public Service No. 1949, was also painted in the Hudson River line colors and was likewise not fitted with snow guards. These cars were stored at the Market St. car house by Public Service and others replaced them on the trip to Passaic River Junction. Public Service found itself short of cars for Paterson local lines, and Superintendent Stone decided to run the

red cars on the Broadway and Park Ave. lines. Hudson River Line passengers were required to change cars at Passaic River Junction during this interval.

Trolley Freight Proposed

Fort Lee and Edgewater boroughs agitated in favor of the NJ&HR carrying freight, especially building materials, as was reported in the press during April 1907. The NJ&HR management refused on the grounds that it would have to build freight stations, and more turnouts and switches. Despite the Hudson River line's position, Edgewater granted a ten-year freight and express franchise to the trolley company in May 1907.

The year 1907 marked the peak of the upward trend in the fortunes of the New Jersey & Hudson River Ry. & Ferry Co. which had been continuous since 1896. The financial depression which began late in 1907 arrested this trend. An anecdote: 1907 was also the peak year for the infant motion picture industry in the Fort Lee area which spanned thirteen years (1902-1914) of production here.

Car 20 (Stephenson, 1906) was part of the last order of cars acquired by the NJ&HR. It was photographed here on Dempsey Ave., apparently when new. The Edgewater power house is to the rear. The track curving to the left immediately behind the car led to the power house coal trestle.

North Jersey Rapid Transit

On 3 June 1908, a proposal was made to build an interurban railway from Passaic River Junction 15 miles northward to Suffern, New York via Ridgewood. The new company set up its office on the fourth floor of the Colt Building in Paterson and was incorporated as the North Jersey Rapid Transit Co. (NJRT) on 8 September 1908. The story of the New Jersey Rapid Transit Co. is covered in chapter 11.

Car 25 was one of eight identical cars built by American Car Co. in 1900 which were used by the NJ&HR to upgrade service on the former Bergen County Traction Co. line. This photograph was taken at Edgewater in 1912 after acquisition by Public Service Railway. The work car to the right rear is Public Service 5606, built by the Cincinnati Car Co. in 1904.

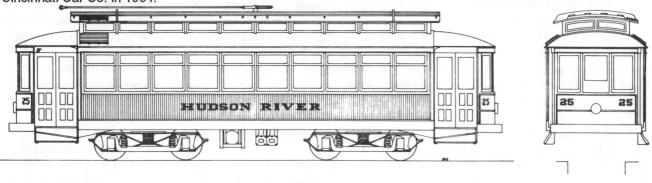

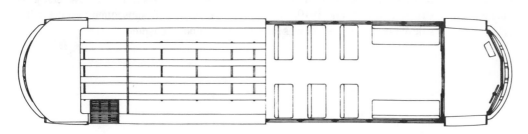

Cars 38-40 were purchased from Brill in 1904 for the Hudson River Traction Co. They were originally built for the Philadelphia, Coatesville and Lancaster Electric Railway, a Pennsylvania line which was never completed. As a result the cars differed from the normal Ford, Bacon and Davis design which characterized the other NJ&HR closed cars.

The 1910 Englewood Extension

During October 1905 a number of Tenafly residents agitated for an automobile service between Tenafly and Englewood to connect with Englewood trolleys at Chestnut St. They wanted the NJ&HR management to pay the expenses as it had previously done for the stage between Bogota and Hackensack during 1899. The company turned down the suggestion because it was deemed too expensive. In May 1906 a private automobile service began conveying passengers from Chestnut St., Englewood to Tenafly for ten cents. This was double the fare on the parallel Northern RR, but passengers felt the excitement of the auto trip was worth the extra nickle. Trips were made hourly from each end of the line connecting with the trolleys. The auto stage was painted black and resembled a cross between a lunch wagon and a small trolley car.

The NJ&HR filed a map on 29 January 1910 for an extension of the Englewood Line from Chestnut St., Englewood, to the Northern RR of New Jersey depot at Tenafly. Franchises were received from Englewood City on 29 April and from Tenafly Borough on 28 June. Construction began on 9 May and was completed to the Highwood Section of Englewood on 22 June 1910. On Saturday, 25 June, all Englewood cars began running from the Edgewater ferry through to Highwood. The extension into Tenafly was completed by Public Service Ry. and opened on 19 November 1910.

Corporate Reorganization

The New Jersey & Hudson River Ry. & Ferry Co. simplified its corporate structure in 1909 and 1910. *The* Riverside & Fort Lee Ferry Co. was formed on 14 April 1909 to take over the property and franchises of Riverside & Fort Lee Ferry Co. The old company was merged into the new on 16 April. In October 1909 the NJ&HR acquired the capital stock of New York Real Estate Co. (organized 7 July 1904) from The Riverside & Fort Lee Ferry Co. A joint agreement for consolidation between the NJ&HR and the Hudson River Traction Co. was filed at Trenton on 31 January 1910. The certificate of consolidation was issued on 25 February. The capital stock of the NJ&HR was increased to $6.0 million of which $2.5 million common and $750,000 preferred stock was outstanding. On 9 May 1910, the Alpine Navigation Co. was organized in New York State to enter navigation business on the Hudson River and was controlled by Highland Improvement Co. Alpine Navigation was dissolved by unanimous consent of the stockholders on 14 July 1911.

As future events revealed, reorganization would shortly be followed by acquisition of the New Jersey & Hudson River and its underliers by the Public Service Corporation of New Jersey. This change and subsequent events will be found in chapter 4.

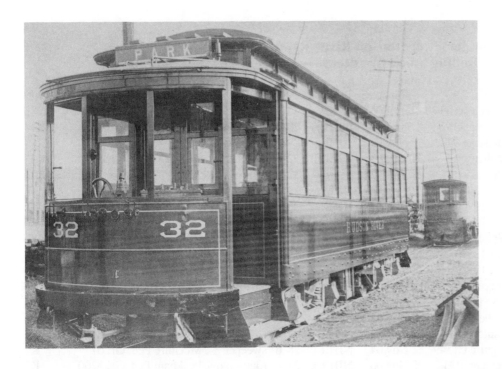

The NJ&HR began using Hunter roll signs with the closed cars built in 1903 and 1904. The roof sign design shown here on car 32 was also used on the older open cars, although the original American-built closed cars were not equipped. The cars built by Stephenson in 1906 (20-21, 44-49) were equipped with window roll signs showing the points reached.

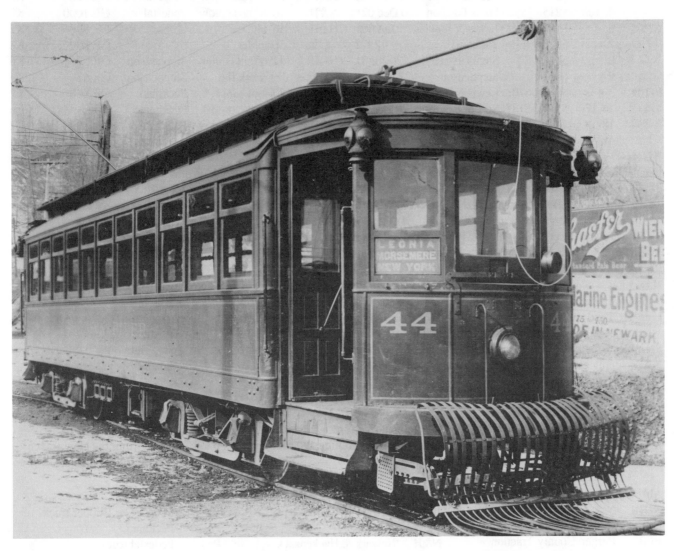

New Jersey & Hudson River Ry. & Ferry Co.
Rolling Stock Inventory — 1 May 1911

BCT	NJHR	PSR	Builder	Shipped	Buyer	Type	Trucks	Motors	Controls
	20-21	1869-1870	Stephenson 1120	Oct 06	NJHR	32-foot closed	FBD MCB*	GE 90A	K28F
	22-26	1847-1851	American 352	25 Oct 00	NJHR	29' 6" semiconv	FBD MCB*	GE 57	K14
	27-29	1852-1854	American 390	7 Nov 01	NJHR	29' 6" semiconv	Peck 14B3	GE 57	K14
	30-31	1855-1856	Stephenson	30 Apr 03	NJHR	32-foot closed	FBD MCB*	GE 57	K14
	32-33	1857-1858	Stephenson	30 Apr 03	JCHP	32-foot closed	FBD MCB*	GE 57	K14
	34-37	1859-1862	Brill 12941	12 Oct 03	HRT	29' 4" semiconv	Peck 14B3	GE 67	K6
	38-40	1863-1865	Brill 13900	22 Oct 04	HRT*	28' semiconv	Peck 14B3	GE 67	K6
	41-43	1866-1868	Brill 13898	28 Nov 04	HRT	29' 4" semiconv	Peck 14B3	GE 67	K6
	44-49	1871-1876	Stephenson 1120	Oct 06	NJHR	32-foot closed	FBD MCB*	GE 90A	K28F
	50-54	1053-1057	Brill 12586	30 May 03	NJHR	14-bench open	Peck 14B3	GE 67	K6
	55-56	1058-1059	Brill 12586 1/2	28 May 03	JCHP	14-bench open	Peck 14B3	GE 67	K6
12-21	57-66	1060-1069	American 333	May 00	BCT	14-bench open	Peck 14B3	GE 67	K6
14-15*	67-68	1070	J&S 904-905	Spring 97	Union	12-bench open	Peck 14B3	GE 1000	K6
10-11	69-70	1071-1072	Stephenson	5 Sep 02	JCHP*	14-bench open	Peck 14B3	GE 67	K6
	1	5169	Taunton	19 Dec 03	NJHR	27' 6" sweeper	Taunton Ped	GE 67*	K2
	2	5170	Maguire C1549	22 Nov 04	NJHR	28' 6" sweeper	McGuire Ped	GE 67*	K2
	2	5216*	Peckham R31	20 Nov 00	NJHR	24' 6" rotary plow	Peckham Ped	GE 1200	K2
	4; 100	5215	Phila Traction	20 Dec 02*	N&H	16' 8" nose plow	Pedestal	GE 1000	K2
6?*	6	None	Lewis & Fowler	Jan 00*	N&H	16' line car*		GE 800	K2
	7	5015	Taunton*	1897?		Sprinkler		GE 800	K2
	8	5668	Stephenson	20 Jul 01	NJHR	41' 6" side dump	Stephenson	GE 57	K6
	9	5667	Stephenson	27 May 01	NJHR	DT work flat	Stephenson	GE 57	K6
9-10*	3-4	5669-5670*	Lewis & Fowler	Jan 01*	N&H	20-foot supply*	Peckham	GE 800	K2
1-6 (-)	14-17	5515-5518*	St. Louis	20 Dec 95	BCT	20-foot closed	Peckham*	None	None
2-3?	18-19	26-27*	St. Louis	20 Dec 95	BCT	20-foot closed	Peckham	GE 1000	K2

* Notes

FBD MCB These trucks were built by Stephenson.

38-40 originally built for the Philadelphia Coatesville & Lancaster Ry. (PA) but not delivered.

14-15 were Union Traction numbers. Not owned by Bergen County Traction. Became Newark & Hackensack 20-21. Car 68 burned in accident on 17 August 1906.

10-11 were purchased by the Jersey City Hoboken & Paterson and were sold to the NJ&HR on 29 February 1904.

Sweepers 1 and 2 each equipped with 1 — GE 1200 broom motor.

Rotary plow 2 numbered PSNJ 5216, then renumbered 5222 in 1913.

Nose plow 4 acquired second-hand in 1902 from Union Traction Co. of Philadelphia where it was numbered 2831. It was renumbered 100, designated as Public Service plow 5215, then rebuilt as Public Service line car 5411.

Line car 6 and supply cars 3 and 4 acquired from Newark & Hackensack. Not owned by Bergen County Traction. Originally purchased second-hand from Brooklyn Heights Railroad in 1900 and 1901. Car 6 also used as sand car.

Sprinkler 7 reported as built by Taunton in Public Service records. NJHE inventory says McGuire. Taunton is likely.

NJHR supply car 3-4 not renumbered 5669-5670 as planned. Car 3 was scrapped. Car 4, which had been used as a line car, was renumbered as line car 5415.

16-17 were listed as stripped of electrical gear in the inventory, 14 and 15 were bodies only. All four were restored to the roster as sand cars 5515-5518.

26 and 27 became sand cars 5540 and 5545 in 1915 and 1917 respectively.

A second-hand flat car numbered 17612 was purchased on 20 June 1900. It is believed to have come from the New Haven Railroad and probably became the underframe of a portable substation which was used at Fort Lee for many years.

Abbreviations

NJHR	New Jersey & Hudson River	JCHP	Jersey City, Hoboken & Paterson	MCB	Master Car Builder truck
HRT	Hudson River Traction			Peck	Peckham
BCT	Bergen County Traction	N&H	Newark & Hackensack	Ped	Pedestal truck
Union	Union Traction	FBD	Ford Bacon & Davis	GE	General Electric

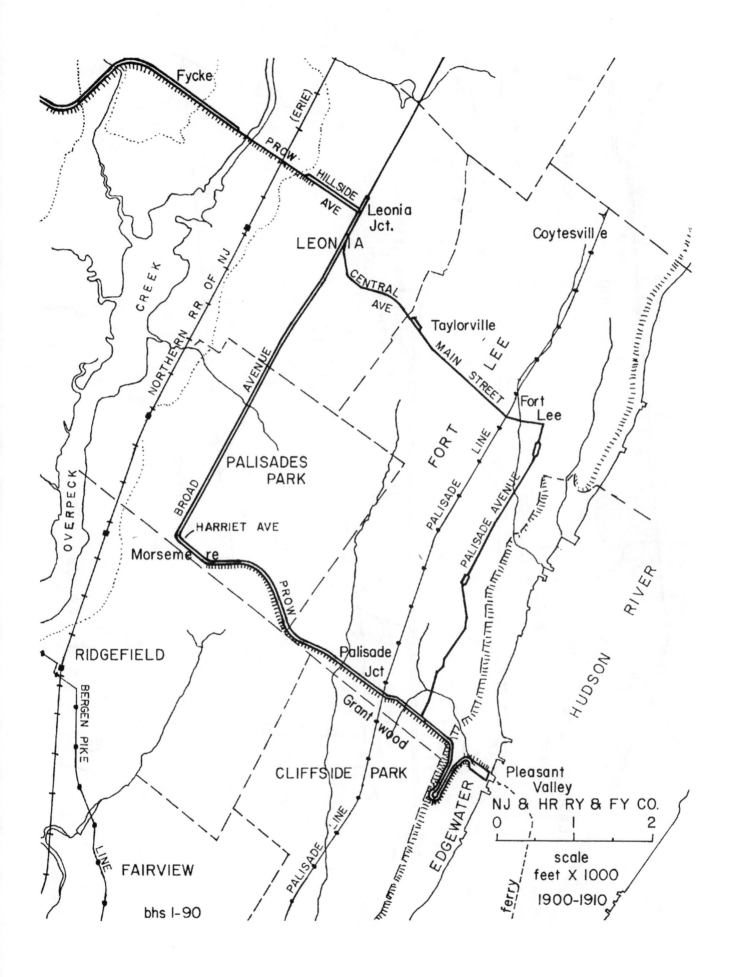

Fycke

(ERIE)

PROW.

HILLSIDE

AVE

Leonia
Jct.

LEONIA

Coytesville

CENTRAL

AVE

Taylorville

MAIN STREET

FORT

LEE

Fort
Lee

NORTHERN RR OF NJ

AVENUE

CREEK

PALISADES
PARK

BROAD

HARRIET AVE

PALISADE

LINE

PALISADE AVENUE

Morseme re

OVERPECK

PROW.

HUDSON

RIVER

RIDGEFIELD

BERGEN PIKE

Palisade
Jct

Grant wood

CLIFFSIDE   PARK

Pleasant
Valley

PALISADE LINE

EDGEWATER

NJ & HR RY & FY CO.

0   1   2

LINE

FAIRVIEW

bhs 1-90

ferry

scale
feet X 1000
1900-1910

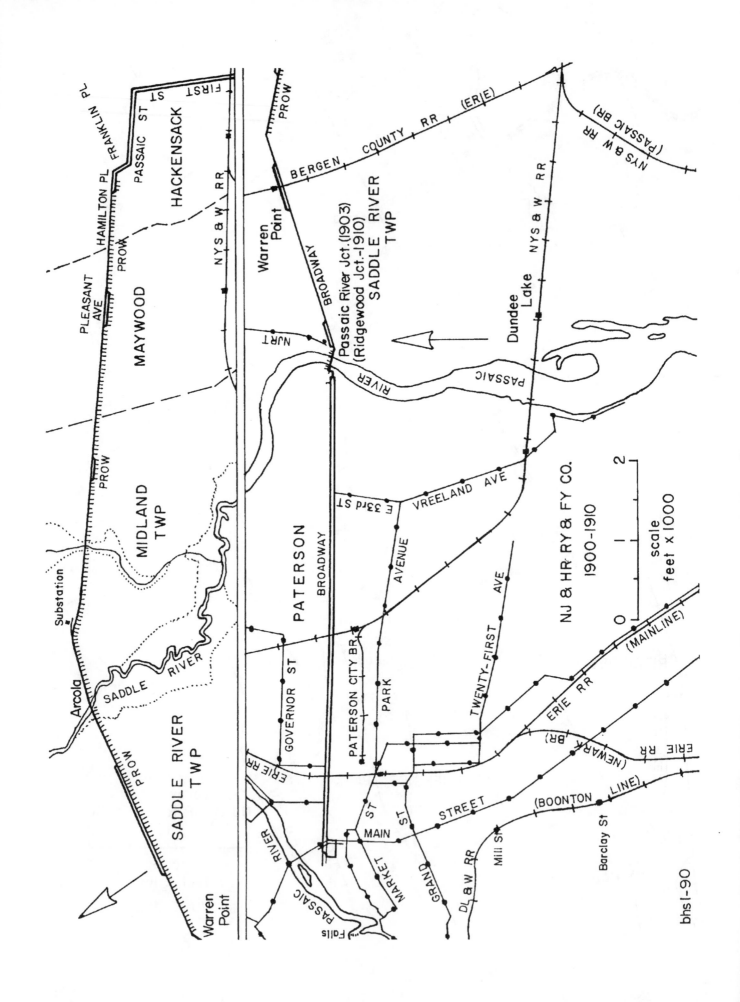

NJ & HR RY & FY CO.
1900-1910

scale
feet x 1000

2   1   0

bhsI-90

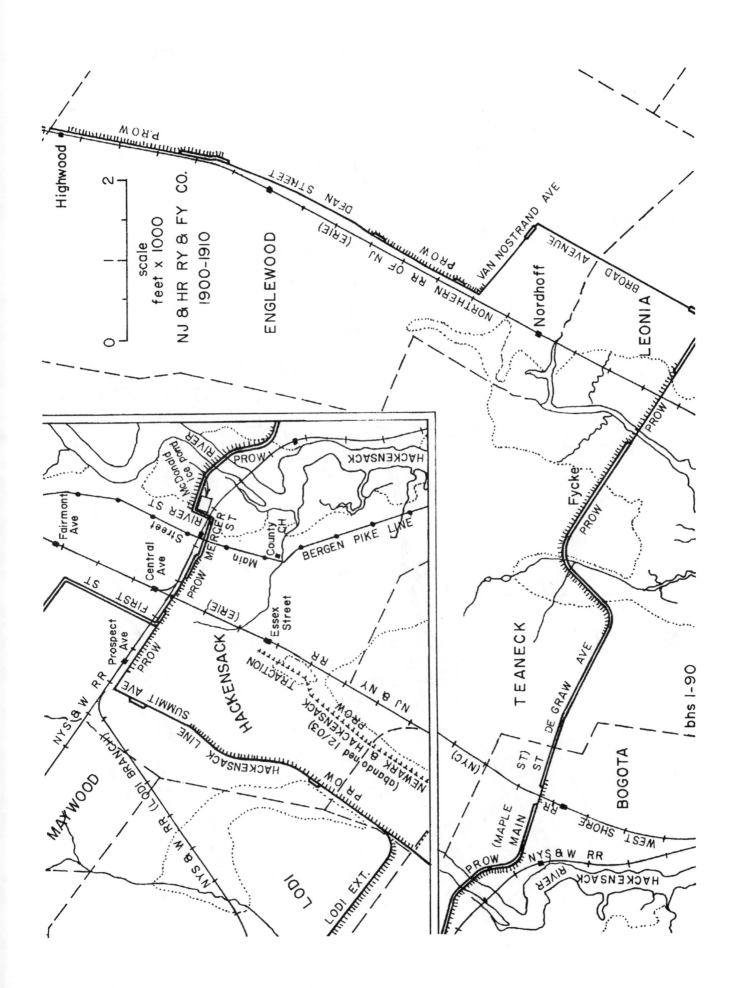

Highwood

P.R.O.W

scale
feet x 1000
NJ & HR RY & FY CO.
1900-1910
ENGLEWOOD

DEAN STREET

(ERIE)

NORTHERN RR OF NJ

P.R.O.W

VAN NOSTRAND AVE

Nordhoff

BROAD AVENUE

LEONIA

PROW

Fycke

PROW

HACKENSACK RIVER

McDonald Ice Pond

RIVER ST

PROW

MERCER ST

River Street

Fairmont Ave

Central Ave

Main

County CH

BERGEN PIKE LINE

PROW

(ERIE)

FIRST ST

Essex Street

Prospect Ave

PROW

NJ & NY

RR

NEWARK & HACKENSACK TRACTION
(abandoned 12/03) PROW

SUMMIT AVE

NYS & W RR

HACKENSACK

HACKENSACK LINE

PROW

TEANECK

DE GRAW AVE

(NYC)

MAPLE ST

MAIN ST

RR

PROW (MAPLE ST)

NYS & W RR

HACKENSACK RIVER

WEST SHORE RR

BOGOTA

bhs I-90

MAXWOOD

NYS & W RR (LODI BRANCH)

LODI

LODI EXT.

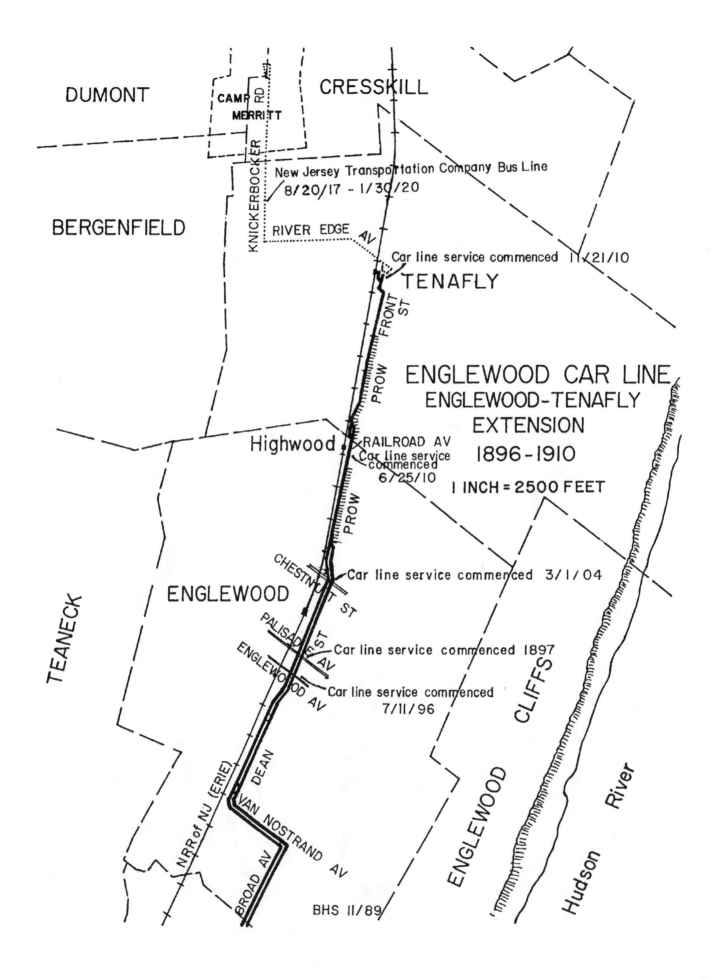

DUMONT

CRESSKILL

CAMP MERRITT

BERGENFIELD

New Jersey Transportation Company Bus Line
8/20/17 - 1/30/20

RIVER EDGE AV

Car line service commenced 11/21/10

TENAFLY

FRONT ST

PROW

ENGLEWOOD CAR LINE
ENGLEWOOD-TENAFLY
EXTENSION
1896-1910

1 INCH = 2500 FEET

Highwood

RAILROAD AV
Car line service
commenced
6/25/10

PROW

CHESTNUT ST

Car line service commenced 3/1/04

ENGLEWOOD

TEANECK

PALISADE AV

ST

Car line service commenced 1897

ENGLEWOOD AV

Car line service commenced
7/11/96

ENGLEWOOD CLIFFS

Hudson River

DEAN

NRR of NJ (ERIE)

VAN NOSTRAND AV

BROAD AV

BHS 11/89

KNICKERBOCKER RD

3

THE HACKENSACK LINE

In south-central Bergen County, Rutherford Borough, a small community formed in 1881 along the south side of the New York, Lake Erie and Western Ry, became a center for trolley companies connecting Newark with Hackensack. These companies eventually became part of the Public Service Railway system.

Rutherford Railway Company

The Rutherford Heights Association had been developing real estate south of Union Ave. and east of Jackson Ave. for over ten years when it incorporated the Rutherford Ry. Co. on 11 February 1891 as a horse railway to encourage Erie RR commuters to settle in Rutherford. Rutherford granted a franchise on 6 April 1891 for a single-track route from the West Rutherford (Carlton Hill) depot of the New York, Lake Erie & Western RR, south on Riverside (Jackson) Ave. to Newell Ave. An amended franchise on 8 September changed the route to run south on Riverside Ave., east on Francisco Ave., and south on Santiago Ave. to Passaic Ave., returning by the same route. By the time the amended franchise was granted, the line had already been completed, service beginning 7 September 1891.

There were several passing turnouts on the single-track line. On arrival at the end of the line the car was not turned around—instead the horses were hitched to the opposite end of the car for the return trip. The horse cars were operated by John Hollenbeck. The company owned two cars, one horse and one mile of standard-gauge track. Henry G. Bell was president and treasurer and David Stoddard was secretary.

The railway was unprofitable as can be seen in the following report:

	1892	1893	1894	1895	1896
Gross Income	$110	186	229	204	137
Operating Expenses	$480	661	746	582	571
Net Deficit	$370	475	517	378	434

The Francisco Horse Car, as it was known locally, had an abrupt ending in 1896. During the dark of night, some teenage boys pushed the horse car down the Francisco Ave. hill. It jumped the rails on the curve at the bottom and bounded into the woods of Riverside Park never to roll again. The Rutherford Ry. Co. was dissolved on 5 January 1898 which was approved by the State of New Jersey on 20 January. Tracks, property and franchises were turned over to the Union Traction Co.

Union Traction Company

During June 1894, Delos E. Culver of Jersey City proposed a trolley line from Arlington through Carlstadt via Polifly Road to Hackensack. Surveys were made through Hackensack and either First St. or State St. was to be selected. Consents were secured from enough property owners along the route in Rutherford and along Polifly Road by August 1894 to carry the project through. Culver had said that he would not apply for a certificate of incorporation under the name Newark, Rutherford and Hackensack Electric Ry., until he had secured the necessary consents. On 7 August, Culver asked the Rutherford Borough Council for a franchise on Park Ave. the full length of the borough, claiming possession of consents from the property owners in Rutherford and Union Township. The proposed franchise called for a five-cent fare, Telford macadam paving from curb-to-curb, street sprinkling by the railway, a double-track railway, and an annual license fee of five dollars per car. During November 1894, the company opened a subscription list for prospective stockholders. Culver still had not applied for a certificate of incorporation and now said it was nec-

essary to ascertain whether or not a franchise would be granted before raising the necessary capital.

Meanwhile, another group of entrepreneurs quietly organized the Union Traction Co. and filed a route map during October 1894 which included the same route Culver had proposed for the Newark, Rutherford and Hackensack. Luther Shafer of Rutherford was the attorney representing the new company which received its certificate of incorporation on 2 November 1894. Because the area encompassing Lyndhurst and North Arlington during 1894 was named Union Township, the traction company used the name "Union." Local names appearing among the original incorporators were Francis J. Callenan, Charles Burrows, Henry G. Bell, Edwin T. Galloway and John M. Bell of Rutherford; Theodore G. Hoster of East Rutherford; and Henry C. Broking of Carlstadt. The remaining incorporators were from New York City and George S. Forbush was from Brookline, Massachusetts. Union Traction officers were George H. Forbush, president; Henry G. Bell, vice president; Henry C. Ellis, secretary; and Francis J. Callenan, treasurer.

The Transit Equipment Co. was incorporated in New York on 2 November 1894, by the incorporators of Union Traction, with offices on Cortlandt St., Manhattan. J. W. Gilmore was president and Gilbert T. Gale, secretary. Transit Equipment was to furnish Union Traction such appurtenances as motors, controllers and trolley poles. It was reported in the December, 1894 *Street Railway Journal* that representatives of Union Traction and the Newark, Rutherford and Hackensack had agreed that the latter company should be absorbed by the former. Delos E. Culver and Henry H. Copeland became members of Union Traction's board of directors.

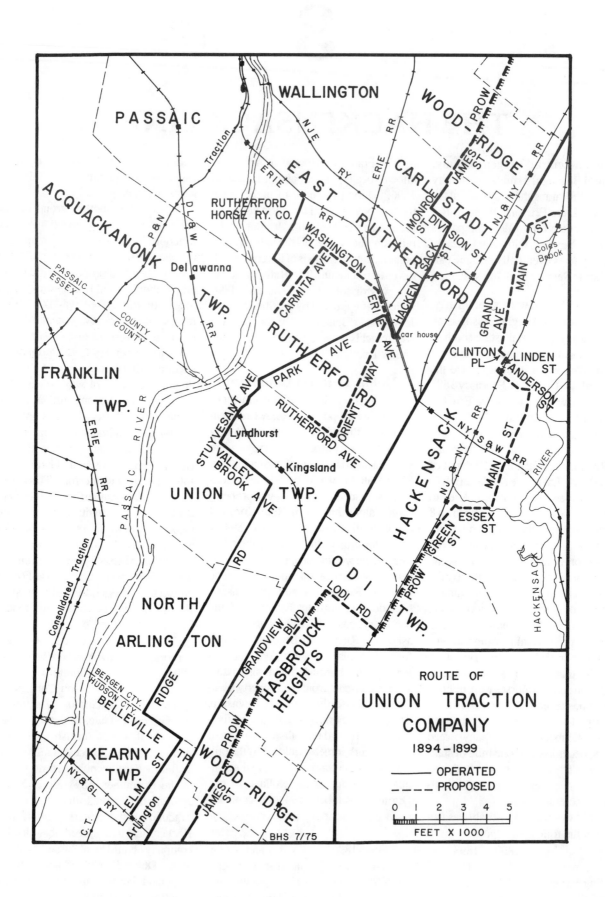

ROUTE OF

UNION TRACTION COMPANY

1894-1899

—————— OPERATED
- - - - - - PROPOSED

0 1 2 3 4 5

FEET X 1000

BHS 7/75

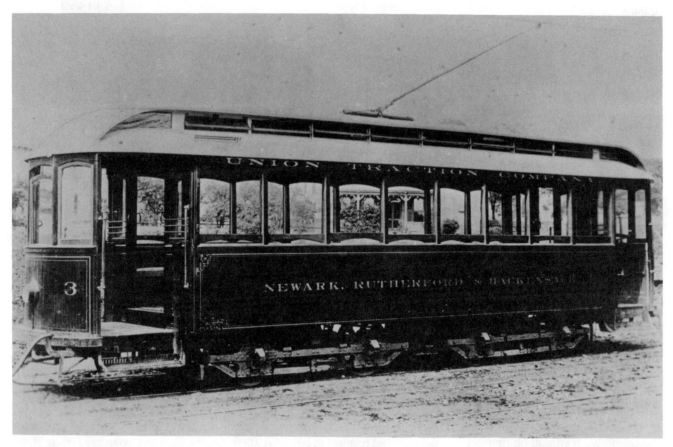

On 26 November 1894, $1 million in Union Traction bonds were sold to the Metropolitan Trust Co. of New York City. The State of New Jersey, on 4 December 1894, issued a Certificate of Entry upon the Rutherford Ry. Co. property to Union Traction. Franchises between Arlington and Carlstadt were sought during December. Rutherford was petitioned on 10 December and Carlstadt on 17 December. The Rutherford petition covered nine different routes with one running the full length of Union Ave. to the Passaic River, a route also sought by the Passaic & Newark Traction Co. Franchises were granted by Union Township on 5 February 1895, Rutherford on 5 March, and Kearny Township on 12 March. East Rutherford denied a franchise because Hackensack St. had recently been macadamized and would be torn up by construction of the railway. Then the company ran out of money. On 8 October, Union Traction's creditors applied for appointment of a receiver. The company filed for receivership on 18 October. To further aggravate the situation, the Rutherford council on 22 Octo-

ber 1895 repealed the franchise. Union Traction offered a $5,000 bond guaranteeing construction if the borough would rescind the repeal. It was reported that a Philadelphia syndicate , headed by Contractor Wilson, were dickering to purchase a controlling interest in the company in late November 1895.

The application for a receiver was heard by Vice-Chancellor Read at Newark on 3 December 1895 when Luther Shafer appeared. Shafer claimed Union Traction owed him $166.66 for rent of a building in Rutherford and $1,000 for legal services. The complaint alleged that Union Traction was an unsuccessful speculative scheme whose sole aim was to secure franchises and then sell them. Read appointed William H. Clark, a director and vice president of Bergen County Traction, as receiver on 14 December and issued an injunction restraining the company from collecting debts or transferring stock. The latter stopped the Philadelphia syndicate from buying Union Traction. New officers elected at a reorganization meeting in early 1896 included Henry C. Adams of Hackensack,

Union Traction ordered many cars but took delivery on few. Ten cars of this type were ordered from Jackson & Sharp but only five were received. In time, even these were sold and replaced by second-hand single-truck cars in order to raise the money to pay Jackson & Sharp's construction bills.

president; David A. Pell of Hackensack, treasurer; and Frank Bourne of New York City, secretary. It was reported on 16 February 1896 that Union Traction had contracted a Philadelphia firm to construct the line. Construction was scheduled to commence on 1 March.

North Arlington Borough was formed out of Union Township on 11 March 1896. On 13 November Union Traction petitioned the borough for a franchise for the same routes granted previously by Union Township. North Arlington adopted the 1895 Union Township ordinance on 15 December 1896 effective on 10 January 1897. Union Township re-

The parlor car *Oritani* was ordered by Union Traction but never ran on the property. It wound up running on the Seaview Railroad in Rhode Island.

vised its franchise ordinance and passed it on 1 September 1896, effective on 5 September. North of Rutherford, Union Traction filed petitions for franchises in Hasbrouck Heights on 18 May and in Wood-Ridge on 21 May 1896. East Rutherford and Carlstadt granted franchises on 3 August, and Carlstadt and Wood-Ridge on 4 September. In September 1896, Union Traction applied to the Belleville Township Committee for a line through the township. In Hackensack, company representatives were busy the week of 27 June 1896 securing signatures on a petition for a franchise on Main St. A number of property owners along Main St. and the famous Oritani Field Club signed in favor of the railway.

Franchises could be expensive. In East Rutherford, Union Traction was required to widen Hackensack St. to 60 feet for the full length of the borough, paying 90 percent of the cost, and to grade and macadamize the street from curb-to-curb.

This required moving several houses. The company was given one year to complete the work and required to post a $10,000 construction bond. A 5-cent fare was mandated and turnouts prohibited except at the carhouse. After 1901, the company was required to pay a percentage of gross earnings to the borough.

The Berlin Iron Bridge Co. of Connecticut commenced the East Rutherford carhouse, adjacent to the Erie RR on the east side of Hackensack St., during August 1896, under the direction of C.J. Field, Chief Engineer. The car house was 97 ft. x 100 ft., adjoining were offices' storeroom and repair shop. Union Traction received the deed to the carhouse property on 9 February 1897. The brick powerhouse was built directly behind and contiguous to the carhouse. The engine room was 50 ft. x 65 ft. and the boiler room was 40 ft. x 65 ft. The corrugated steel roof was supported by steel trusses. The powerhouse housed three 320 horsepower Stirling Consolidated water tube boilers, three McIntosh & Seymour steam engines and three 200-kw Crocker Wheeler belt-driven generators.

Contractor Cullin of Paterson began construction between Arlington and East Rutherford car house on 5 October 1896.

The track was completed during the week of 22 November. Construction continued to the Carlstadt boundary, where it was halted from 1 December until the spring of 1897 by a Carstadt ordinance forbidding tearing up of streets during winter.

Union Traction concluded an agreement with the Jersey City, Hoboken & Rutherford for a grade crossing at Hackensack St. and Paterson Ave., East Rutherford. The JCH&R began service to East Rutherford in 2 June 1895 from Jersey City, and the Paterson Passaic & Rutherford commenced running between Paterson and East Rutherford on 3 July 1894.

Ten closed cars with 23-foot 2-inch bodies were ordered from the Jackson & Sharp Co. of Wilmington, Delaware. The cars were painted carmine red with light-yellow trim and lettered "Newark, Rutherford and Hackensack." The cars had 8 windows on each side, were 33 feet long overall, were equipped with two GE1000 motors, two K-2 controllers, and two Peckham No.14B3 swivel trucks, and were capable of negotiating the 30-foot-radius curves on the line. The cars were equipped with longitudinal seats and lighted with three clusters of three bulbs each. A second order changed one of the

48

coaches to a parlor car named *Oritani* and ordered a replacement coach, plus five 12-bench open cars. Construction delays and financial problems reduced the number of cars finally delivered in April and May 1897 to only five closed cars, numbered 1-5, and two opens numbered 14 and 15. The remaining five coaches and the *Oritani* were sold to the Seaview RR, a line serving Narragansett Pier in Rhode Island. The three surplus open cars were sold to the New Haven RR for electrification of its New Canaan branch in Stamford, Connecticut. An effort to buy nine more identical open cars for the 1898 summer season was no more successful. By delivery time Union Traction was in receivership and the cars became New Haven RR numbers 3513-3521.

Union Traction decorated its open cars for special occasions. A newspaper in July 1898 reported that Superintendent Gale "has arranged a patriotic display on one of the open cars. In place of the incandescent lights in the car, red, white and blue globes were placed alternately, and instead of a headlight, there is a glowing American flag made of red, white and blue lights at the front of the car. The effect is heightened by a real American flag stretched behind the lights."

The Hasbrouck Heights borough council delayed a franchise, demanding that Union Traction build a spur on Franklin Ave. to the New Jersey & New York RR depot. The company agreed provided a right-of-way was secured. It was reported Messrs. Van Gilder, Van Bussum and others had offered a right-of-way from the junction of Passaic Ave. and Terrace Ave. through the Van Bussum ravine to the depot, but nothing happened. By March 1897 the company had decided to avoid the borough and reroute its line from Wood-Ridge to Lodi, then following the old Lodi RR right-of-way to the New Jersey & New York RR and then north into Hackensack. An ordinance was finally signed by Mayor Lawrence on 22 May, omitting the disputed spur.

The Union Traction line was tested on 7 May 1897 between the New York & Greenwood Lake Ry.'s Arlington Depot and Hoboken Road in East Rutherford, a distance of 6.5 miles. On 13 May, the line officially opened when three cars filled with officials from communities along the route left the East Rutherford car house at 10:00 a.m. Mayor Turner of Rutherford acted as conductor to Arlington and as a motorman on the return trip.

Union Traction ordered fourteen open cars like number 12 in 1897 and 1898, but only two, numbers 14 and 15, were delivered. The other twelve were sent to the NYNH&H RR New Canaan electric line in Stamford, Connecticut. Credit Delaware State Archives.

The trip was repeated on 19 May. One-way running time was scheduled at 25 minutes with a 15-minute headway, requiring four cars. Fare was 5 cents and at the Arlington depot on Elm St., by walking across the Greenwood Lake Ry., a transfer could be made to Consolidated Traction cars for a 25-minute ride to Broad St., Newark. On 3 May 1897 Union Traction petitioned the Hackensack Commission for a franchise on Green, Essex, and Main streets and over a route to Cherry Hill identical to that granted to the Bergen Turnpike Co. for a horse railway in 1875. After a summer of heated discussions, the company turned down the franchise offered in August because it felt the annual fee of $50,000 was excessive and a route on Kansas St. instead of Essex St. was undesirable. The petition was withdrawn by the company on 15 November 1897.

Construction was completed through Carlstadt to the Wood-Ridge boundary on 1 July. On July 4th Union Traction began service between Arlington and Carlstadt's north boundary — a distance of 7.2 miles. The cost of building the line from Arlington to Carlstadt had been $852,000 — approximately $12,000 per mile. In Wood-Ridge, the company was unable to obtain a right-of-way across the Elizabeth Ann Anderson, Henry Schoonmaker, Henry E. Brinkerhoff and William Brinkerhoff properties. In September 1897 Union Traction instituted litigation to condemn a right-of-way. During November a settlement was reached with Union Traction paying Mrs. Anderson $445 and Mr. Schoonmaker $550 for a right-of-way.

Still financially weak, Union Traction defaulted on its bond interest in December 1897 and was declared insolvent. Senator William M. Johnson of Hackensack was appointed receiver for Union Traction and the Transit Equipment Co. He took possession on 8 January 1898. On 11 November 1898, the suit filed by the Metropolitan Trust Co. to foreclose Union Traction was heard by Vice-Chancellor Pitney in Chancery Chambers. General Electric Co. and Crocker-Wheeler Electric Co. also were attempting to collect $50,049. The litigants were aligned thusly: Metropolitan Trust Co. versus the Union Traction Co., the Pierce & Miller Engineering Co., the Stirling Co., the Berlin Iron Bridge Co. and Crocker-Wheeler Electric Co.; and General Electric Co. versus the Transit Equipment Co., the Union Traction Co., the Berlin Iron Bridge Co., the Pierce & Miller Engineering Co., and the Metropolitan Trust Co. The case was decided on 19 December and filed on 10 June 1899. The records were sealed and are not available to this day. On 24 December 1898 the Chancery Court ordered Receiver Johnson to sell all property belonging to Union Traction. It was rumored that at least four competitors were to bid at the foreclosure sale which was set for 27 January 1899.

Until 1899 Union Traction was stymied in its efforts to reach Hackensack because it had no right-of-way through Wood-Ridge and no franchise in Hackensack. The line was mostly single-track except in Rutherford where there was double-track for the full length of the borough. The route, beginning at Arlington depot of the New York & Greenwood Lake Ry., ran on the east side of Elm St. to Belleville Turnpike, west along the north side of the turnpike and north on the west side of Ridge Road through North Arlington. It crossed to the east side of Ridge Road through Union Township to Valley Brook Ave., then ran west to Stuyvesant Ave. and north to Park Ave., Rutherford. The double-track on Park Ave. and Erie Ave. to the East Rutherford car house was about 1.4 miles long. North of the car house the single-track ran on Hackensack St., west on Division St. in Carlstadt, and north on Monroe to the Wood-Ridge boundary.

Newark & Hackensack Traction Company

Early in January 1899 a committee was formed to restructure Union Traction. William C. Giles, secretary of the committee, represented 90 per cent of the bondholders. The other committee members were W.G. McCormick and W.G. Street, both of the New York Stock Exchange; F.N. Pierce, a large creditor; and J.H. Coon, a large bondholder. The $1 million bonded debt was reduced to $500,000. Bondholders received new bonds at 40 percent of face value of the old bonds and the creditors received 65 percent of their claims, paid in new bonds. Union Traction and Transit Equipment were sold at foreclosure on 27 January 1899 to the reorganization committee by Metropolitan Trust Co. for $20,000. The deed, signed by Senator Johnson on 10 February, was transferred to Giles and wife, of Brooklyn, New York.

The committee met in Hackensack on 20 February 1899 to establish the Newark & Hackensack Traction Co. Giles and his wife deeded Union Traction to the N&H for $1.00. William G. McCormick of Chicago was elected president: William C. Giles of Brooklyn, vice-president and general manager; and John H. Coon of Brooklyn, treasurer. The Newark & Hackensack received its certificate of incorporation on 23 February with a capital stock of $700,000 issued in 14,000 shares. By 1900, Giles was president; Daniel W. Coon of Mt. Vernon, NY, vice president;

John H. Coon, treasurer; and John H. Coon, Jr. of Glen Ridge, N.J., secretary.

When Giles acquired Union Traction, Superintendent G. T. Gale was fired and replaced by Assistant Superintendent Ernest E. Foote, and a wage cut was announced. Conductors were reduced from $2.00 to $1.50 per day, and there were similar reductions in other jobs. The employees struck on 12 February. Giles brought 75 men from New York to the East Rutherford car house on 14 February, but when they learned there was a strike, they refused to work and left. The strikers, after consultation with Superintendent Foote, returned to work on 15 February for 18 cents per hour.

Effective 1 April 1899, the Newark & Hackensack reduced its fare to five cents between Carlstadt and Arlington. This enabled passengers to make the trip to Newark for 10 cents. A 15-minute headway was established by running six cars instead of three, a schedule which would have left only one spare car from the five closed and two open cars on hand. N&H records are fragmentary. However, surviving reports indicate that the closed Jackson & Sharp cars were sold to an unknown purchaser for $8000 in the spring of 1900, allowing payment of outstanding bills to Jackson & Sharp for the cars and Peckham for the trucks. They were replaced by six decaying 16-foot Lewis & Fowler single-truck closed cars (1-6) purchased second hand from Giles S. Allison, sales agent for the Brooklyn Heights Ry., and delivered between December 1899 and March 1900. Four additional Lewis & Fowlers — two 16-foot (7-8) and two 20-foot (9-10) — were acquired from Allison in January 1901. Second-hand cars from the same source were operated by the Elizabeth, Plainfield and Central Jersey St. Ry. Co. The ex-Brooklyn cars were equipped with roof-mounted headlights, whereas the Union Traction double-truck cars had dash-mounted lights. All N&H cars had hand brakes only. The closed cars were heated electrically. The two Union Traction opens, renumbered 20 and 21, remained in service. By 1902, the N&H reported two work cars, one a trailer, but owned no plows or sweepers.

The roof headlights caused one fatality. A newspaper reported on 6 Decem-

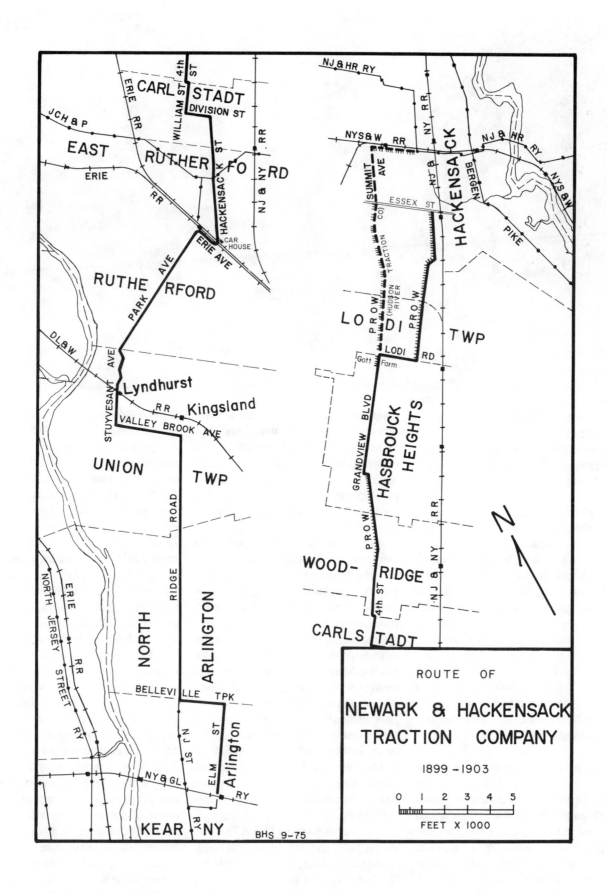

ROUTE OF

NEWARK & HACKENSACK TRACTION COMPANY

1899 - 1903

0 1 2 3 4 5

FEET X 1000

Newark & Hackensack cars 5 and 7 in front of the Erie RR depot at Station Square, Rutherford. These cars served the N&H line between 1900 and 1903.

ber 1899 that motorman Clarence Smith of Carlstadt was killed by his own car as he was leaving the East Rutherford car house at 6 a.m. It seems that Smith, as he took his car out of the car house into Hackensack St., looked up toward the headlight on the roof of the car, and his conductor saw him catch hold of the roof and raise himself by his hands. He wore a pair of gloves and just as his head reached the level of the roof, he lost his hold and fell backward over the front of the car. The motorbox struck Smith's head as he fell under the car and became wedged so that the car had to be raised by jacks.

The new management set out to continue the advance to Hackensack and applied to the Hasbrouck Heights council on 13 May 1899 to revise its franchise on the Boulevard to Madison Ave., then east on Madison and north on Terrace Ave. into Hackensack. Because consents had not been obtained from Madison Ave. property owners and the borough op-

posed use of Terrace Ave., the application was denied on 19 June. Finally, on 19 January 1900, the Hasbrouck Heights council granted a franchise to operate on the Boulevard, east on Lodi Ave. to a point 250 feet east of Terrace Ave., then north across open land on a private right-of-way into Hackensack.

During May 1899 it was reported that there were three companies attempting to secure a franchise on Main St., Hackensack. These were Bergen County Traction, building towards Hackensack from Leonia; the Newark & Hackensack; and the Saddle River Traction Co. interests who proposed a line between Passaic and Hackensack via Lodi. The first meeting between the Hackensack Commission and the N&H took place on 9 June 1900 when a route on Essex and Main streets was discussed, but no action taken. In the meantime, Edward E. Poor granted the N&H permission to run through his property, located west of the NJ&NY RR, from his south property line to Essex St.

For over three years Union Traction and the N&H had difficulties with North Arlington Borough. On 6 July 1897 the North Arlington Council had notified Union Traction to repair streets over which

it ran within five days. The notice was ignored despite repeated threats. The company also failed to pay a one percent franchise tax and the council notified the company that unless it paid the $441 due for 1897 and 1898 the franchise would be revoked. In July 1899, borough authorities under Mayor Bayliss' orders seized and sold several of the company's cars, buying them in at $1.00 each, there being no other bidders. Notice was also given that the trolleys would be halted until the taxes were paid. The N&H secured an injunction on 24 July 1899 restraining the borough from seizing the cars.

The N&H again went before Vice-Chancellor Pitney on 4 June 1900 to get an injunction preventing Mayor Bayliss and the North Arlington council from interfering with the company's repairing of tracks and improving its roadbed. The council contended that the company had forfeited its franchise as it had failed to pay for its privileges and its taxes,to run cars properly, and to keep its tracks in repair. It was also alleged that the company was changing the grade of its roadbed on Belleville Turnpike.

During October, 1899 representatives of the Saddle River Traction Co. and the N&H appeared before the Lodi Town-

ship Committee to apply for a franchise to operate on or near Polifly Road. No action was taken, but at a subsequent meeting the Committee refused to grant a franchise to either company.

At the Hasbrouck Heights Council meeting of 25 October 1899 the views of the Saddle River Traction Co., represented by counsellor Moore, Gilbert Bogert and David Young, and the Newark & Hackensack, represented by counsellor Thompson and William C. Giles, were heard. David Young appeared first and stated that the Saddle River Traction Co. would build from Lodi to the NJ&NY RR on Lodi Road, then north into Hackensack; and a second route from Lodi Road south on the Boulevard to the boundary with Wood-Ridge provided his company received the franchise. Young said his railway would be completed by 1 August 1900 using grooved girder rails and block pavement between the rails. William C. Giles of the N&H argued that no other traction company could receive a franchise from Wood-Ridge and that his company needed the Hasbrouck Heights franchise in order to reach Hackensack. Public sentiment seemed to favor the Saddle River Traction Co. because of the N&H's delays in starting

construction north of Carlstadt. However, the mayor and council felt the N&H offered the much-needed access to Erie RR trains at Rutherford and granted the N&H a franchise on 19 January 1900. This required operation within six months after 1 March 1900 under a penalty of $3,000.

The Hasbrouck Heights franchise closed the gap between Wood-Ridge and Hackensack. In Wood-Ridge, the N&H was deeded rights-of-way across the Elizabeth Ann Anderson estate on 8 February 1900, the Henry Schoonmaker estate on 10 February and the Henry E. Brinkerhoff estate on 26 February. A condemnation proceeding against William Brinckerhoff, executor for the Hiram W. Davis estate, was settled on 10 June 1901. During the last week of March, 1900 the N&H began grading its right-of-way through Wood-Ridge. In Hasbrouck Heights Mayor Lawrence shoveled the first spade of dirt on 24 March 1900 to commence construction there; 50 men and 10 teams went to work building the line between Wood-Ridge and the Gott Farm in Hasbrouck Heights. Construction of the railway and overhead was completed through Wood-Ridge and on 12 May 1900 N&H cars began running

This view of N&H car 3 at the Franklin Ave. turnout on the Boulevard, Hasbrouck Heights is an example of the decaying ex-Brooklyn cars which were used on the line between 1900 and 1903.

from Arlington to the north end of Wood-Ridge.

The Jersey City, Hoboken & Paterson St. Ry. Co. which had consolidated the Saddle River Traction Co. on 1 November 1899 obtained a writ of certiorari on 3 April 1900 temporarily delaying the N&H's progress through Hasbrouck Heights. Saddle River Traction's application alleged the ordinance granting a franchise to the N&H was not passed in accordance with a law which required that such an ordinance first be read at a public meeting of the borough council.

The N&H also had difficulty in obtaining a right-of-way across the Enoch Vreeland, Kingsland and Gott farms in Hasbrouck Heights. On 23 May 1900, 200 laborers laid tracks across the Kingsland farm at the south end of Hasbrouck Heights in a preemptive strike which began at 11:45 p.m. At 8:30 a.m. Mayor Lawrence, cheered by 500 spectators, guided the first N&H car to Passaic Ave. in Hasbrouck Heights. An application was made on 2 June 1900 for condemnation of a right-of- way across the Kingsland farm. Construction advanced rapidly. By 9 June cars were running to Kipp Ave. and reached Central Ave. by 3 July. A force of men started construction at Essex St., Hackensack opposite the W. C. Thomas' house on 4 June grading a private right-of-way.

By July 1900 the track was completed on the Boulevard to the south property line of the Gott Farm. An injunction filed on 5 July and served on the N&H on 27 July, restrained the company from erecting poles across the Gott Farm to carry feed wires to the tracks on Lodi Road. The 500-foot gap in the track required passengers to walk to the next car ahead and Outwater, the tenant on the Gott Farm, granted permission for this procedure. The newspapers reported that on the evening of 14 September 1900 the Newark & Hackensack erected a tall pole on each side of the Gott Farm to suspend

Newark and Hackensack Traction Co.

WEEK DAY SCHEDULE.

In effect Saturday, Nov. 9, 1901

CARS GOING NORTH

Leave Power House. A. M. 5.0), 5:30 and 6 00.

Leave Rutherford Depot 6:30 a m. and every half hour thereafter until 12 p. m. Last car 12:45 a. m.

Special cars for Hasbrouck Heights 5:42 p. m., 6:15 p. m. and 6:45 p. m.

CARS GOING SOUTH.

Leave Hackensack every half hour from 5:30 a. m. to 12:30 a. m. Last car leaves 1:15 a. m.

Leave Rutherford Depot at 5:30 a. m. 6:00 a. m. and every half hour thereafter until 11:30 p. m.

Sunday Schedule.—The same schedule will be observed on Sundays that is in effect week days, with the exception that the first car for Arlington will leave Rutherford depot at 6.00 and Arlington at 6:30 a. m.; the first car leaving Rutherford depot for Hackensack 6:00 a m., leaving Hackensack at 6:30 a. m.

Special Hasbrouck Heights cars will not be run on Sundays.

the trolley feedwire 500 feet across the farm. On the same night beginning at 11:00 p.m. a force of 100 men went to work constructing the line north of Lodi Road on a proposed street named Crescent Ave. across lands of E.B. Merritt, Mortimer Sanford's "consolidated farm" and the Myers property into Hackensack. A trolley car was hauled across the Gott Farm to the track on Lodi Road.

A different version of the pole crossing was given in a Court of Chancery hearing on 4 February 1901: "An injunction was served upon the Newark & Hackensack Traction Co. on 27 July 1900 which had been filed on 5 July 1900. The present litigation is for violation of the injunction when on 12 September 1900, Giles conveyed to the traction company the one-fourth interest in the 80-foot strip which had been conveyed to him by Gott's executrix. On 20 September 1900, Outwater, the tenant in possession of the farm, gave the Newark & Hackensack Traction Co. his consent to suspend over the farm, where the right-of-way of the N&H crossed, two feedwires from poles erected at points north and south of the farm boundaries. On 5 October 1900, Outwater assigned his lease to the Newark & Hackensack Traction Co. and the Newark & Hackensack Traction Co. relet to Outwater the use of the farm and buildings except for the 80-foot wide strip. Before making the leases, the Newark & Hackensack Traction Co. on the night of Saturday 22 September 1900 and Sunday 23 September 1900, strung and suspended two feedwires across the strip from poles outside the farm boundaries."

N&H President Giles swore out a warrant for the arrest of Captain Addison Ely, President of the Bergen County Herald Publishing Co., and Henry H. Copeland and Edward J. Luce, of the law firm of Copeland, Luce and Kipp, on 20 June 1900 on a charge of conspiring to publish a libel against the traction company in the *Bergen County Herald*. Giles filed a law suit on 31 May against Captain Ely and the paper

asking damages of $50,000. Giles cited statements by Ely printed in the *Herald* alleging that the Union Traction reorganization committee had elected themselves officers of the N&H, voted themselves stocks to the disparagement of the large bondholders and managed the affairs of the railway inequitably.

One of the obstacles to the entrance into Hackensack was the 18-foot high embankment of the abandoned Lodi Branch RR. On Sunday evening, 16 September 1900, the N&H construction force cut through the embankment without permission from the railroad and at 4:30 a.m. on 17 September, the first car ran on the new track through the cut to follow the track laying forces into Hackensack. The New Jersey & New York RR, at 3:00 a.m. on 4 October, commenced tearing up the traction company's track in the cut and filled in the breach. The railroad enclosed its property with wire fences and put up warning notices against trespassers. An agreement between the railroad and traction company was reached several days later and the trolley tracks were restored in a new cut.

On 18 September 1900, Mortimer Sanford obtained an injunction restraining the N&H from crossing his farm. The farm was referred to as the "Consolidated Farm" because it was reportededly owned by the Jersey City, Hoboken & Paterson St. Ry. which was formed by consolidation of several street railways. On 2 October an N&H car was hauled across the "Consolidated Farm" to Hackensack and the next morning, the N&H commenced through service between Arlington and Hackensack to within 450 feet of the Essex St. railroad station. Passengers had to transfer cars twice due to track gaps at Gott Farm and the "Consolidated Farm." The *Rutherford American* reported that an N&H car carried five passengers in the Hackensack Commission on the morning of 18 September 1900 and that tracks would be completed to Essex St. by 22 September.

As a result of a hearing on 4 February 1901, the N&H settled with the heirs of the Gott farm by payment of $1,000 for a 25-foot-wide right-of-way. On 18 March 1901, the N&H commenced construction across the farm and began running cars on the new track on 26 March.

Union Traction car 15 was retained by the Newark & Hackensack, probably as car 21 and eventually wound up on Public Service Railway. Shown here on Park Ave. near Addison St. in 1898.

David Young of the JCH&P and William C. Giles of the N&H, rivals for entry into Hackensack, had a second encounter before the Lodi council on 5 November 1900. Young wanted to extend the Saddle River line from Garfield into Lodi. Giles, already possessing property owners' consents on his proposed route, wanted to extend the N&H from Hasbrouck Heights west on Lodi Road and south on Main St. to Garfield. It was reported that Giles was purposely "bottling up" the JCH&P in Lodi as a response to the JCH&P's efforts to stop the N&H from crossing the Sanford farm.

In December 1900, the N&H announced fare and schedule changes: "On and after 11 December 1900, the rates of fares are as follows: Arlington to Lyndhurst, 5 cents; Lyndhurst to Carlstadt, 5 cents; and Carlstadt to Hackensack, 5 cents. Transfers will be given over the Gott Farm and Sanford farm. For the accomodation of those desiring to attend court, passengers will be carried to and from Hackensack between 6:55 a.m. and 9:55 a.m. and 2:55 p.m. and 6:35 p.m. On and after Tuesday, 11 December 1900, cars will leave Hackensack on a 20-min-ute headway in the above hours. Regular service will begin as the work on the track is completed." The Hackensack terminus was located at the intersection of South Newman and Essex streets, 400 feet west of the Essex St. railroad station.

An application was made by the JCH&P on 19 April 1901 for a receiver for the Newark & Hackensack. At a hearing on 7 May, Giles laughed at what he said was a last ditch attempt of the JCH&P to force him out of Hackensack. In another action, Bergen Turnpike Co., a wholly-owned JCH&P subsidiary, filed for a franchise in Hackensack on 4 March 1901 to prevent the N&H from extending beyond Essex St. over the same route wanted by the Bergen Pike trolley line.

The gross receipts of the Newark & Hackensack were $19,873 in 1899; $27,692 in 1900; and $47,393 in 1901. Despite the substantial increase in receipts, the N&H was unable to meet its commitments for improvements and extensions. It was necessary to sell $500,000 in bonds to the Guarantee Trust Co. of New York on 1 July 1901.

The franchise granted by Rutherford to Union Traction in 1895, required construction of a line within five years on Rutherford Ave., Orient Way, Washington Ave., Cedar St., Carmita Ave., and part of Erie Ave. west of Park Ave. which formed a "U." By March, 1901 the five years had elapsed and the N&H was called upon to appear before the Rutherford borough council on 2 July 1901 to show why the part of the franchise referring to the above route should not be repealed. That portion of the franchise was repealed by the council on 1 October.

The final gap in the N&H's track was closed in August 1901, when the company paid Mortimer Sanford $500 for a 240-foot long right-of-way across the "Consolidated Farm." The company had applied for commissioners to examine and appraise Sanford's land and assess damages for condemnation under eminent domain. The arguments were heard by Circuit Court Judge Gray on 24 June 1901. The first through cars between Arlington and Hackensack began operation across the "Sanford Strip" on 25 August 1901. The "dinky" car shuttling between Essex St. and Sanford's property was discontinued.

During October and November 1901 the Hasbrouck Heights council considered amending the N&H's franchise to include the right-of-way across the Gott Farm. This involved a franchise to cross Lodi Road for a new route into Hackensack and opening up the Boulevard across the Gott Farm.

With track gaps and shuttle cars eliminated, two dinky cars became available as waiting-rooms at each end of the line. On 6 December 1901 it was reported that the N&H was reluctant to provide a pot-belly stove for the waiting room car at the Essex St. terminus since the stove at the Arlington terminus had been stolen by several boys.

On 24 January 1902, sometime after midnight, thieves cut away 1500 feet of copper wire over the Gott Farm and the Boulevard and cars had to coast between Washington Ave. and Lodi Road. The first car to Hackensack discovered the gap at 5:30 a.m. and sent word to Superintendent Allen. Later in the day it was necessary for passengers to walk across the Gott Farm as cars from Hackensack could not gain sufficient momentum to coast across the gap due to the sharp curve at Lodi Road. The missing feed wire was replaced on 26 January with wire bought from the New Jersey & Hudson River Ry. & Ferry Co. Thieves struck again on 21 February when 800 feet of trolley wire was stolen above Lodi Road at Hasbrouck Heights.

The Rutherford car house was built in 1897 and is shown here in 1911 or 1912. NJ&HR car 25 is signed for Hackensack. PSRy sprinkler 5015, built by Taunton, formerly NJ&HR 7 is in the far right bay.

The N&H employed a "police car" to catch the thieves. The men in charge of the car sneaked over the line after midnight without lights in hope of catching the marauders unawares. The car never succeeded in getting on the track of the thieves, but did manage to get off its own track several times. On 10 March 1902 a passenger on an N&H trolley had to walk from Lodi Road at Hasbrouck Heights to Hackensack early in the morning while other passengers waited in the car until the "obstruction" was cleared away. The "obstruction" was the "police car" which had derailed because the motorman had not seen a switch in the wrong position. The night before, the "police car" crashed into a bakery wagon, causing one witness to the accident to remark: "If the trolley Hawkshaws couldn't see an object as large as a bakery wagon, how in the name of goodness could they be expected to see

wire thieves." On 10 March 1903, the N&H again placed two "police cars" into service to catch wire thieves in North Arlington.

Heavy snowstorms hit Bergen County during February 1902, particularly on 18 February when it seems the storm was more severe in the vicinity of Rutherford than Hackensack. The N&H was closed for almost a week in an effort to clear snowdrifts along the tracks reported to be 6 to 7 feet deep in Wood-Ridge, Rutherford and Kingsland.

The familiar trick of motormen "stealing" a switch was tried unsuccessfully on the N&H on the morning of 3 March 1902. Two cars crashed head-on in the early morning fog in Wood-Ridge on the private right-of-way. It was reported that northbound car 4 with motorman Weller at the controller left the turnout at Carlstadt on Monroe St. five minutes late. Southbound car 2 with motorman Weldman at the controller had the right of way and because it was foggy, it proceeded slowly south from the Harrison Ave. turnout at Hasbrouck Heights on the single-track line when car 4 came into sight. Car 2 was stopped immedi-

ately and put into reverse, but 4 crashed into 2 tearing off the vestibules of both cars. Weller's left foot was crushed and Weldman's head was severely cut, but none of the few passengers were injured. The N&H had discharged Weller in 1901 for carelessness, but had rehired him after a period of probation.

The N&H never received good publicity from the *Bergen Record* and the paper was ready to amplify any misfortune which beset the trolley line. The editor of the *Bergen Record* newspaper devised the name "Nappy and Hackneyed Tackey Co., the rag-time trolley line which wends its way over a jagged course through vales, ravines and jungles from Arlington to the County Seat." The N&H was apparently unable to employ sufficient manpower to operate the cars on regular schedules; "nothing better than rag-time can be made." The employees running the cars were sometimes obliged to work up to 18 hours per day. This was especially true during the Winter of 1901-02 when the slightest amount of snow would disrupt schedules completely: Sometimes N&H cars wouldn't run for a few days because of deep snow drifts.

The Rutherford power house was located behind the car house and erected at the same time. Photo taken on 28 January 1916.

Excitement for N&H passengers seemed endless. An incident on 13 May 1902 gave the passengers on car 7 a bad scare when, near Hackensack, the trolley wire broke and fell across the car setting it on fire. The repair car was sent for and the wire was speedily restored.

The *Bergen Record* of 6 September 1902 noticed the passing of the N&H water sprinkler thusly: "For the first time since its construction, for the first time since its dirty cars first passed through Hasbrouck Heights raising clouds of dust, for the first time after innumerable appeals for help, the sprinkling cart has at last appeared on the N&H."

Hudson River Traction Co.

In 1902, the New Jersey & Hudson River set out to gain control of the financially-troubled N&H. The NJ&HR management organized the Hudson River Traction Co. and received its incorporation certificate on 21 March 1902. The officers were A. Merritt Taylor of Philadelphia, president; Frank R. Ford of New York City, vice president; and William N. Barrows of New York City, treasurer and secretary. The office was located in the Edgewater ferry house at the foot of Dempsey Ave. Following negotiations between Hudson River Traction and N&H managements, Hudson River Traction purchased the interests of a majority of N&H bond and stockholders, and took control of the property by the election of a new Board of Directors on 20 November 1902. This caused general rejoicing in the areas served by the old company.

The N&H had defaulted on the bond interest due on 1 July 1902 to the Guarantee Trust Co. of New York which applied through its counsel for a receiver. On 12 January 1903, State Senator Edmund W. Wakelee was appointed.

Frank R. Ford, of the engineering firm of Ford, Bacon & Davis, examined the roadway, track and equipment of the Newark & Hackensack Traction Co., and issued a report dated 6 January 1903, stating that "The said railway, its road and property is dilapidated and out of repair, and greatly in need of reconstruction and improvement. That it is inadequately furnished with properly constructed cars and equipment to enable it to render proper service and meet the demand of the public, and by that reason of its condition, want of repair, maintenance and equipment, its income is largely diminished and it will require more money to place it in suitable condition and equip it properly so as to serve the public as it should, than it would probably receive from its tolls and income after deducting the expense of running cars.

"The portion of the track between Essex St., Hackensack and the junction of Terrace Ave. in Hasbrouck Heights, being single track a distance of 7000 feet, is in extremely bad condition for comfortable and economical running of the cars. This portion of the track was constructed of second-hand rails, and is in the worst condition of any of the track of the Company, as practically all of the joints of this section are low and the rail is surface bent, making it impractical to remedy this condition without largely renewing the rails.

57

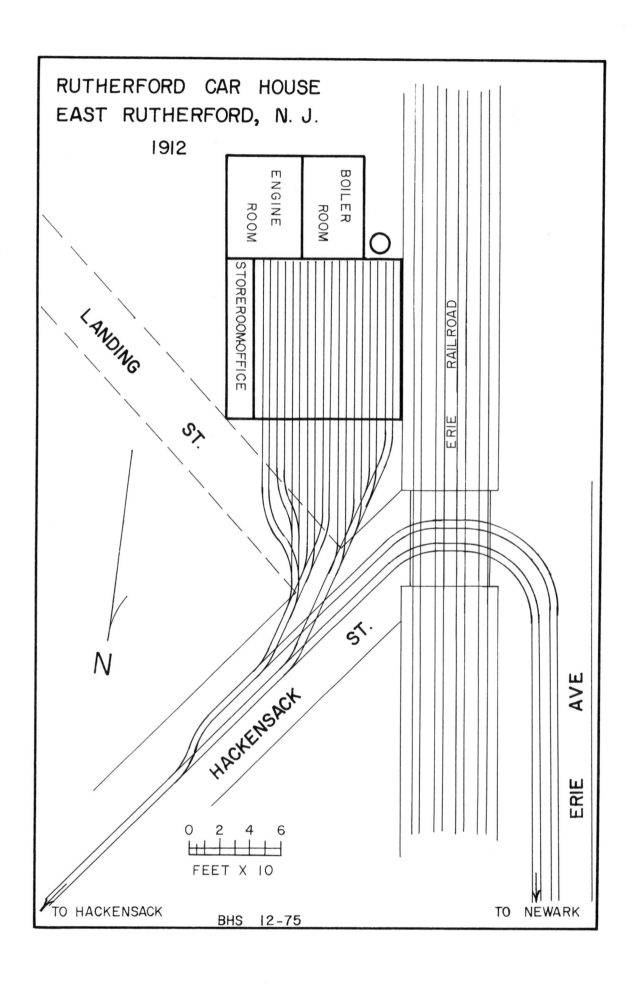

RUTHERFORD CAR HOUSE
EAST RUTHERFORD, N. J.
1912

ENGINE ROOM

BOILER ROOM

STOREROOM·OFFICE

ERIE RAILROAD

LANDING ST.

N

HACKENSACK ST.

ERIE AVE

0 2 4 6
FEET X 10

TO HACKENSACK

TO NEWARK

BHS 12-75

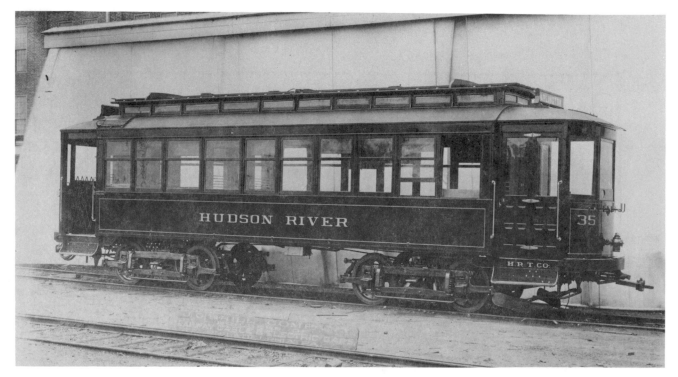

"At the Hasbrouck Heights end of this section of track, on private property east of Terrace Ave., there is located a curve of short radius at the foot of a steep grade. The conditions at this point are such as to render it dangerous to operate cars, as they are liable to derailment. [A northbound N&H car toppled over on its side here on 2 December 1902 without injuring its occupants.]

"At a number of other points on the line from Hasbrouck Heights to Arlington, it is necessary to renew ties, and to resurface and reline the track in order to enable cars to be run safely and comfortably. There are also curves and switches which should be renewed.

"The car and power house of the Company, located at East Rutherford, and constructed of galvanized iron, has not been painted since it was erected in 1897. As a result, the iron is rusting, and so causing serious leaks. This should be repaired and the building painted.

"The car equipment consists of short single-truck cars, which were purchased about 3 years ago, secondhand. These are in poor repair, and are extremely uncomfortable to ride in, due to the fact that in some cars the window sashes are loose, permitting the entrance of cold air, and the doors and flooring are also loose, causing the car to rack, and being single-truck cars and not in good repair, any motion of the car at a fair rate of speed will cause them to jolt severely. The platforms of many of these cars are in such condition as to be liable to drop with a heavy load. These cars are wholly unfit for modern first class operation. The condition of the cars and track is notorious among the residents of the section served, and has been also severely condemned by various newspapers published in that section. There are only two first class cars on the road, these are summer cars, the others being of the description above set forth.

"Although this road operates over fourteen miles of track, it is insufficiently provided with equipment for removing snow, and should be furnished with a snow-sweeper."

The N&H was sold at the office of the County Sheriff at Hackensack on Tuesday, 1 September 1903 at 3:00 p.m. The line was bought for $60,000 by Henry C. Everdell of New York City, one of the three original incorporators of Hudson River Traction, who conveyed the title to the new company. The acquisition was approved on 29 September 1903. The New Jersey & Hudson River Ry. & Ferry Co. formally leased the Hudson River Traction Co. effective on 15 April 1904. N&H motormen and conductors had already begun wearing Hudson River line uniforms in March.

Car 35, shown at the Brill plant in 1903, was one of four cars bought by Hudson River Traction to replace the old N&H single-truck cars.

Hackensack Heights Exten.

One of the first goals of the new company was construction of a new line into Hackensack from Hasbrouck Heights. On 15 October 1902 Hudson River Traction applied to the Hackensack Commission for a route beginning at First St., Hackensack to run alongside of the NYS&W RR, south on Summit to Beech St. and over a private right-of-way to Essex St. continuing southeast to Prospect Ave. and curving southwest over a private right-of-way to a connection with the N&H at Lodi Road and the Boulevard in Hasbrouck Heights. The franchise was granted on 12 January 1903 and construction began on 13 April. The new route was named the Hackensack Heights extension by newspapers and was completed on 30 July.

Hudson River Traction and the NJ&NY RR concluded an agreement on 23 September 1903 permitting the Hackensack Heights extension to cross the

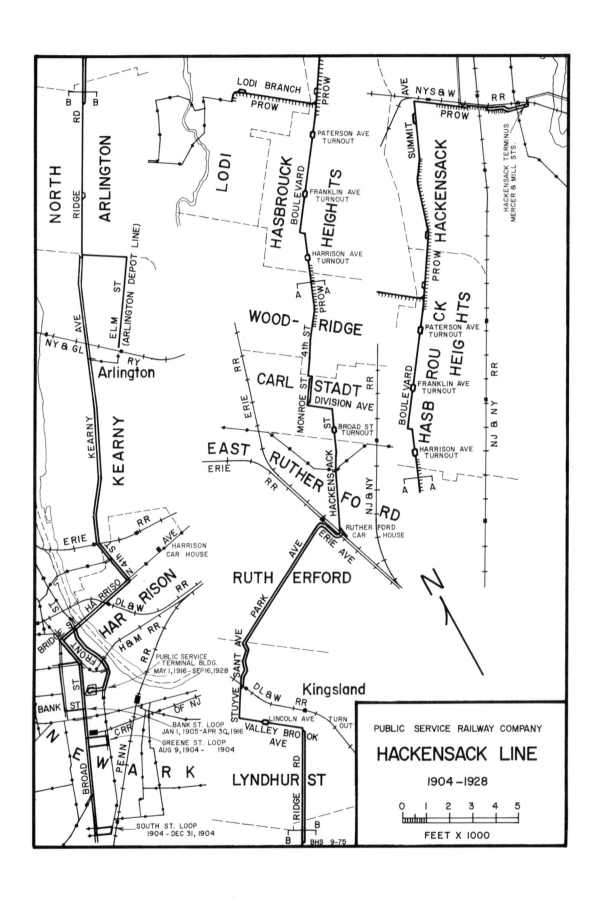

NORTH ARLINGTON

LODI

LODI BRANCH
PROW
PROW

NYS&W
PROW

RR

B B
RD
RIDGE

ARLINGTON

PATERSON AVE
TURNOUT

SUMMIT AVE

HACKENSACK TERMINUS
MERCER & MILL STS.

ELM ST
(ARLINGTON DEPOT LINE)

HASBROUCK BOULEVARD

HEIGHTS

FRANKLIN AVE
TURNOUT

HACKENSACK PROW

NY & GL
AVE
KEARNY
RY
Arlington

HARRISON AVE
TURNOUT

HASBROUCK HEIGHTS

KEARNY

WOOD- RIDGE

A PROW A
4th ST

PATERSON AVE
TURNOUT

CARL STADT

DIVISION AVE

ERIE RR

MONROE ST

ST

RR

FRANKLIN AVE
TURNOUT

BOULEVARD

NJ & NY RR

EAST RUTHER FO RD

ERIE

BROAD ST
TURNOUT

HARRISON AVE
TURNOUT

ERIE RR

HACKENSACK

NJ & NY

A A

AVE
HARRISON
CAR HOUSE

RUTHER FORD
CAR HOUSE

ERIE
N 4th ST

HARRISO

RUTH ERFORD

ERIE AVE

HAR RISON

DL&W RR

RR

PARK AVE

N

BRIDGE ST
FRONT ST
H&M RR
RR

PUBLIC SERVICE
TERMINAL BLDG.
MAY 1,1916-SEP16,1928

BANK ST

STUYVESANT AVE

Kingsland

DL&W RR
TURN OUT

CRR
OF NJ

BANK ST. LOOP
JAN 1, 1905-APR 30, 1916

LINCOLN AVE

N E W

GREENE ST. LOOP
AUG 9,1904-   1904

VALLEY BROOK
AVE

PENN

PUBLIC SERVICE RAILWAY COMPANY

A R K

HACKENSACK LINE

BROAD ST

RIDGE RD

LYNDHURST

1904-1928

SOUTH ST. LOOP
1904 - DEC 31, 1904

B B

0 1 2 3 4 5

B

BHS 9-75

FEET X 1000

abandoned Lodi Branch RR. The first car over the extension ran on the morning of 29 September. It was one of the N&H open cars which carried Hudson River line officials and ran through from Hackensack to the East Rutherford car house. Following directly behind the official car was a construction car with a number of laborers who, after arriving at the East Rutherford car house, started work on changing the tracks and making improvements in and around the property.

On 11 July 1903, Hudson River Traction ordered four cars (#34-37) from J.G. Brill Co. (Order 12941) for the extension. However, regular service was delayed when a test run on 2 October 1903 revealed that the turnouts were too short and the double tracks too close together to allow the new cars to pass each other. Further delays resulted from demands by Rutherford that the company pave Park Ave. at a cost of $60,000 after respacing the tracks, and by East Rutherford to widen and dress down Hackensack St. at a cost of $40,000. Local papers reported that regular service would commence at 5:40 a.m. on 3 December 1903. However, because agreement between Hudson River Traction and the two Rutherfords had not been reached, the opening was delayed until 7 December. The Hackensack terminal was established on Mercer St. at the NYS&W RR depot.

Because of delays in track changes required for use of the new cars, it was necessary to keep the old N&H cars running, but on a faster schedule, until the trackwork was completed. Car 2 was taken to Leonia Junction on the NJ&HR during January 1903 for use as a waiting-room. In April, it was taken to the Edgewater terminal where it was laid up and described as almost a wreck. On 11 May 1903, car 1 was laid up for two weeks for repairs, and car 7 was equipped with new springs, wheels and electric gear.

Several days after the Hackensack Heights extension opened, a *Bergen Record* reporter made the following comments after a ride on one of the old cars: "If we continue to run these old cars at the rate of speed they have been running the last three days," remarked the N&H trolley conductor, "there won't be anything left of them in a couple of weeks but

the wheels." The car was humping itself at a lively clip over the Hackensack Heights extension at the time and the anxious expression worn by the *Record* reporter who was nervously watching the motorman no doubt occasioned the remark.

"Don't you think these cars will stand the pace?" inquired the reporter without taking his eyes off the motorman and the track ahead.

"Hardly," said the conductor. "Why, yesterday the moulding and a piece of the roof fell off my car at Carlstadt. The shaking up the old things are now getting is something awful and I expect to see them disappear in installments." By this time the car was whizzing down the hill south of Essex St. on the private right-of-way with the swiftness of a toboggan on an icy slide.

"You see, we have to run this way in order to maintain schedule time," said the conductor. "We are only allowed a half-hour between the Susquehanna depot and the Rutherford depot, and it just keeps these old hasbeen arrangements hustling to get there. You don't notice the strain on them so much while they're running over those new heavy rails, but wait till we hit the crooked worn-out tracks on the old line, then you'll hear the creaking and feel the rocking."

"Well, now just watch the difference," said the conductor, as the car ran across Lodi Road and onto the old rails on Grandview Boulevard in Hasbrouck Heights. Instantly there was a slammety-bang, humpety-bumpety, whangety-whang movement that caused every timber in the car to creak and groan and made it very difficult for the *Record* reporter to keep from sliding along the slippery cane seat into the lap of a stout woman who had braced her shoulder against the rear platform of the car. "Its a new roadbed we need on this end of the route," said the conductor, "and then even these old dinkys would run smoothly."

The accelerated schedule took its toll upon the old N&H cars. Car No. 7 derailed at First St., Hackensack on 1 January 1904 and tied up the Arlington and Lodi cars. Car 9 dropped a motor on Valley Brook Ave. a short distance east of Stuyvesant Ave. in Union township on 17 March. The old cars were finally

replaced by the new Hudson River Traction cars. The first new car to run on a regular schedule was No. 37 on 2 May 1904. The two 12-bench open cars continued in use and were renumbered 67 and 68.

For the accomodation of passengers to the lower end of Hackensack, one of the old cars operated as a shuttle over the old line through the swamp from Essex St. to a connection with the Hackensack-Arlington cars at Lodi Road, Hasbrouck Heights. The Swamp line car did not run for several days after Christmas 1903, and it was reported that service was not resumed because of a lack of patronage.

New fare zones were established: Hackensack to Cleveland Ave., Hasbrouck Heights, 5 cents; Cleveland Ave. to Kingsland, 5 cents; Rutherford to Arlington, 5 cents. Previously, the second fare from Hackensack was collected at Paterson Ave., East Rutherford. On 28 December 1903 the first zone boundary was moved south from Cleveland Ave. to Passaic (Fritsch) Ave., Wood-Ridge.

Since commuters who lived on the ridge in Wood-Ridge and Hasbrouck Heights used Erie RR trains between Rutherford and Jersey City rather than make the mile-long walk to the NJ&NY RR trains at the bottom of the ridge, extra cars were operated beginning in September 1903 to connect with Erie trains at Rutherford. In November additional rush-hour cars were also provided between Rutherford and Kingsland to connect with three Erie commuter trains in the P.M.

The Lodi Extension

Hudson River Traction in January 1904 proposed a connecting branch from its line in Lodi Township between Hackensack and Hasbrouck Heights to join with the Public Service Corporation's Saddle River line at Lodi Borough. Hudson River Traction purchased Mortimer Sanford's "Consolidated Farm" which was 6000 feet long by 250 feet wide. Construction began on 6 April 1904 and was completed on 10 May. The new track diverged from the Hudson River Traction track 500 feet north of Lodi Road and connected with Public Service track at Union St. about 1300 feet east of Main St., Lodi. The right-of-way was shown on maps for many years as St.

HRT car 39 (Brill, 1904) on the Boulevard at Washington Place, Hasbrouck Heights, on the way to Newark.

Joseph Boulevard. The first car over the line left the Susquehanna depot at Hackensack at 6:00 a.m. on 16 May 1904. Public Service cars numbered in the low 1900s were assigned and the route was named Main St. line. The cars ran between Hackensack, Lodi, Garfield, Passaic, Clifton and Paterson on a half-hour headway. The through fare was 10 cents. Hudson River Traction crews operated the Public Service cars between Hackensack and Lodi.

No sooner was the Lodi route opened than protests were heard about the double 5-cent fare charged between Hackensack and Lodi. A loophole in the franchise permitted conductors to collect a second fare after the car crossed West St. The Lodi council resolved the matter and, beginning on 24 May 1904, conductors were not permitted to collect a second fare in Lodi until the car turned the corner just beyond the Post Office.

The Newark-Hackensack Line

Hudson River Traction and the North Jersey St. Ry. (Public Service) agreed to a track connection at Belleville Turnpike on Ridge Road, North Arlington in March 1903. It was completed during the first week of August 1904. Through service between Hackensack and Newark commenced on 9 August using Public Service crews south of Belleville Turnpike. When the Hudson River cars ran through from Hackensack to Newark the crews swapped cars at Belleville Turnpike. The Hudson River conductor on leaving the southbound car took the fare registering clock from the case and the Public Service conductor hung his fare-registering clock in the case and hung the Newark license in the Newark-bound car. On northbound trips the procedure was reversed.

The first Newark terminus was at Broad and Green streets, then it was moved to the Pennsylvania RR's South St. Station. On 1 January 1905, cars began using the Bank St. loop. Hackensack cars entered Newark via Clay St., Broad St. and Central Ave., then south on

Washington St., east on Bank St. and north on Broad St. to Clay. The old Arlington depot line via Belleville Turnpike and Elm St. was continued as a shuttle line and two former Bergen County Traction cars (5 & 6) were renumbered as Hudson River line 18 & 19 and assigned to the shuttle. A Newark newspaper reported in May 1905 that the most spectacular thing in Newark at night are the electric headlights on the Hackensack cars; "They are more powerful than many locomotive headlights and dazzle the eyes that gaze at them."

The Newark cars began running through to Edgewater via Fort Lee and the Hudson River line on Sundays and Holidays commencing on 2 July 1905 between the hours of 10:00 a.m. and 10:00 p.m. Daily through service began on 11 July 1905 on a half-hour headway between 7:25 a.m. and 7:55 p.m. This continued until some time around 1916 when it was reduced to Saturdays, Sundays and Holidays only. On 11 June 1906 Newark & Hackensack cars began running to Edgewater via Morsemere.

During July 1905 the City of Newark stopped Hudson River Traction cars from using the Clay St. bridge spanning the Passaic River claiming it was unsafe for the heavy cars. Hackensack line cars temporarily turned back at Belleville Turnpike, requiring Newark passengers to transfer to Public Service cars at that point. On 2 August 1905 the Hackensack line cars resumed running through Kearny to the Clay St. bridge, where passengers transferred to Kearny line cars to reach downtown Newark. Beginning on 25 May 1907 Hackensack cars resumed service to Bank St. loop over the Bridge St. bridge, leaving Newark's Prudential Building on the hour and half-hour. The Newark Board of Works made an inquiry on 31 July 1907 questioning the right of the Public Service Corporation to make a deal with a company that had no right by any local grant to operate cars and do business within the city limits.

When the low numbered 1900 series cars were taken off the Main St. line in August 1905, they were assigned to the Englewood-Weehawken Joint line. In their place on the Main St. line Public

Service assigned low numbered 1700s.

In the spring of 1906, Public Service Corporation's North Jersey St. Ry. proposed a belt line in Kearny and North Arlington. The North Jersey cars would have run on the Hudson River Traction tracks from Arlington depot to Kearny Ave. and then on North Jersey tracks south on Kearny Ave., east on Midland Ave. and north on Elm St. to the Arlington depot on the south side of the NY&GL Ry. tracks. It was thought that the belt line would benefit residents of the Arlington Heights section. However, on 6 May 1906, the North Arlington borough council refused to allow a 13-foot track connection between the Hudson River Traction on Belleville Turnpike and Public Service on Kearny Ave. and the plan was dropped.

Hudson River Traction had been using an old car body for a waiting room at Belleville Turnpike and Kearny Ave. On 9 April 1906, Mrs. L. G. Calhoun of New York City, owner of the land on which the car body sat, ordered the removal of the car body or the payment of rent. Superintendent Allen of the Hudson River

HRT car 37 (Brill, 1904) at Franklin Ave. Switch, Hasbrouck Heights, ca. 1903-1904. Note the differences from car 39 on the opposite page, which was not built to Ford Bacon & Davis standards.

Traction said the Kearny Board of Aldermen had advised the company to place the carbody there where it would be under the care of Kearny authorities. The traction company did not feel it was justifiable to pay rent for a public convenience and moved the carbody to the northeast corner of the intersection in North Arlington where vandals had previously destroyed company property.

Open car 68 running northbound and due at Hackensack at 6:30 a.m. on 17 August 1906 had arrived at the Cleveland Ave. turnout in Hasbrouck Heights when flames were noticed issuing through the flooring. The local fire department did what it could after extending 1000 feet of hose to the nearest hydrant. However, No. 68 was totally destroyed by the fire leaving nothing but the trucks and steel framework.

The Public Service Terminal in Newark became the terminus of the Newark-Hackensack line after its opening on 30 April 1916. Public Service car 1875, formerly NJ&HR 48, is shown below loading at the terminal on opening day.

At Hackensack about 7:30 a.m. on 13 February 1908 a Newark-bound Hackensack line car collided headon with a Public Service Main St. line car bound for Hackensack. The accident occured on the single-track private right-of-way at the east end of the bridge spanning the NJ&NY RR. The yellow car of the Main St. line, although lighter than the red Hudson River Traction car, had greater speed and telescoped through the platform into the smoking compartment of the Hackensack line car. The crash between the two cars was the worst experienced in Hackensack. The vestibule of the Main St. line car was crushed, but motorman Harry Stephens escaped injury. It was foggy at the time of the collision and it was believed that the Hackensack line motorman, Michael Egan, missed the red signal; he succumbed to his injuries the next evening.

In East Rutherford on 14 November 1907, residents saw the unusual sight of a trolley speeding along through town without either motorman, conductor or passengers. The story goes that the car was standing in front of the car house in East Rutherford where it was left by the crew while they went inside and waited for their regular schedule. When the time came for the car to leave, the crew emerged from the car house only to find the car missing. Believing someone had run it into the car house, they searched but were unable to locate it. The crew became alarmed and notified the assistant superintendent that their car had been stolen. For fifteen minutes there was no end of excitement. Men were sent in every direction to round up the runaway car. The telephone was worked with more alacrity than ever before. Several persons along the route to the White Line crossing at Paterson Ave. reported having seen the car go by, but none dared to stop its progress. Even the police were telephoned to keep an eye out for the missing trolley. Finally the car hove into sight in charge of a former employee. He said that while he was standing near the White Line crossing the car came along. Seeing that it was without a crew, he jumped aboard and took charge. The car was running at half speed when picked up. The mystery of how the car was set in motion was never solved.

The New Jersey & Hudson River reorganized in early 1910 to consolidate its operations. The Hudson River Traction Co., which had been operating as lessee of the NJ&HR since 1904, was merged into the lessor on 25 February 1910. Prior to this action, the principal office of Hudson River Traction was moved from Edgewater and relocated to the East Rutherford car house on 31 January 1910. At this time the Hudson River Traction Co. had outstanding $631,000 in 5 percent mortgage bonds sold to the United States Mortgage and Trust Co. The Riverside & Fort Lee Ferry Co. owned $67,000 of the bonds and the remainder were in public hands.

Public Service Railway Co.

As is discussed in chapter 4, the NJ&HR was acquired by Public Service Corporation on 2 July 1910, and became the Public Service Ry.'s Bergen Division. Beginning 4 August 1910 Main St. line crews began running through between Paterson and Hackensack. On 30 September, Hackensack line crews began running through between Hackensack and Newark.

The Hackensack terminus of the Main St. line was changed from the Susquehanna depot to the corner of State and Gamwell (Trinity) streets during July 1911. Single-end cars were able to reverse directions on a wye on the Gamewell property. This became the site of Pubic Service Coordinated Transport's Hackensack bus garage in 1927. During the winter of 1910-1911, Public Service assigned six 1900-series semi-convertibles to the Hackensack line. Hudson River Traction had previously assigned ten closed and one open car. The two NJ&HR cars, 18 and 19, assigned to the Arlington Depot line, were renumbered by Public Service as 26 and 27.

The railway's East Rutherford power house was leased to the Public Service Electric Co. on 1 March 1913. While under railway operation, its use was limited due to the more efficient generating units of the larger and newer generating stations in Jersey City and Newark. After acquisition by Public Service it operated for two months in 1910, three in 1911, four in 1912 and one in 1913 before being shut down in March. The boilers and

machinery remained in place until it was officially abandoned on 1 March 1921. Public Service had installed a new 13,200-volt feeder from Hackensack to the East Rutherford sub-station located on Van Winkle St. and installed a 300-kw rotary convertor in 1907 to feed power to the Hackensack line.

Beginning on 8 June 1911 Bergen Division lines operating in Hackensack issued free transfers to passengers wishing to travel on connecting lines to points within Hackensack. Effective 1 November 1912, the Hackensack line had its free transfer limit extended to Hasbrouck Heights. A trolley pole designating the transfer limit was marked "T.L." at the corner of Harrison Ave. and the Boulevard. The Main St. line's terminus in Hackensack was changed back to the Susquehanna depot on 11 August 1913 and low-numbered, double-end 1100s replaced the single-end 1700s. Under Public Service Ry., Hackensack line crews and cars operated out of both Harrison and East Rutherford car houses until 22 January 1918 when all operations were transferred to East Rutherford.

The Harrison car line was started on 4 August 1913, duplicating Hackensack line service between Newark and Kearny and terminating at Belleville Turnpike. On 10 July 1916 the Kearny terminus was changed to the south side of the NY&GL Ry.'s Arlington depot on Elm St.

Competition for the trolleys appeared when a bus known as the Blue Line jitney was completed on 18 November 1915 in the Herman T. Backhus shop on Paterson Ave., East Rutherford for a new Hackensack and Newark bus route. The vehicle was described as being of beautiful design, steam heated, and electrically lighted, with a double row of seats, all facing forward, accomodating 25 passengers without crowding. Service over the new bus route, established by Fred Kuhnert of Hackensack and George Leghnig, his nephew, commenced in late November 1915.

Public Service began construction of a new office and terminal building in 1914 at Park Place facing Military Park in Newark. The Hackensack line's Newark terminus was relocated to the upper level of the new Public Service Terminal Building on 30 April 1916. Hackensack

line cars departed from track 4, which it shared with Trenton Fast Line cars. This was the first track to be removed when buses began using the second floor terminal in 1929. Delos F. Wilcox in his book *Analysis of The Electric Railway Problem* disparagingly described the new terminal building thusly: "Out of the desire to decongest the Market and Broad corners during rush hours, to house itself and its subsidiaries conveniently and conspicuously, to secure ample railway facilities on private property adjacent to the Morris Canal, against the day when the canal would be abandoned and its right of way could be secured for rapid transit purposes, grew the Public Service Newark Terminal project splendid, expensive and, from the point of view of Public Service, unsatisfactory. The Public Service Terminal did not solve the problem of adequate trolley service in Newark. It gave partial relief to Broad and Market corners, but failed to provide adequate street car facilities for handling the immense traffic that originates at the Hudson Tubes station on Park Place."

The old Hiram Davis estate in Wood-Ridge was sold on 15 March 1917 to Charles H. Reis by real estate broker Albert Gorab. Gorab convinced Reis that the farm could be sold for residences. The result in 1928 was Sunshine City, a development of over 800 houses on approximately 110 acres on both sides of the Hackensack line right-of-way between Highland Ave. and the Hasbrouck Heights boundary.

At Main Ave., Wood-Ridge, on 5 February 1921 two Hackensack line cars (# 1861 and 1865) crashed headon. The southbound car crashed into the northbound car which was standing still. The injuries of the southbound car's motorman were fatal due to loss of blood.

During the six-day strike of Public Service Ry. employees which commenced on 12 March 1919, the Hackensack line operated intermittently between Hackensack and Rutherford only. On 1 August 1923 railway employees again struck. Service was resumed on the Hackensack line at 1:00 p.m. on 20 September. Main St. line cars resumed service to Hackensack on 21 September, the first car arriving at the Susquehanna depot at 4:00 p.m. During the strike a bus line

The Arlington shuttle was served by a succession of small cars and was one of the first lines converted to one-man operation in 1913. Public Service car 369 (Brill, 1895), a former Consolidated Traction (Newark) car, was used on the shuttle from 1913 to 1923.

Rutherford line was reported as a losing operation and deficits were made up from profits of the Kearny-Arlington lines. There were 34 vehicles on these lines which operated on a 4-minute headway between Newark and Arlington and a 15-minute headway between Newark and Rutherford. The fare between Newark and Rutherford was 15 cents. During the 1923 railway strike the Kearny-Arlington Bus Line reportedly carried 36.5 per cent more passengers. The Hackensack car line began one-man operation on 23 December 1923, as a result of the strike.

began operating between the County Court House in Hackensack and Newark hourly commencing on 2 August 1923. It was not verified, but this service was probably an extension of the bus line which had started service between Hackensack and East Rutherford on 5 April 1922 with one vehicle making 15 trips per day on an irregular schedule which took 30 minutes per trip.

The Kearny-Arlington Bus Line which operated between those places and Newark ran trial service to Rutherford for one year during 1921 and 1922. The Newark-

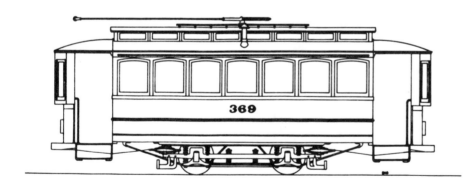

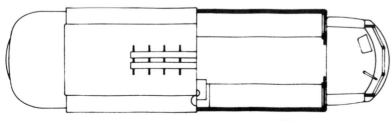

66

NJ&HR cars remained in service on the Newark-Hackensack line throughout the Public Service era. Car 1870 (Stephenson, 1906) was originally NJ&HR 21.

Lyndhurst Township and Public Service Ry. agreed on 23 June 1922 to the removal of the double-track built during 1912 on narrow Stuyvesant Ave. and replacement with single-track. The township approved new turnouts at the Lyndhurst depot of the DL&W RR and at Lincoln Ave. on Valley Brook Ave.

Arlington Depot Line

The Arlington Depot shuttle car resembled the famous Fontaine Fox cartoon "Toonerville Trolley" and was given a lengthy write-up in the 11 March 1923 issue of the *Newark Sunday Call:*: "Joseph C. Yahle of Carlstadt has for nineteen full years commendably filled the role of conductor, motorman, supervisor, inspector and official trolley pole shifter of the Public Service "dinky." Surely the only one in captivity, [it] runs from the New York & Greenwood Lake Ry. depot at Arlington to the Belleville Turnpike and Kearny Ave., North Arlington . . . on a regular 15-minute schedule . . . all for 8 cents [a round trip ride]. . .The conductor-motorman brings his car out at 6:46 a.m. [and] at exactly 12:50 p.m. . . . starts his passengerless car home . . . Joe parks his friend (No. 369) at the East Rutherford car house and goes to dinner at his home

. . . Between 1 and 4 O'Clock then there is no service on the line . . . [Then from] 4 O'Clock . . . until about 7 O'Clock it is a case of drive and prod again until all the weary toilers by day have been lifted to their respective homes." Public Service assigned four cars to the Arlington Depot line — Nos. 38, 174, 184 and 369. Car 369 ran from 1913 until the discontinuance of the 1.12-mile-long line during the 1923 strike. The 38- Kearny-Newark bus line was extended to replace the discontinued shuttle. On 15 May 1924 Kearny announced it proposed to improve Elm St. from the NY&GL depot to Belleville Turnpike by covering the rails of the old car line. Bergen and Hudson counties proposed to improve Belleville Turnpike in the same manner.

Bus Substitution Begins

After formation of the Public Service Transportation Co. on 15 May 1923, Public Service began purchasing competing bus lines and acquired new buses to replace unprofitable trolley lines and those where expensive track repairs were required. Public Service Transportation began service to Rutherford by the 38-Kearny-Newark bus line on 14 July 1924 after purchasing seven independent

buses. In February 1925 PST placed 32 new White model 50-A buses from the 140-175 and 180-193 groups on the 36—Kearny-Arlington and 38—Kearny-Newark bus lines to replace the independent buses. During 1925 the former East Rutherford power house was converted into a bus garage.

Operation of the Rutherford-East Rutherford-Hackensack Bus Co. which had been running since 1 April 1922 was assumed by Public Service on 4 May 1926 as the 12-Hackensack-Rutherford line. The original route avoided the steep hill on Hackensack St. at Carlstadt and traversed the back streets from Summit Ave. via 2nd St. and Boiling Springs Ave. to the Triangle Park near the Rutherford Depot of the Erie RR. The bus company owned six buses — two Garfords, two Whites and one Pierce Arrow — which were renumbered 1708-1713 by Public Service and scrapped in 1928, and one Reo traded in for a Yellow Coach bus. During May, June and July 1928, Public Service placed the 2500-series gasoline-electric buses in service and Nos. 2580-2584 were assigned to the 12-Hackensack-Rutherford line. The 12—Hackensack-Rutherford line was extended to Ten Eyck Ave., Lyndhurst on 9 August 1931. On 20 May 1934 the line was merged into the 102—Hackensack-Newark bus line.

The city of Passaic on 13 May 1924 said it desired to install sewers under Passaic St. from State St. to Wall St., the route used by the Main St. cars to reach the bridge spanning the Passaic River to Garfield. In response, Public Service applied to the PUC in July 1924 for permission to substitute buses for trol-

The #102 bus led to abandonment of the Newark-Hackensack trolley. Bus 5622 (Yellow Coach, 1928) is shown at Public Service Terminal. It was rebuilt as an all-service vehicle in 1938 and ran until 1947.

leys between Passaic and Hackensack. Approval was granted on 28 August and the Main St. cars ceased running on 31 August. On 3 September, the PUC authorized the No. 44—Lodi bus line between Passaic and Williams Ave. and the Boulevard in Hasbrouck Heights, where a connection was provided with Hackensack line cars. Through tickets were sold between Passaic and Hackensack.

Until the 1950s, when garden apartments were built on the site of the former junction between the Hackensack and Main St. lines in Hasbrouck Heights, 44—Lodi buses terminated and laid over there.

On 5 February 1927, the PUC granted Public Service Transportation permission to operate deluxe express bus service between Hackensack and Newark, the

first such service in Bergen County. This heralded the demise of the Hackensack trolley. The 102—Hackensack-Newark bus line commenced service on 13 February 1927 with four new duco red-painted Yellow Coach type Z gas-mechanical buses with Yellow Coach bodies, numbered 5000-5005. The 5000s were replaced early in 1927 by buses from the 5521-5540 group. The buses operated on a half-hour headway between 7 a.m. and 11 p.m. from Branford Place and Halsey St., Newark, and 8 a.m. and 12 midnight from Moore and Mercer streets, Hackensack. The buses stopped at 3 points in North Arlington, 3 in Lyndhurst, 3 in Rutherford, 1 in East Rutherford, 1 in Carlstadt, 3 in Wood-Ridge, 3 in Hasbrouck Heights and 3 in Hackensack. Through fare was 50 cents and the running time was 50 minutes. In 1928 the 5500-series buses were replaced by 5600-series Yellow Coach, 6-cylinder, type Z gas-electric buses with red-painted Public Service Newark Shop bodies.

Public Service Ry. Co. and Public Service Transportation Co. were merged on 10 January 1928 to form the Public Service Coordinated Transport Co. In July 1929 Public Service Coordinated

Transport announced it would renovate the second floor of the Newark Terminal Building to provide space for a bus terminal. Buses now entered the second floor terminal on track 1 and looped around the Park Place end of the building, terminating at the center of the building where a 50 x 250-foot unloading and loading area was provided. Part of the bus terminal area occupied the former location of track No. 4 formerly used by Hackensack cars. The new upper-level bus terminal was put into use on 29 December 1929 and the 102—Hackensack-Newark bus line's Newark terminus was relocated there on the same date.

Hackensack Line Discontinued

The opening of the 102 bus line made it possible for Public Service Coordinated Transport to discontinue the Hackensack trolley. The first cut-back occurred on 18 September 1928 when the Hackensack line began operating only between Hackensack and Rutherford and the Harrison line was extended north of Belleville Turnpike to the East Rutherford car house. While Ridge Road was being rebuilt into State Highway No. 2 (now 17), Harrison cars turned back at

Van Amburg's original line car was NJ&HR supply car 4. It was one of two 20-foot cars bought from the Brooklyn Heights RR in 1901. It was retired from passenger service in 1903.

Van Amburg's Line Cars

There were several line cars on the Hackensack line and all were in charge of Tom Van Amburg of Lyndhurst who was the line foreman. Van Amburg, a veteran of Hudson River Traction days, was knicknamed the "sky pilot" on the Hackensack line and night or day he was ready to do his share towards keeping the cars rolling. Van Amburg's wife frequently aided in keeping the headway of the line straight by giving the time of passing cars to the station master at the East Rutherford car house. Van Amburg used Hudson River car No. 4 for a line car. This was a second-hand, single-truck 20-foot car having 8 windows on each side and the platform inclosed by portable vestibule windows. Originally bought by the Newark & Hackensack from the Brooklyn Heights Ry., it was carried on the NJ&HR books as a supply car. The car was renumbered 5415 by Public Service and continued working out of the East Rutherford car house until July 1914 when it was sent to the Plank Road shops. It was scrapped in August 1915. No. 5415 was replaced by 5417 in June 1914. This was rebuilt from 20-foot single-truck car No. 373 which had 7 windows on each side and was built by J.G. Brill for Consolidated Traction in 1895. No. 5417 was retired in March 1923, sent to the Newark shops and scrapped in April 1924. Van Amburg received his third and final line car on 27 February 1923 when No. 5412, built in February 1911 by the Plank Road Shops, was transferred from the Hudson River line to the Hackensack line. A Newark newspaper reported that "Thomas Van Emburgh of Lyndhurst, long the trolley fixit, sported a new bright red repair car." Jokingly the paper reported the new car was a birthday present from the company. The car was fitted up completely for rapid repairs to the trolley system, and was such an improvement over the old trolley that "Van" feels very proud of himself as he rides through the township. Van's 5412 operated from the East Rutherford car house until the end of Hackensack line service and in 1928 was reassigned to the Union City car house. It operated on the Hudson Division until it was scrapped on 5 August 1949 at the Greenville car house.

Belleville Turnpike starting on 23 September 1928 and a shuttle car furnished service between Belleville Turnpike and Rutherford. Hackensack cars were extended to Valley Brook Ave. and Ridge Road on 25 October 1928 and the shuttle car terminated at that point. On 29 October the shuttle car was discontinued after P.M. rush hours and all service between Belleville Turnpike and Hackensack was operated by the Hackensack line. Hackensack cars ran for the last time between Hackensack and North Arlington on Sunday, 2 December 1928. On 4 December track removal commenced on Valley Boulevard in Wood-Ridge.

On 3 December without fanfare the 20-Grandview bus replaced the trolleys between Hackensack and East Rutherford on a 20-minute headway, using 1927 AL gas-mechanical Mack buses, numbered 1070-1074. The buses operated via Polifly Road between Essex St., Hackensack, and Williams Ave., Hasbrouck Heights, until the extension of the Boulevard from Hasbrouck Heights to Summit Ave., Hackensack was completed. The Rutherford terminus was at the triangle park by the Erie RR depot on Park Ave.

Public Service Coordinated Transport operated a shuttle bus between Belleville Turnpike and Rutherford from 2 December until 16 December 1928 while Ridge Road reconstruction was in progress. The road was relaid with double trolley tracks

from Belleville Turnpike to Valley Brook Ave. and was paved curb-to-curb with concrete. Harrison cars resumed running between Newark and East Rutherford car house on 16 December 1928 but were cut back to the intersection of Ridge Road and Valley Brook Ave. on 9 August 1931. The last Harrison cars ran on 4 September 1937. The next day "all-service" vehicles (ASVs), which were electric buses that could be operated either as trackless trolleys or as self-propelled vehicles, began service on the 39—Harrison line between Newark and Hedden Terrace in North Arlington, the only area that ASVs operated in Bergen County. The ASVs were Yellow Coach model 729 gas-electric trolley coaches and 21 were assigned to the 39-Harrison route. The ASVs were assigned gradually with the first electric vehicles replacing temporary bus service on 7 January 1938 and all ASV service starting on 23 August.

The last eleven Bergen Division cars assigned to the Hackensack line during the Fall of 1928 were: 1849-1852, 1859-1861 and 1864-1867. After the Hackensack line service ceased the cars were sent to the Passaic Wharf at Newark for scrapping. The last Harrison line cars assigned to the East Rutherford car house in 1931 were 2674, 2681, 2683, 2706, 2709, 2710, 2711, 2717, 2722, 2724, 2725, 2752, 2753, 2754, 2756, 2759, 2762, 2763, 2764, 2766 and 2769.

Line car 5412 is shown on the scrap track in 1949. This was the last surviving car which saw service in Bergen County.

Reminiscing

Thomas P. Vaughn, a resident of Hasbrouck Heights for 42 years, wrote to the author several years ago and reminisced on the old Hackensack line trolleys. Some of Mr. Vaughn's items of interest were: "I can remember walking what was left of the old right-of-way going down below Terrace Ave., as the ties were still down there until the thirties. There was also a time during the Summer of the trolley strike when the town covered all the tracks with asphalt and the franchise car had a tough time wending its way north... The old movie house (Strand Theater) was built ... next to Roth's shop. When I was a kid projectionist there, our films used to come up on the 2:50 P.M. car, and if it was late so was the show... I was very proud of the Heights until progress forced it up from a handful of people to what it is today. Always liked my hometown, from the horse troughs on Terrace Ave. to the birch roots we could dig up and brew. These grew in profusion near Oak Grove as did fresh horseradish on First St., that was covered over by the athletic field. . . "

The author was a resident of Wood-Ridge for 30 years and remembers well the 1000-series Mack buses on the 20 Grandview bus line whose rear windows rattled violently until they almost shattered while bumping along Monroe St. through Carlstadt. Also remembered was the hard straining of the motors on the No. 12 and No. 102 buses as they climbed the Hackensack St. hill in Carlstadt while the passengers hoped that no passenger desired to get off at Central Ave. lest the bus would stall upon pulling away from the curb and have to back down the hill for a restart. The author can still recall the ding-ding-ding of the fare register boxes on the red "camel-back" 102 buses as the driver recorded his fares. Some years later while attending College, a chemistry professor who had lived his youth in Carlstadt during the 1920s told the class a story of how he and his friends saved their father's left-over paints, then took the paint, all mixed together in one container, into Wood-Ridge and hid in the bushes along the private right-of-way. When one of the Hackensack line's bright yellow trolleys came by they would thrust out a broom that had been dipped into the paint and smear the full length of the car with an ugly colored stripe.

4

BERGEN DIVISION
Public Service Railway Company

Public Service Corporation of New Jersey

The momentum for street railway mergers started by B. M. Shanley in 1899 carried into the 1900s. In May 1902, the Prudential Insurance, Fidelity Trust, and United Gas Improvement companies formed a committee to explore forming a corporation to acquire and lease gas, electric and street railway properties in New Jersey. The numerous small utility companies had neither the revenues nor assets to raise capital needed for modernization and growth. By October 1902 the committee, called a syndicate by newspapers, had secured options on over 50 percent of the capital stock of the JCH&P, North Jersey, Orange and Passaic Valley, and Elizabeth, Plainfield and Central Jersey street railways. A deal was consummated a few weeks later.

On 12 March 1903, a joint committee was appointed by the directors of the participating traction companies to recommend a final corporate plan. The committee included A. J. Cassatt, President of the Pennsylvania RR (1899-1906); John D. Crimmins; Thomas Nesbitt McCarter; Randall Morgan; John I. Waterbury, President of the Manhattan Trust Co.; and E. F. C. Young. In April the committee unanimously approved the proposition of the Fidelity Trust Co. whose president, Uzal H. McCarter, was the older brother of Thomas N. McCarter. The McCarters were both directors of Fidelity Trust and Prudential Insurance, which had been controlled by Fidelity before becoming a mutual company.

The proposition called for formation of a corporation with an authorized capital stock of $25 million, of which $10 million would be immediately issued at par and underwitten by Fidelity Trust. The corporation would purchase the traction companies' stock in exchange for perpetual interest-bearing certificates. JCH&P shareholders who delivered their stock to the new corporation would receive new certificates worth $35 per share and a cash payment of one percent on the par value of the certificates when issued. The stock was deposited on 27 April 1903 with Fidelity Trust in Newark or its agents in Jersey City, New York, and Philadelphia.

Public Service Corporation received its certificate of incorporation on 6 May 1903. On 16 May, David Young sold his controlling interest in the JCH&P and its subsidiaries, including the Bergen Turnpike, to Public Service. Thomas N. McCarter was elected president and is credited with naming the corporation. Previously he had been a judge on Newark's First District Court, state senator from Essex County, and New Jersey attorney general. As attorney general and as general counsel for Fidelity Trust, McCarter had become aware of the shaky finances of the traction and utility companies and perceived the opportunity for someone with vision to resolve the situation and, over a period of time, reap a nice profit.

During 1903, Public Service acquired the Jersey City, Hoboken & Paterson St. Ry. Co., North Jersey St. Ry. Co., Orange & Passaic Valley Ry. Co. and United St. Ry. Co. of Central Jersey. These proper-

ties continued their identities as separate operating divisions of the Corporation's Railway Department until 20 August 1907 when the Public Service Ry. Co. was formed to operate the street railways as a single entity.

The Bergen Division Formed

On 1 July 1910 the Public Service Corporation of New Jersey acquired 97.79 per cent of the securities of New Jersey & Hudson River Ry. & Ferry Co., ending sixteen years of control by Philadelphians and Ford, Bacon and Davis. The NJ&HR Board of Directors met in New York City on 2 July to resign their positions, Public Service officials taking their places. The acquisition included several NJ&HR underliers: The Riverside & Fort Lee Ferry Co., dissolved on 15 November 1949; Highland Improvement Co., merged into Public Service Coordinated Transport on 30 November 1940; and New York Harbor Real Estate Co., dissolved on 18 December 1930. Public Service assumed the $5 million 4% fifty-year mortgage of the NJ&HR due 1 March 1950 made by United States Mortgage & Trust Co., of which $3,911,000 was outstanding, and Hudson River Traction Co.'s 5% $1 million first mortgage due March 1, 1950 made by United States Mortgage & Trust Co., of which $63,000 was outstanding.

The office of the NJ&HR was moved from Edgewater to the Public Service corporate offices at 759 Broad St., Newark, on 7 December 1910. A 900-year lease of NJ&HR to Public Service Ry. received New Jersey PUC approval on 20 April 1911, effective on 1 May. On 10

The lines crossing at Palisades Junction were first connected in 1911. This picture of the location was taken in the mid-1930s.

May, Public Service Ry. received a certificate of entry upon the NJ&HR, which thereafter operated as the Public Service Ry.'s Bergen Division.

The acquisition was designed to complement existing Public Service operations. According to Public Service's 1910 annual report, the lines connected "with the existing lines of Public Service at Paterson on the west, Kearny near Newark on the south, and intersecting other lines of Public Service at Hackensack, Grantwood and Fort Lee. This property thus complements the existing lines of Public Service, and, it is believed, will form a most valuable acquisition to its railway system. Furthermore, it was the only substantial railway property in the northern section of the State not already controlled by Public Service."

The acquisition of the Hudson River system by Public Service came as a complete surprise to the employees as well as citizens of Bergen County. The officers, heads of departments, and many of the employees had been connected with the company for years. The officers were known personally in all the towns through which the line passed. Most of the Hudson River line's employees were retained by Public Service. Henry Wissel, who was serving his fifth term as Mayor of Edgewater, continued as chief engineer of the Edgewater power house. John W. Greer remained to become superintendent of the Public Service Bergen Division after Louis P. Bauerhenn transferred to the Newark headquarters.

With acquisition of the NJ&HR by Public Service Ry., the last independent electric railway in Bergen County was the North Jersey Rapid Transit Co. NJRT would finally be acquired in 1926.

The Tenafly Extension

Public Service continued the extension of the Englewood line towards Tenafly. By 16 November 1910 track construction had reached the terminus in front of the Tenafly railroad depot, but had not been ballasted. The extension officially opened on 19 November when Tenafly's mayor and council made the initial trip. When the car reached Tenafly it was met by a cheering throng. Andrew De Packes, a New York artist, sketched the scene and it was reported that as a painting it was sold later for $120. After the ceremonies, an elaborate dinner was served at Shenkel's Hotel (Clinton Hotel). An unofficial opening trip had been instigated by a group of teenage boys the night before. They took up a collection and paid the motorman to ride through to Tenafly from Englewood. However, their stout hearts gave way to fear and apprehension when they reached Phelps Ave. on the Tenafly boundary. They implored the motorman to let them off and walked to the Tenafly depot. Regular service to Tenafly began at 5 a.m. on Monday, 21 November 1910. Schedule time from Tenafly to Edgewater ferry was 40 minutes and cars ran on a 20-minute headway. Although in 1911 Rockland County, New York, residents were still hoping

that the Rockland Ry. would build southward from Nyack to connect with the Englewood line in Tenafly before winter, the Tenafly extension was the last northward extension of the Bergen Division.

Bergen Division cars began stopping on the "near side" of street intersections in February 1911. That is, the cars stopped to discharge or pick up passengers before crossing the intersection.

In the Grantwood area of Cliffside Park and Fort Lee, the Palisade line from Weehawken crossed the Hudson River Line at grade at Palisade Junction. A connection was completed on 14 March 1911, enabling Palisade line cars from Weehawken to continue over the Hudson River line to Palisades Amusement Park and the Edgewater ferry terminal. The service commenced with alternate cars from Weehawken running to Palisades Park instead of Coytesville.

Commencing on 8 June 1911 free transfers were issued to passengers between the Hudson River, Bergen Pike, Hackensack and Main St. trolleys in Hackensack. The transfers were good only within the Hackensack Commission limits. Transfer stations were established at Main and Mercer streets, and First St. at the private right-of-way.

On 13 June 1910 the Public Service Electric Co. was formed to operate the electric properties that had been acquired by the Public Service Corporation. The Edgewater power house was leased by Public Service Ry. to Public Service Electric on 1 March 1913. The year 1913 was also the first year that the annual electric lighting and power load surpassed the electric railway load for the Public Service Corporation.

The photograph of cars 3519 and 3520 arranged for train service was taken on Broad Ave., Leonia, in September 1912.

Double Track to Paterson

Until 1912 the Hudson River car line between Hackensack and Paterson was double-tracked from Edgewater to a point 0.25 mile east of the Maywood-Hackensack boundary, except for single-track sections at the several railroad trestles. The remainder of the line to the Passaic river, a distance of 4.0 miles, was single-track with passing turnouts totaling about 1.52 miles. Increasing traffic generated rumors after 1912 that Public Service would extend the second track to Paterson. On 30 December 1915 Public Service was informed that it did not require NJPUC permission for the second track, but it was not completed until 1923. The single-track wooden trestle over the Saddle river was replaced with a new double-track steel-plate girder bridge.

Car 3522, built at Plank Road in 1913, pauses in front of the Tenafly Station on the Englewood line on 21 June 1936.

Multiple Unit and Blizzard Operations

During June 1914 Public Service Ry. officials determined that the heavy Sunday traffic on the Hudson River line required additional capacity and they experimented with two-car multiple-unit trains, using two conductors and one motorman. A photograph of cars 3519 and 3520 coupled together in MU service received wide circulation in trade publications. The 3510-3521 series cars were originally equipped with type HL multiple-unit controllers which were replaced by K35 controllers in 1928. The trial runs were not successful because of slow loading and train line difficulties and MU operation was discontinued.

On the evening of 1 March 1914 a blizzard struck Bergen County with winds up to 75 miles per hour. During the night trolley service was halted to prevent marooning of cars in remote areas. Scheduled service resumed between Edgewater and Leonia on March 3rd. A shuttle car ran between Leonia Junction and Hackensack with only one track cleared of snow. The first car reached Hackensack at 10 a.m. Service to Paterson did not resume until that afternoon. The NJ&HR owned a rotary snow plow (No. 2) built by Peckham. It was renumbered 5222 by Public Service Ry. The plow was capable of hurling stones and debris through windows of the buildings it passed, and was restricted to use on private right-of-way. Since it was impractical for use in urbanized areas, No. 5222 was withdrawn and stored at Secaucus car house in 1916 and scrapped in 1924.

RELIABLE BUS SERVICE

BETWEEN

CAMP MERRITT AND TENAFLY

NEW JERSEY TRANSPORTATION COMPANY

Comfortable Motor Busses will make Regular Connections with Street Cars at Railroad Depot, Tenafly, on and after Saturday, November 17, 1917.

FARE, 10 CTS. EACH WAY

On 13 March 1915 Leonia granted Public Service Ry. permission to relocate its track on Central Ave. from the side of the road to the center. Track reconstruction was underway on 26 October and the Fort Lee car line was temporarily cut back to the Leonia-Fort Lee boundary. The track relocation was completed on 1 December 1915 and the Fort Lee car line resumed running through to Leonia Junction on 11 December.

New Jersey Transportation Company

As early as 1912, the US Army had considered establishing a camp in Bergen County. When the United States entered World War I, Camp Merritt was developed in the Cresskill and Dumont area as a staging area for troops destined for and returning from Europe. Construction began on 20 August 1917 in a 770-acre area described as barren fields with scattered homes. Troops began arriving on 30 August.

John Greer, Bergen Division Supervisor for Public Service Coordinated Transport, in 1937 recalled the World War I period as the high spot in the history of the Englewood car line. "It was a regular thing to load as many as sixty cars an hour right here in Edgewater, most of them on the Englewood line. First it was the great crowd of workmen building the camp. Many of them lived in New York and came over on the ferry. We used to carry them back and forth to work at the camp. Then there were thousands of soldiers. They rode with us whenever they had time off on furloughs. And after the war, Camp Merritt was used by the Army as a point for discharging soldiers who had returned from France. Yes sir, we carried them before, during and after the war." A total of 1,088,081 troops passed through Camp Merritt before the camp was finally closed on 30 January 1920.

The need for transportation to the camp caused Public Service to offer bus service for the first time. The New Jersey Transportation Co. was incorporated on 13 November 1917 to provide bus service between the Englewood line's Tenafly terminus and Camp Merritt via River Edge Ave. and Knickerbocker Road — a one-way distance of 1.75 miles. The fleet consisted of ten motor buses built by Kelly-Springfield in 1917 and numbered 1 to 10. These were primitive vehicles on 1 1/2-ton truck chassis and were originally operated with both a driver and a conductor. They were apparently rebuilt in the spring of 1918 to allow one-man operation.

A second bus line was placed in service on or about 5 January 1918, from the Park Place Hudson & Manhattan Station to Port Newark. Buses 4, 6 and 10 were replaced by 1919 with buses 15, 16, and 19 from the Port Newark service, the higher-numbered buses having been bought from a bankrupt operator for use on the Port Newark line. These were also Kelly-Springfields. The Port Newark service was discontinued in September 1918 because of government restrictions on gasoline. The Camp Merritt bus was discontinued on 30 March 1919.

The original New Jersey Transportation buses were built on Kelly-Springfield chassis.

Although the Englewood line was the primary provider of trolley service to Tenafly, the Fort Lee line provided additional service during World War I. It was extended north of Leonia Junction on 15 July 1918 to the end of double-track in Englewood, and on to Tenafly on 26 August 1918 to help handle the traffic generated by Camp Merritt. Following the subsiding of wartime traffic, the Fort Lee line was cut back to Leonia Junction on 29 October 1919. Because of heavy power demands imposed on the Public Service Electric system by the Tenafly service, a rotary converter was installed in the Dean St. substation, located in Englewood north of Chestnut St., and placed in service during August 1918.

One may have wondered if a trolley ever ran away down the incline from the top of the Palisades to the ferry terminal. One did on 2 January 1918 when an 1800-series car on the Fort Lee line got out of control just as it was starting down the steep incline. In some miraculous fashion the car remained on the track until it reached the last sharp turn directly in front of the ferryhouse. There the car derailed and plunged into the building. A ferry was just discharging a crowd of passengers when the errant car hurtled into their midst. A number of men were knocked down and badly bruised, two were severely injured and were taken to the Englewood Hospital. The car was winched out of the ferryhouse. On 7 January 1919 a similar incident occurred when an early morning ferry-bound Fort Lee car containing 70 passengers derailed on Dempsey Ave. at the curve where the track crossed River Road and crashed into the First National Bank building. There were no fatalities, but seven passengers were injured, none seriously.

Labor Strife 1918-1923

Since the Trolley Car Men's Association strike which began in the afternoon of 24 September 1903 at Newark, Public Service Ry. had been relatively free of labor problems. On 7 June 1918 a wildcat strike over wages by motormen and conductors affected car lines in Essex, Passaic, Hudson and Union counties. The Hudson River line did not operate into Paterson during the strike. In some areas 56 women, who had been trained in the Public Service Ry. school for motormen and conductors, were summoned to work. The union members were furious over this action as it had protested two weeks before against the employment of women in car service.

On 12 March 1919 recently formed locals of the Amalgamated Association of Street and Electric Railway Workers of America representing Public Service Ry. employees went on a six-day strike. During the strike Hudson River cars ran on a half-hour headway between Edgewater and Rochelle Park with no service to Paterson; Englewood cars operated a complete schedule; Hackensack cars operated on an intermittent schedule between Hackensack and Rutherford with no service to Newark; the Main St. (Lodi) line, a Passaic Division route, and the Bergen Pike line, a Hudson Division route, were completely shut down; and the Palisade line, a Hudson Division route, operated an infrequent schedule between Coytesville and Union Hill.

During January 1921 the union and the railway agreed to a 10-hour instead of a 9-hour work day. Prior to this agreement, trolley operators worked a 9-hour day with time and one-half for overtime. The Union agreed to 50 cents per hour straight time for a 10-hour day with time and one-half for overtime.

Labor unrest struck again on 1 August 1923 when a strike brought the entire trolley system to a halt. There were two principal issues. Public Service Ry. had been instituting one-man operation since the early 1920s and the union felt the problems of operating a big trolley car in city traffic plus collecting fares was making a tough job tougher for the motorman. In addition the union pressed for a thirty-percent wage increase. On 17 September 1923 Chancellor Walker ordered the railway to restore normal service before 24 September. The 51-day strike was settled with the union agreeing to one-man operation of all cars and the company to a 20 percent wage increase.

During the strike the only trolley operating on the system was the U.S. Mail car on the Palisade line between Hoboken and Coytesville. Private jitneys were pressed into service all over the state. In the Bergen Division area, James S. Mead operated six vehicles between Hack-

ensack and Edgewater on no particular schedule, running whenever there was a sufficient load. William Brady also operated two buses over the route hourly. Both operators began their trips at Main and Mercer streets in Hackensack.

When the strike continued beyond 1 September, many municipalities grew impatient over the lack of service. Englewood covered the tracks on South Dean St. between Palisade and Englewood avenues with a mixture of tar and small stones on 14 September. The Hudson River, Englewood and Fort Lee lines resumed normal service after the strike settlement at 12:12 p.m. and the Hackensack car line at 1:00 p.m. on 20 September. The first Main St. car from Passaic and Lodi arrived at its Hackensack terminus at 4:00 p.m. on 21 September.

The Jitney Problem

The "jitney" was not as prominent in Bergen County as in the urbanized areas

The Edgewater terminal in April 1917. From the left, Fort Lee car 1875 signed as a special car, Hudson River car 3516, Tenafly car 3502, and car 3506 with a blank sign. The last two were so-called "jumbo" cars.

of Essex, Hudson and Passaic counties. They became a serious problem for Public Service following World War I when every sort of motor vehicle was brought into use from the nondescript flivver to decrepit limousines that had seen better days. Jitneys were free of regulations regarding standards of service, franchise fees and most of the taxes that the street railway was required to pay. It was a favorite practice of jitney drivers to travel just ahead of the trolleys, capturing much of the passenger business from the cars. It soon became apparent that the railway company would have to enter the bus business in order to compete.

Public Service already had a corporate structure for bus operation. The New Jersey Transportation Co. had wound up its affairs and transferred all of its funds to Public Service Corporation in January 1921. However, the NJT was not dissolved and was revived and renamed The Public Service Transportation Co. on 7 June 1923 to purchase the rights of independent bus operators who were doing business in direct competition with street car lines. It assumed operation of many of these buses in 1923 and 1924. A secondary effort was directed towards replacing unprofitable car lines with buses. The first car line replaced in Bergen County was the Passaic Division's Main St. line between Passaic, Lodi and Hackensack on 31 August 1924.

On 8 July 1921 the Fort Lee line was extended from Leonia Junction to First St., Hackensack. The extended service operated only on weekdays with the first car leaving Hackensack at 8:15 a.m. and arriving at Edgewater ferry at 8:57 a.m., then continuing on a 15-minute headway until 7:57 p.m. On Saturdays, Sundays and Holidays, substitute service was provided by the Hackensack line running through to Edgewater ferry. On 1 February 1924 the Fort Lee line schedule was

reduced to rush hours only. The line was cut back to Leonia Junction again on 25 January 1926 and completely discontinued on 10 July 1927.

Paterson's Board of Public Works in 1923 recommended rerouting buses and trolleys so that as much of this traffic as possible was removed from Main St. where the various lines looped around the downtown area on city streets. On 23 December 1923 the Hudson River line's Paterson terminal was changed from a street loop encircling Broadway Terminal to a new loop on the terminal property. Effective 1 August 1924 the Broadway Terminal car yard was closed and the lines operating therefrom transferred to the Market St. car house.

The surging development of communities in the Bergen Division area following World War I increased passenger traffic. To provide enhanced facilities for the increased patronage, Public Service Ry., during June 1923, erected two shelters over the loading and unloading platforms at the Edgewater ferry terminal which were erected by the Stillman-Delehanty-Ferris Co. The shelter over the unloading tracks measured 82 feet long by 33 feet wide while that over the loading tracks measured 122 feet long by 33

The Palisades Amusement Park entrance was lavishly decorated with flags during the annual county fair. The picture is believed to have been taken in 1909 during the Hudson-Fulton Celebration. Note the car tracks in the lower left corner of the picture.

feet wide. The terminal tracks were realigned and concrete platforms installed by John J. McGarry of Edgewater.

Many complaints were received by Public Service Ry. from angry church parisioners during 1923 and 1924. Therefore, the railway issued a general order to all divisions requiring all cars to slow down and refrain from ringing the gong while passing churches of all denominations during Divine services on Sundays.

Coytesville Car Line

On 1 July 1925, Public Service Ry. discontinued Palisade line service to the Coytesville section of Fort Lee and established the Coytesville line between the Edgewater ferry and Coytesville via Palisade Junction. The Palisade line continued to operate "owl" service to Coytesville until 10 July 1927 when all Palisade line trolleys were terminated at Palisade

Hudson River car 3510 is shown bound for Paterson entering Broadway from private right-of-way in Fair Lawn. The gas station to the left of the trolley is advertising gasoline at 15 cents a gallon.

Junction. Coytesville line service was reduced to rush hours only on 10 July 1927 (6-9 a.m. and 4:07-6:57 p.m). Public Service Transportation provided non-rush hour service with the No. 10 bus line between the Edgewater ferry terminal and Englewood. The Palisade car line resumed "owl" service to Coytesville on 6 October 1930. In the beginning four cars handled the Coytesville line schedule, but was reduced to three cars in 1928.

The Coytesville line ceased operating on 1 June 1933, although special cars carried high school students from Edgewater to the Fort Lee High School and the Palisade line continued to provide owl service until 4 September 1938. Cars assigned to the Coytesville car line changed often: 2000 and 2100-series in the beginning; 1800-series from 1928 to 1931; and 2400-series from 1931 to 1933. Double-end 1400-series open cars were assigned during the summers of 1928, 29 and 30.

Edgewater Power House Closed

After 31 years of supplying electric power, the Edgewater power house was permanently shut down on 10 March 1926. Former NJ&HR Superintendent Louis P. Bauerhenn, in 1926 the General Superintendent of Public Service Ry., was present when the the last generator, the 500-kw, 500-volt D.C./375-volt A.C., 3-phase unit, made its final revolutions. Former Edgewater Mayor Henry Wissel

had been chief engineer at the power house and had started as a fireman there in May 1910. The former power house was converted into a bus garage for Public Service Transportation in 1927.

Power for Bergen Division trolleys was henceforth supplied from the Fort Lee, Arcola, Dean St. (Englewood) and East Rutherford substations. Power generated at the new electric generating stations of the Public Service Electric and Gas Co. supplied 13,000-volt 60-Hz A.C. power over transmission lines to the rotary converters in the substations, which produced 500-volt D.C. power for the railway feeders. The size of the rotary converters were: Fort Lee, 850-kw; Arcola and Dean St., 600-kw; and East Rutherford, 300-kw.

Local Paterson Car Lines Discontinued

Local Paterson car lines were mostly slow single-track routes with average speeds between six and seven miles per hour. In contrast, the Hudson River car line schedule called for an average speed of 12.4 miles per hour within Paterson and 13.9 miles per hour in Bergen County. Slow speed was a primary cause of the growth of independent bus lines which duplicated the lethargic trolley routes. Most of the car lines needed heavy repairs by 1919, but low revenues discouraged expenditures. Public Service Ry. believed the use of lightweight Birney cars were a solution and purchased 200

Birneys in 1920. It equipped many of its worn-out car lines in northern New Jersey with these cars. The Paterson lines were the first to be equipped with Birneys, the Riverside car line being the very first on 5 September 1920.

Birneys did not solve the schedule problem and the loss of patronage to buses. Thus, Public Service Transportation set out to purchase the 19 independent operators in Paterson and Passaic and by the spring of 1925 acquired nearly all of the permits. The first Paterson car line replaced by buses was the City Hall to Sixth Ave. portion of the Governor line on 5 June 1925. The City Hall to Lincoln Bridge portion continued as the Grand car line. During 1925 Public Service placed eight new White model 50-A motor buses into local Paterson service that were numbered in an interrupted series beginning with 638 and ending with 653. During the summer of 1926 Public Service Transportation assigned Yellow Coach Type Z-AL gas-electric buses to Paterson, replacing the decrepit buses acquired from the independent operators. In the spring of 1927 new 4500-series Mack Type AL gas-electric buses were assigned to Paterson and Passaic bus lines, completing modernization of the Passaic Division bus fleet and enabling Public Service Ry. to discontinue the last local car lines in Paterson.

During 1926 Public Service Transportation introduced its first deluxe interurban buses Nos. 5500-5510 on the No.

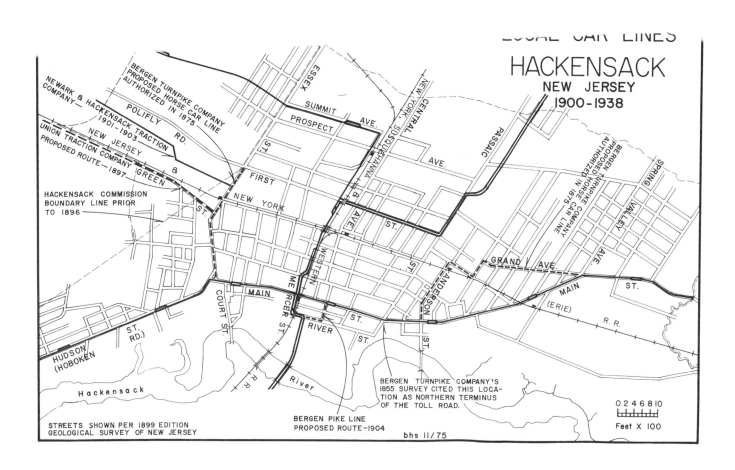

LOCAL CAR LINES

HACKENSACK
NEW JERSEY
1900-1938

NEWARK & HACKENSACK TRACTION
COMPANY — 1901-1903

BERGEN TURNPIKE COMPANY
PROPOSED HORSE CAR LINE
AUTHORIZED IN 1875

POLIFLY RD.

UNION TRACTION COMPANY
PROPOSED ROUTE—1897

NEW JERSEY & GREEN

HACKENSACK COMMISSION
BOUNDARY LINE PRIOR
TO 1896

HUDSON
(HOBOKEN

Hackensack

STREETS SHOWN PER 1899 EDITION
GEOLOGICAL SURVEY OF NEW JERSEY

BERGEN PIKE LINE
PROPOSED ROUTE—1904

BERGEN TURNPIKE COMPANY'S
1855 SURVEY CITED THIS LOCA-
TION AS NORTHERN TERMINUS
OF THE TOLL ROAD.

BERGEN TURNPIKE COMPANY
PROPOSED HORSE CAR LINE
AUTHORIZED IN 1875

bhs 11/75

0 2 4 6 8 10

Feet X 100

The interior of the Edgewater power house taken on 8 February 1916 showing the belt-driven engines.

Car 3525 was inbound to the Edgewater Ferry from Palisades Park on 21 June 1936. The car barn is to the right and the ferry terminal is straight ahead.

70 Paterson-Suffern bus line. This route was acquired through purchase of Stoddard's Arrow Bus Lines. Operation of suburban bus lines from downtown Paterson over extended routes accelerated the demise of the remaining interurban car lines operating into Paterson.

The last day of operation for the local Paterson car lines was as follows:

Cedar Lawn	6 April 1924
Hawthorne	11 August 1926
Lakeview	22 February 1925
Grand	9 June 1927
Governor	5 June 1925
Singac	14 July 1927
Riverside	1 August 1926
Totowa	15 September 1927
Broadway	3 August 1926
Haledon	5 November 1927
Park	1 October 1928

The Cedar Lawn car line was replaced by extensions of the Broadway and Totowa car lines. The other local car lines were replaced by buses.

Erie Railroad Eliminates Grade Crossings in Paterson

Between 1924 and 1931 the Erie RR eliminated all grade crossings in Paterson between River St. on the north and 21st Ave. on the south. The grade separation was the result of many years of agitation by the City of Paterson and the Erie's desire to avoid increased accidents resulting from the growth of automobile traffic. Incidents involving Erie trains and Hudson River cars occurred during the early days of Hudson River line operations into the city. A Hudson River car had its first encounter with the Erie RR on 27 November 1903 when 25 passengers on the car had a hair-raising scare at the Broadway grade crossing. When the car was on the railroad crossing, the trolley pole came off the overhead wire. As the conductor was trying to get the pole back on the wire, an express train bound for Jersey City rounded the bend and bore down on the car. The passengers saw the train, the motorman yelled, and everybody made a jump for windows and doors, clothing being torn in the struggle. All of the trolley's passengers managed to get out safely and the locomotive engineer, by applying emergency brakes, brought the express train to a standstill less than a car's length from the trolley.

Another incident occurred on 6 January 1905 when Hudson River car 27 heading into downtown Paterson on Broadway approached the Erie crossing as the gates were being lowered for a westbound train. The derail switch was out of order and the trolley tracks were slippery with ice and snow. Car 27 crashed through the gate and slid onto the railroad track in front of the fast approaching train before the motorman realized the danger. The conductor had left the trolley to flag it across the railroad, and promptly raised the gate on the other side of the crossing. Car 27 cleared the railroad tracks just in time with less than three feet between the rear of the trolley and the passing train.

A Hudson River car, number unknown, was struck and demolished by the Erie RR Chicago Express on 1 September 1909 at the Broadway crossing. The car had stopped as it approached the crossing. The conductor went ahead and seeing no train coming, set the derail switch for the car to cross the railroad. Just as the car was on the crossing the trolley pole came off the overhead wire leaving the car in darkness. Erie train No. 5, the Chicago Express, had departed Paterson

80

at 8:24 p.m. to head west. The motorman saw the locomotive headlight and shouted for the passengers to get out quickly. The car was emptied just in time as the passengers scurried to safety.

More Buses, Fewer Car Lines

Public Service Transportation bus route extensions continued into 1927 with the 10—Englewood Cliffs bus line between Englewood and Edgewater on 10 July, the 2—Fort Lee bus line on 20 June, and the extension of the 14—Edgewater-Hackensack bus line on 20 November. Public Service Transportation assigned 40 gas-mechanical Mack Type AL buses (1038-1077) in 1927 and three Mack Type AL buses (1078-1080) in 1928 to most of the Bergen Division lines. 1927 was the year in which Public Service Ry. and Public Service Transportation replaced the corporate name "Public Service" on the sides of its vehicles with the blue circle enclosing a red triangle logo.

In a step to promote better customer relations between vehicle operators and passengers, Public Service equipped each of its drivers and motormen with a name plate beginning in 1927. The plate provided the operator's name and badge number and was hung above the windshield in full view of the passengers. In July 1932, bus drivers and trolley motormen were redesignated as "salesmen" in order to encourage employees to be more active in generating business.

The Palisade car line, a Hudson Division route, extended operations from Palisade Junction to Edgewater ferry on 6 February 1927. The extension was reduced to rush hours only on 6 May 1927. Service to Edgewater ferry was discontinued on 15 June 1928 and Weehawken cars resumed terminating at Palisade Junction. On 10 July 1927 the Fort Lee car line was discontinued and the original Bergen County route via Palisade Ave. and East Main St. in Fort Lee was abandoned. The Englewood car line, which had been operating via Morsemere since May 1905, was re-routed over the Palisade line tracks between Palisade Junction in Grantwood and Main St., Fort Lee, and thence via Main St. to Broad Ave., Leonia.

During 1927 Public Service Transportation erected a new garage on the Gamewell property adjacent to the NYS&W RR, through which the Hudson River car line travelled between State St.

Car 3535, on the Hudson River Line on 28 August 1937, bound for Hackensack, leaving Main St. at the River Road in Bogota.

and Union St. The Public Service Production Co. constructed the garage which was originally designed to house 43 motor buses. The Gamewell property had been used for a wye to reverse the Main St. cars from Lodi and Passaic between July 1911 and August 1913.

Public Service Interstate Transportation Co. was formed on 17 September 1927 to operate interstate bus routes into New York and Pennsylvania for Public Service Transportation. Public Service Ry. and Public Service Transportation were merged on 10 January 1928 to form Public Service Coordinated Transport Co. which was approved by the New Jersey PUC on 31 January 1928. The purpose was to consolidate trolley and motor bus operations into the hands of one company, permitting the full coordination of 56 street car and 150 motor bus lines.

The Hackensack car line was discontinued between Hackensack and Rutherford on 2 December 1928 and the Bergen

Division was reduced to three trolley routes handled by 46 cars. Before abandonment of the Fort Lee and Hackensack lines, 70 cars had been assigned during the winter of 1926-1927 and 84 in the summer of 1927.

Summer patronage on the Paterson extension of the Hudson River line was stimulated by the incorporation of the Arcola Amusement Park on 7 May 1928. The amusement park's swimming pool on Passaic St. in Rochelle Park Township lasted into the 1950s and eventually became the site of exit 160 of the Garden State Parkway.

During 1931, all street cars and motor buses operated by Public Service were equipped with illuminated signal arms which indicated turns or stops.

January and February, 1933 was an unusually harsh winter period due to four blizzard-like snow storms. A more than usual amount of slush and ice wore out snow sweeper brooms so that 20 tons of rattan was consumed by Public Service for rebuilding 636 broom sections. By comparison, the winter of 1932 required 121 broom sections to be rebuilt and over the previous five winters, an average of 70 broom sections were rebuilt. All of this work was performed by twenty men in the Newark Shops for all of Public Service's railway divisions. The rattan was imported from India and the Malayan States and was the strongest and most effective material found by Public Service for use in sweeper brooms.

New ASVs and Buses

In 1934 Public Service Coordinated Transport's engineers developed the all-service vehicle (ASV), a gas-electric bus which could operate from overhead wires like a trackless trolley in urban areas and function as a self-propelled motor bus where the wires did not exist. It was tested successfully on the Pershing Ave. hill in Weehawken in 1934. Between 1936 and 1938, Public Service purchased 356 new Yellow Coach & Truck Model 729 ASVs and rebuilt 227 old Yellow Coach Type Z buses into ASVs for a fleet total of 583 vehicles. All-service vehicles were never used in the Bergen Division area although wires were strung above Paterson Plank Road from the Hackensack River bridge to the Passaic River bridge where the Passaic car line trolleys once operated.

By the last years of Bergen Division trolley operation, the area lying at the foot of the Palisades below the horseshoe had become highly urbanized as can be seen in this picture of car 3515 on the curve with Edgewater spread out below taken about 1938.

Public Service, in its desire to economize and modernize its suburban routes, purchased 390 Yellow Coach & Truck 21-passenger Model 733 buses between September 1936 and March 1938. These had Chevrolet engines mounted over the front axle inside the passenger compartment. About 138 Model 733s were assigned to the Bergen Division, replacing Mack Type ALs and Yellow Coach Type Zs delivered in the late 1920s.

Englewood Cars Discontinued

The Englewood car line was cut back from Tenafly to Leonia Junction on 20 March 1937. The last car on the section left Tenafly at 8:20 a.m. on 21 March 1937, operated by John A. Macken. Service between Leonia and Tenafly was provided by rerouting the 54—Dumont-Weehawken bus line. Englewood cars

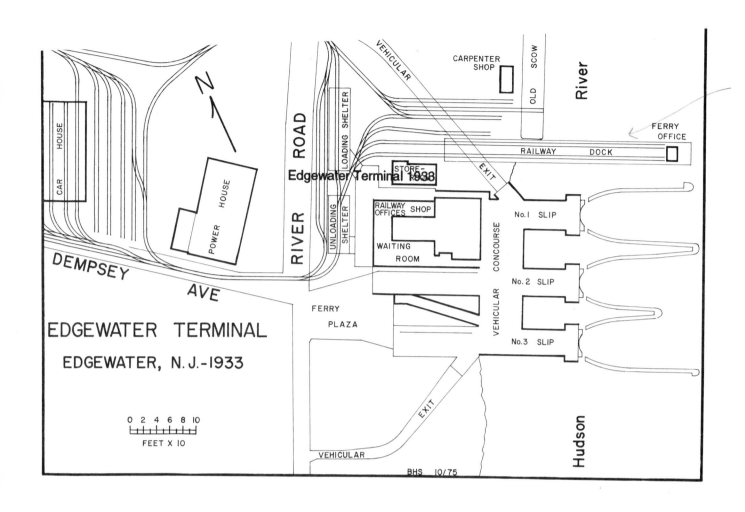

EDGEWATER TERMINAL

EDGEWATER, N.J.-1933

VEHICULAR

CARPENTER SHOP

OLD SCOW

River

FERRY OFFICE

RAILWAY DOCK

RIVER ROAD

LOADING SHELTER

UNLOADING SHELTER

STORE-

Edgewater Terminal 1933

EXIT

RAILWAY OFFICES SHOP

WAITING ROOM

No.1 SLIP

No.2 SLIP

No.3 SLIP

VEHICULAR CONCOURSE

CAR HOUSE

POWER HOUSE

DEMPSEY AVE

FERRY PLAZA

EXIT

VEHICULAR

Hudson

BHS 10/75

0 2 4 6 8 10
FEET X 10

Car 3604 (Brill, 1916) was one of three former Trenton Fast Line cars used on the Englewood line in the early 1930s. It is shown beside the Edgewater car barn in the summer of 1932.

83

The little Model 1204 Yellow Coaches which replaced the Hudson River cars were an unimpressive for the large deluxe cars which they supplanted.

continued operating between Edgewater and Leonia Junction pending a decision by the New Jersey PUC allowing bus substitution. This service was discontinued on 20 June 1937 and 2—Edgewater-Hackensack buses were substituted. Prior to the cutback to Leonia Junction, the Englewood line was assigned eight 3500-series cars. Afterwards five cars were assigned, Nos. 3536 to 3540.

The Hudson River line was now the last Bergen Division trolley line, using 22 assigned 3500-series cars including 3584 and 3588 which continued operating as school cars between Edgewater and the Fort Lee High School and as Palisade Amusement Park trippers. The Palisade line, a Hudson Division route, continued operating between Weehawken and Palisade Junction at Grantwood until 3 September 1938. In 1937 the two other car lines operating in Paterson were discontinued. The Passaic line which once ran through to Hoboken was discontinued on 19 March 1937 and the Paterson line to Newark on 18 July 1937.

Hudson River Car Line Discontinued

A new highway, NJ Route 4, was completed between the George Washington Bridge and Broadway, Paterson early in 1931. The Hudson River car line tracks were relocated from the old wooden trestle to the new concrete highway bridge across the Passaic River.

On 5 August 1938 the last scheduled Hudson River line trolley with salesman Joe Nolan at the controller departed from the Paterson terminal at 3:28 a.m. and arrived at Edgewater ferry at 4:45 a.m. Later that day, Public Service noted the passing of the Hudson River line by an unusual celebration. Car 3540 was decorated with patriotic bunting and a banner stretched the full length of the car body proclaiming, "Last Trolley off Hudson River Line." No. 3540 left the Broadway terminal, Paterson, at 10:15 a.m. preceded by a Yellow Coach Model 1204 bus carrying an 18-piece band. Following behind car 3540 were additional new buses which Public Service assigned as replacements for the trolleys. They carried guests picked up at points along the line in Bergen County. All along the

route from Paterson to Edgewater thousands of persons saluted the parade and many cameras clicked from street and doorstep. At Edgewater the celebrities aboard car 3540 were transported on three of the new buses to the Swiss Chalet in Rochelle Park Township where luncheon was served. At the luncheon the speakers were Vice President Edmund W. Wakelee of Public Service; Harry B. Haines, Publisher of the *Paterson Evening News;* and John Borg, Publisher of the *Bergen Evening Record.* Among the guests were Harry Knight who operated the first Hudson River car to Paterson in 1903, William Dougherty who operated the first work car over the line and John Greer, former Superintendent of the Bergen Division, who had retired in 1937 after almost 50 years of employment with Public Service and its predecessors.

During 1938, twenty cars (3510-3517, 3519-3521 and 3532-3540) were assigned to the Hudson River car line. During the summer of 1938, cars 3584 and 3588, operated as Palisades Amusement Park trippers from the ferry. The 32 Yellow Coach Model 1204 buses that replaced the trolleys were 24-passenger lightweight vehicles, 159 of which were pur-

The abandonment notice above was posted in Hudson River cars to herald the end of electric railway service.

chased by Public Service. They were numbered 3200-3358 and buses in the low 3300-series were assigned to the No. 1 — Hudson River line. The buses were painted chrome yellow with light cream trim and black lettering, and adorned with a Public Service logo with bright red wings beneath the windshield. The gasoline motors were installed under the rear seat. The little chrome yellow buses were a dashing contrast to the big red 3500-series trolley cars.

In Bogota, the trolley trestle that had spanned the New York Central Railroad's West Shore line since 1899 was replaced with a motor vehicle overpass. The Main St. overpass was dedicated on 3 June 1939. The abandoned double-track bridge and private rights-of-way leading thereto at the Hackensack River were also acquired by Bergen County for future use by motor vehicles. The county rebuilt the bridge and right-of-way after World War II and it was dubbed Midtown Bridge.

In Manhattan the Third Avenue Ry. (Third Avenue Transit System) continued operating three trolley car lines to 125th St. ferry terminal until 1946. The three car lines were: Car line X, 125th St. Cross Town; Car line 10th Ave. Tenth Avenue to the 42nd St. West Shore ferry terminal; and Car line W, Willis Avenue to Third Avenue and Fordham Road in the Bronx. Also about two blocks up 125th St., the IRT Seventh Avenue-Broadway subway line was available. By this time, Amsterdam Ave. had been renamed W. 125th St. and old 125th St. was renamed LaSalle St.

New Jersey & Hudson River Railway & Ferry Co. Dissolved

Beginning in 1934, Public Service Corporation of New Jersey and its subsidiaries appointed a committee to study the corporate structure with a goal of eliminating as many underliers as possible. In the spring of 1936 the committee submitted its report. The electric and gas corporate structure was simplified first and was completed in 1939.

Restructuring of the transportation companies commenced in 1937. The New Jersey & Hudson River Ry. & Ferry Co.'s six percent cumulative preferred capital stock was redeemed for $115 per share on 15 April 1938. The funds ($750,000) were provided by Public Service Coordinated Transport from money advanced by Public Service Corporation. This reduced the annual rental payments by Transport to Corporation by $45,000. On 21 November 1939 the NJ&HR was further integrated into Public Service Coordinated Transport by the issuance of new transport bonds to replace NJ&HR's dividend-paying stock. The NJ&HR was formally merged into Transport on 28 June 1940. Another vestige of the NJ&HR disappeared when the Highland Improvement Co. was merged into Transport on 30 November 1940.

The last NJ&HR property under Transport control was the Riverside & Fort Lee Ferry Co. The ferry company's corporate existence was terminated when Transport filed a certificate of dissolution at Albany, NY on 15 November 1949.

Public Service Car Route Numbering System

During early 1927 trolleys on urban lines in Essex and Hudson counties began displaying route numbers in addition to destination signs. A sign with numbers in white on a blue background was placed on the right hand front corner of the roof of each car, one number facing the front and another the side. Bergen Division cars did not display route numbers.

Public Service bus lines had been carrying route numbers for some time prior to 1927 and were designated by even numbers. Street car lines were designated by odd numbers. Car lines operating through Bergen County were assigned the following route numbers in 1927:

Hudson River	1	Palisade	23
Englewood	5	Main Street	M
Fort Lee	3	Bergen Pike	33
Hackensack	37	Passaic	15
Harrison	39		

Bus lines that directly replaced car lines carried the same route numbers and names as the car lines.

85

Cars 1286 and 1854 in front of the entrance to Palisades Amusement Park on the Hudson River line.

BERGEN DIVISION
EQUIPMENT NOTES

Rolling stock acquired by Public Service from the NJ&HR in 1910 included 2 single-truck closed cars, 28 double-truck closed cars, 18 double-truck open cars, 9 utility cars, one rotary snow plow and the ferryboats Edgewater, Englewood and Leonia. When Public Service assumed operation, there were five lines: Englewood, Hudson River, Fort Lee, Hackensack, and Arlington Depot. Normal assignments for the winter of 1911-1912 were: Englewood, 9 cars; Hudson River, 11 cars; Fort Lee, 5 cars; Hackensack, 11 cars; and Arlington Depot, 2 cars; totalling 38 cars. Public Service Ry. as-

signed a variety of trolleys to Bergen Division car houses, located at Edgewater and East Rutherford. At times, some cars were stored at the western terminus in Paterson and in the south at Harrison. The following describes the car assignments:

Single Truck Cars

Public Service assigned several single-truck cars to Rutherford car house for the Arlington Depot line, the only Bergen Division line to use single-truck cars. NJ&HR cars 18 and 19, which were on the line when Public Service Ry. assumed control, remained there until 1914. Public Service renumbered No. 18 to 26, and No. 19 to 27 in 1911. No. 26 was converted to sand car 5540 in February 1915 and, after assignment to Pavonia Car House, was scrapped in 1924. No. 27 was converted to sand car 5545 in January 1917 and, after assignment to Big Tree Car House, was scrapped in 1924.

During 1913 Public Service assigned cars 37 (May), 38 (May-September), 39 (March-September), and 359 (December) to the line. Car 359 remained until September 1917. During 1914, car 369 was assigned to the line and remained at East Rutherford until March 1924. Public Service assigned other single-truck cars to the line for short durations thusly:

322	12/14-02/15
167,168,181,187	05/16-12/16
174	05/16-11/16,01/17-09/17, 01/18-01/19
325,327	01/18-12/18
172	05/18-09/18
38	05/18-09/18,01/19-06/19
184	05/19-04/20
350	05/20-03/23
369	?/14-3/24

Car 369 was the last passenger car to operate on the Arlington Depot line when the car line stopped running during the 1923 strike. It was returned to the Newark Shops in March 1924.

Car 1487 at the Edgewater Terminal after it was rebuilt for one man operation in 1926.

Double Truck Open Cars
Cars 1053-1072

NJ&HR open cars 50-70, lacking 68 which had been destroyed in 1906, were renumbered by Public Service to 1053-1072. Two cars, 55 and 56, were owned by the Jersey City, Hoboken & Paterson St. Ry. for Hudson River line service. All were 14-bench cars except 1070, which had 12 benches. No. 1070 was originally Union Traction car 15, then Newark & Hackensack 21 and next NJ&HR 67. In 1914 the open vestibules were enclosed with window panels above the front dash. In 1916 the original Providence fenders were replaced by HB "life guard" fenders.

Cars 1053-1072 remained in Bergen Division service through the summer of 1925. Car 1072 was reassigned in the summer of 1920 to the Central Ave. (Newark) car house where it remained until the summer of 1923. Winter storage was at the Secaucus car house from 1911 through 1916, and Newark Shops from 1917 through 1926. While on the Bergen Division, the cars were assigned to the Hudson River and Englewood lines and as Amusement Park trippers to the ferry. The cars were not rebuilt for one-man operation and were scrapped at Passaic Wharf during 1926 and 1927. They were originally equipped with two Peckham 14B3 trucks and four GE 67 motors totalling 152 horsepower. In 1920 the trucks were replaced by Standard 0-50 trucks.

Cars 1286-1298

Public Service assigned 12-bench open cars 1286-1298 to the Edgewater car house each summer from 1920 through 1925. They were originally built for Public Service by John Stephenson in 1905 and were equipped with two Standard 0-50 trucks and four GE 200J motors. As single-ended cars, they were assigned only to the Hudson River line which had loops at the Paterson and Edgewater terminals. They were scrapped between January and March 1927.

Cars 1400-1499

In 1904 Public Service received two batches of 12-bench open cars: Nos. 1400-1459 from J.G. Brill and Nos. 1460-1499 from John Stephenson. The Brills were equipped for single-end control and the Stephensons for double-end control. The Hudson River line, with loop termini, utilized the Brills. Three double-end 1400s were assigned for runs that turned back at Hackensack and Maywood to the Edgewater ferry. Usually ten single-end 1400s served the Hudson River line in the summer. The 1400s were also assigned to the Englewood (5 cars), Fort Lee (6), and Coytesville (4) lines, and the Amusement Park trippers (8).

Public Service rebuilt the 1400s as one-man cars, completing the work at the Newark Shops in May 1926. The 1400s were assigned each summer from 1926 through 1930 to Edgewater car house. While on the Bergen Division the 1400s used Standard C50P trucks borrowed from 2600-series cars with four Westinghouse 307 motors totalling 160 horsepower. They were the last open cars to operate on the Bergen Division in 1930.

Double Truck Closed Cars
Cars 1847-1876

The New Jersey & Hudson River Ry. & Ferry Co., Hudson River Traction Co. and Jersey City, Hoboken & Paterson St. Ry. Co. Hudson River Line cars 20-49 were acquired by Public Service in 1910. During 1911-1912 they were repaint*ed chrome yellow with l*ight cream trim, black lettering and striping and renumbered 1847-1876. The cars were equipped for double-end operation. An assortment of trucks were used, usually Standard C50P, Peckham 14B3 or Ford, Bacon & Davis MCB. The MCB trucks were built by John Stephenson from the designs of Charles F. Uebelacher. Uebelacher was an early partner in FB&D and its first Chairman of the Board. His son, David A., became a director of FB&D and the family lived in Hackensack for many years. Illustrations of Uebelacher's design appeared in Street Railway Journal, XXI:744 (1903). Motors were mainly GE 67s totalling 152 horsepower. Every car line on the Bergen Division except Arlington Depot had 1800s assigned to it. A few were reassigned to other Public Service Ry. divisions thusly:

1847,1848 to Elizabeth car house for Carteret line,

1859 to Dunellen car house 12/13; Milltown car house 7/14 for Raritan car line service.

1860 to Milltown and Dunellen from 11/3/13 to 10/21/16

1862 to Milltown and Bound Brook car houses from 12/5/13 to 5/8/16, then returned to Rutherford car house.

1866 to Milltown, Dunellen and Bound Brook car houses from 12/4/13 to 10/21/16, then to Newark Shops and to the Paterson car house on 12/2/16.

1869, 1873 to Elizabeth car house in 1931 for Carteret line.

1855 was destroyed by fire in September 1926 while operating from Edgewater car house.

The last of the group operating on the Hackensack line were cars 1849-1852, 1859-1861 and 1864-1867. These eleven were assigned to Rutherford car house until the end of Hackensack line service on 2 December 1928, after which they were sent to the Passaic Wharf for storage. The last on the Hudson River line were cars 1871-1876 in the winter of 1930-1931. The final Bergen Division assignment of the group was during the summer of 1931 when 1853, 1869, 1870 and 1873 operated on the Coytesville line. The last to operate on the Public Service system was car 1869 which was assigned to Elizabeth car house for the Carteret line from 23 April 1931 to 3 November 1934.

Six Niles interurban cars, including car 28, shown at Trenton in 1912, were acquired by Public Service from the Elizabeth & Trenton RR. Car 28 became PS 1882 and ran out of Edgewater car house from 1913 to 1916 and 1921 to 1927.

Cars 1878-1882

Public Service Ry. acquired six Niles interurban cars in 1913 through acquisition of the Trenton & New Brunswick RR which became part of the Trenton Fast Line. The cars were equipped with two Standard C55P trucks and four Westinghouse 307C motors totalling 160 horsepower. Car 1878 was built by Niles with a baggage compartment that was removed by Public Service on 15 October 1917. Renumbered by Public Service, cars 1878-1882 were assigned to the Edgewater car house in 1913 thusly: 1881 on 7/12, 1882 on 7/31, 1880 on 8/13, 1879 on 11/17 and 1878 on 11/27. Car 1877 remained on the Fast Line at New Brunswick.

Being equipped for double-end control, the cars were assigned to the Englewood line. During the summer of 1916 they were reassigned to the Paterson car house for Hawthorne line service, but were returned to Edgewater on 20 September 1921. Cars 1878-1882 remained in Englewood service from September 1921 until January-March 1927.

For the most part Public Service cars had spartan interiors with rattan-covered seats. This view shows the interior of car 3526, built at the Newark Shops in early 1913.

Cars 1900-1949

When the Public Service Corporation was formed in 1903, the street railway properties over which it gained control were in dire need of new rolling stock. One of the first actions taken was the purchase of fifty double-truck semi-convertible cars, numbered 1900-1949, from J.G. Brill in 1903. Semi-convertibles had windows that could be rolled up into the ceiling, making a partially-open car. This enabled the car to be used both summer and winter with equal comfort. They were widely assigned in Hudson, Passaic, Essex and Union counties. Cars from this series first appeared in Bergen County on the White Line (Hoboken-Paterson) in December 1903. They first appeared in Hackensack on the Main St. line which opened on 16 May 1904 into Hackensack from Lodi, Passaic and Paterson. Main St. cars used NJ&HR tracks between Lodi and Hackensack.

From August to October 1905, several 1900s were assigned to the Englewood-Weehawken Joint Line operated over NJ&HR tracks via the Englewood line, Chestnut St., Englewood to the Palisade line at Main St., Fort Lee. On the eve of commencing the Joint Line service,

Public Service stored several 1900s at the NJ&HR Edgewater car house.

Public Service Ry. assigned cars 1941, 1943, 1944, 1945, 1946 and 1948 to the Hackensack line operating out of the Rutherford car house during the winter of 1910-1911. These were replaced in the early summer of 1911 by cars 1906, 1907, 1908, 1910 and 1911 which remained until late 1912. Car 1941 operated on the Hackensack line from January 1911 until 1913. During the summer of 1917 cars 1918, 1919, 1927 and 1931 were assigned to the line. Cars No. 1919 (5/19 to 7/19), 1927 (4/18 to 10/19) and 1931 (4/18 to 10/19) were the last 1900s to be assigned to the Bergen Division. The cars were suitable for the Hackensack line's many short-radius curves because of their short (20 feet) center-line distance between truck centers.

Before Public Service took control of the NJ&HR, Public Service Ry. painted Car 1949 in Hudson River Line carmine red with Hudson River-style extra extended Gothic lettering on the car sides and numbers on the front and rear dash boards. It operated out of the Paterson car house on the Hudson River line at the time.

Cars 2050-2199

Public Service Ry. ordered 150 cars (2050-2199) from Cincinnati Car Co. in 1908. Six (2051, 2099, 2157, 2178, 2190 and 2194) were assigned to Edgewater car house from the summer of 1926 through the summer of 1927 for Coytesville line service. These cars had double-end controls, Brill B27G trucks and four Westinghouse 101B motors totaling 160 horsepower.

Cars 2400-2475

These cars were built in 1912, 2400-2425 being built by Public Service Ry. in the Newark Shops and cars 2426-2475 by the Cincinnati Car Co. Three Newark Shop cars (2406, 2416 and 2421) and eight Cincinnati cars (2427, 2432, 2446, 2451, 2456, 2460, 2462 and 2468) were assigned to the Edgewater car house in 1928 for Hudson River line service. An additional Cincinnati car (2451) was assigned to Edgewater in 1931. In addition to Hudson River line service, four cars were used on the Coytesville line in 1932 and 1933 as substitutes for 3500s being rebuilt as deluxe cars. In 1932 Public Service reassigned cars 2432 and 2468. Cars 2406, 2416. 2427, and 2446 were

Jumbo car 3500, shown here at Edgewater, had a checkered career. It began as Camden & Suburban 127 in 1899, was lengthened and renumbered 256 in 1904 Two jumbos were sent to the Bergen Division in 1911 and six more in 1912.

reassigned in 1933, leaving five 2400s at Edgewater. The last 2400s (2421, 2451, 2456, 2460 and 2462) to operate on the Bergen Division ran during the winter of 1933-1934.

Car 2431, which did not operate on the Bergen Division, is preserved by the Branford Electric Railway Association at East Haven, CT. Car No. 2431 has been stored at the museum since 1947, and is currently being refurbished. It is the lone operating survivor of the Public Service system that once numbered 2575 trolley cars and 897 track miles.

Cars 2651-2700 and 2701-2775

Fourteen days after the shutdown of the Hackensack line on 16 December 1928, Public Service extended the 39 — Harrison car line to the Rutherford car house. Cars of the Harrison line were assigned at Rutherford from December 1928 until August 1931. Public Service assigned 21 cars to the Harrison line which were housed at the Rutherford and Harrison car houses. From 1929 until 1931 any of following Harrison car line cars could have been at Rutherford: 2674, 2681, 2683, 2706, 2709-2711, 2717, 2722, 2724, 2725, 2752-2754, 2756, 2759, 2762-2764, 2766 and 2769. The cars from the 2651-2700 group were built by the Public Service Newark Shops in 1917. Cars from the 2701-2725 and 2751-2775 groups were built by Cincinnati Car Co. in 1917. Cars from the 2751-2775 group were renumbered from 3225-3249 in the late 1920s after operating for ten years on the Southern (Camden) Division.

A sister car, No. 2760, was preserved in operating condition at the Branford Electric Railvay Association museum in East Haven, CT., but was sold for scrap in the late 1940s. A sister car, No. 2651, was rescued from a New Jersey farm and restored, but is not in operating condition at this time. It is the property of the North Jersey Electric Ry. Historical Society at Ringoes, NJ.

Cars 3500-3507

Early in Public Service history it was customary to number cars in North Jersey from 1 through 2999 and in South Jersey from 3000 up. As the car fleet grew in the 1920s, higher numbers were given to Northern Division cars, e.g. 4000-4196 open cars, 7000-7199 Birneys and 8000-8019 Newark subway cars. The 3500s were the first cars to break the customary numbering practice. Cars 3500-3507 were transferred from Camden to the Newark Shops in 1911, and assigned to the Englewood line in October. They remained there until the spring of 1927, then were sent to Passaic Wharf for scrapping. Car 3503 was burned on 20 December 1912 while it was in the wooded area east of Morsemere. The fire was the result of a short circuit, as was a second fire at 5:30 a.m. on 1 April 1922. Car 3502 burned on Broad Ave. south of Lakeview Ave. in Leonia and was totally destroyed.

The 3500s were originally 28-foot cars for the Camden & Suburban Ry. built by the St. Louis Car Co. in 1899. Eight (originally Nos. 127-134, then 252-266, even numbers) were lengthened in 1904 and at 53 feet 4 inches overall with 41-foot 8-inch bodies, were the longest cars on the Public Service Ry. roster. They were referred to as the "Jumbo Cars." They were advertised for sale in 1907 described as "high-speed interurban electric cars, fully-equipped; 75 h.p. motors, mahogany finish; style, St. Louis interurban. Cars can be seen at Camden." The advertisement circulated for almost a year but the cars were not sold. A unique feature of these cars was that they originally carried a Public Service Corporation of New Jersey logo on their front dashes. Painted red at Camden, they

were repainted into Public Service chrome yellow and light cream with black lettering and maroon striping upon transfer to the Bergen Division. They were equipped with two Standard C50P trucks and four motors.

Cars 3510-3541

These were, perhaps, the best-remembered trolleys on the Bergen Divison and the Trenton Fast Line. They were built in several batches at the Public Service Newark Shops: 3510-3521 in 1912 for the Bergen Division; 3522-3531 in early 1913 for the Trenton Fast Line; 3532-3541 in late 1913 for the Trenton Fast Line; and 3585-3599 in 1914 for the Trenton-Camden Riverside line. Cars 3510-3521 were delivered to Edgewater car house in August 1912 and were assigned to the Hudson River line. The cars seated 52 passengers whereas the 1800-series cars they replaced seated 40 to 44.

Six Fast Line cars (3537-3541) were repainted yellow and assigned to Edgewater in September 1917 to cope with the wartime traffic on the Englewood line generated by Camp Merritt. No. 3536 was assigned to the Bergen Division in October 1917 and returned to the Fast Line in December. It was the first of

several green Fast Line cars on the Bergen Division. Fast Line schedules were reduced during the mid- and late-1920s, enabling transfer of the remaining Fast Line 3510-series cars to the Bergen Division in the winter of 1925-1926. The last car sent to the Bergen Division was 3524 in July 1931. The Fast Line schedule thereafter was handled by cars 3600-3609.

Public Service had introduced "super service" bus routes in 1927 utilizing buses painted duco red instead of the customary Public Service chrome yellow and equipped with parlor car interiors. This idea was also applied to the Bergen Division 3510-series cars. Between 1927 and 1931 cars 3510, 3513, 3515, 3528, 3531, 3532, 3533, 3535, 3538, 3539 and 3540 were refurbished with deluxe cross seats and interiors at the Newark Shops. Car 3540 was the first refurbished in 1927 for the Hudson River line. All Bergen Division 3510-series cars were repainted duco red with light cream trim during this period. While the 3500s were in the Newark Shops for renovation, eleven 2400-series cars operated on the Bergen Division.

Cars 3510-3541 were equipped with two Standard C55P trucks and four Westinghouse 310C2 motors for a total

Car 3536 was photographed on 21 May 1937 on the Hudson River line at the junction with the former Fort Lee line near Palisades Park.

of 240 horsepower. Car 3541 was destroyed by a short-circuit fire in 1918. The remaining cars were scrapped at Passaic Wharf during 1938 and 1939.

Cars 3584, 3585-3599

Public Service Ry. built cars 3585-3599 at its Newark Shops in 1914 and assigned them to the Riverside line operating between Camden and Trenton. Car 3584 was built in the Newark Shops in 1919 from the remnants of car 3612 that was destroyed by fire after a collision with car 3610 at Delair, NJ in June 1919. Cars 3584 and 3588 were stored at the Newton Avenue car house in Camden following closure of the Riverside line on 18 April 1931. They were transferred to Newark in November 1933, repainted from chrome yellow to duco red, then assigned to Edgewater car house in January 1934. Eight other cars from this group were assigned to the Hudson Division and operated on the 15—Passaic and 31—Grove St. lines.

Cars 3584 and 3588 were assigned at various times to the Hudson River and Englewood lines. Their principal assignment was the school run between Edgewater and Fort Lee High School and to the Palisades Amusement Park trippers to the ferry. They were scrapped at Passaic Wharf in August and October 1940 respectively. The cars were equipped with two Standard C50P trucks and double-end control. No. 3584 had four Westinghouse 307 motors totalling 160 horsepower while 3588 had four Westinghouse 310 motors totalling 240 horsepower.

Cars 3600-3609

These cars was built in 1916 by J. G. Brill and the wiring, controllers and trucks were installed by Public Service at the Newark Shops. The 3600s were assigned

to the Trenton Fast Line and its Perth Amboy branch. When Fast Line service was reduced, three were transferred to the Edgewater car house — 3603 on 18 December 1930; 3604 on 8 March 1931; and 3607 on 26 February 31. They operated on the Englewood line until December 1932/March 1933, then were sent to the Newark Shops for storage.

Cars 3604 and 3607 were equipped with Standard C55P trucks and 3603 was equipped with Ford, Bacon & Davis (Stephenson) MCB trucks while on the Bergen Division. The C55P trucks had Westinghouse 307CV3 motors totalling 160 horsepower. The MCB trucks had GE67 motors totalling 152 horsepower. The entire series was equipped for double-end operation.

The yard alongside the Edgewater ferry terminal was used for storage for cars laying over between runs and for some service equipment. This view looks west from near the waterfront towards the power plant. Note the roller coaster in the amusement park at the top of the cliff. From the left, the cars on the storage tracks are one of the NJ&HR cars signed for Hudson River; a 3500-series jumbo car signed for Tenafly; car 1855, formerly NJ&HR 30, signed for Fort Lee and a partially obscured car; sand car 5500, an ex-passenger car built by Brill for Consolidated Traction; and the NJ&HR's Peckham rotary plow. A jumbo car on the street to the rear is outbound for Englewood. The picture was taken between 1913 and 1919.

5

THE RIVERSIDE AND FORT LEE FERRY COMPANY

Early Ferry Lines

The earliest known Hudson River ferry in the Fort Lee area was operated in 1750 by Peter Bourdette, a French Huguenot. Bourdette's ferry landed at a location identified as the first natural break in the Palisades south of the New York State boundary, later named Fort Lee bluff. The landing was in Hackensack Township, formed on 31 December 1693 and subsequently subdivided into smaller incorporated areas. Reginald McMahon, Bergen County historian, in his search for.the earliest settlements along the Jersey shore of the Hudson River in this area uncovered a Dutch colony named Vriessendael which was settled in 1640. McMahon estimated the northern extent of Vriessendael to be at the Fort Lee bluff.

As early as the 1830s the west bank of the Hudson near Edgewater's northern boundary became a popular resort. Some historians consider it to be the equivalent of the modern Jersey seashore. Mansions and hotels, especially the lavish Octagon Hotel, drew a steady stream of visitors from New York City.

The first steamboat on the Hudson was Fulton's *North River Steamboat* of 1809, the first of many steamboats passing the Fort Lee bluff. *Matilda*, built in 1825 was the earliest steamboat running from lower Manhattan to Fort Lee.

The incorporators of the Paterson and Fort Lee Railroad received a charter for the Fort Lee and New York Steamboat Company on 15 March 1832. The company was authorized capital stock of $50,000 in $25 shares. The directors were empowered increase capitalization to $100,000 and to regulate rates charged by the boat line. The railroad was never built and it is probable that the steamboat line never commenced operation.

A large estate in the Fort Lee area named Tilletudlum, was owned by Francis R. Tillou of New York City. The estate reportedly became a weekend retreat for Tammany Hall boss William Tweed during the Civil War. The New Jersey Legislature granted Tillou a charter on 1 March 1849 to maintain a ferry between Fort Lee and New York City. He was authorized to build docks for a ferry landing in Fort Lee and to provide one or more steamboats. Bergen County was authorized to establish the rates for the line. A map of Bergen County dated 1867 located at the Bergen Museum of Art and Science at Paramus showed Tillou's dock on the Edgewater shore directly opposite West 140th Street, Manhattan.

On 10 February 1854 the State of New Jersey granted a charter to Robert Annett for a ferry from his dock in Fort Lee to such places in New York City that he might deem proper The State fixed the following tolls:

Passengers over 12	12 cents
Passengers under 12	6 cents
One horse rode or led	18 cents
One mule rode or led	18 cents
One head of cattle rode or led	18 cents
One swine, sheep or lamb	10 cents
Load of hay and two horses	$1.00
Load of hay and one horse	62 cents
Wagon and two horses	50 cents
Wagon and one horse	37 cents
Two-horse carriage or pleasure wagon	62 cents
One-horse carriage or pleasure wagon	50 cents

On the New York side of the river the Harlem Stage and Ferry Co. was incorporated on 17 April 1860 and authorized to establish a ferry from the foot of West 125th Street to Edgewater and to run a line of stages from the ferry through 125th Street to Third Avenue, then north to the Harlem Bridge. On 13 September 1860 the Board of Aldermen of New York adopted a resolution to establish a ferry from West 130th Street to a point on the Jersey shore nearly opposite, and to direct the Comptroller to advertise for proposals.

On 11 March 1862, the State of New Jersey granted James Aird Dempsey and Allan Melville a charter for a ferry from any landing in the Edgewater area to Manhattanville, the area at the foot of 130th Street, Manhattan. The tolls were to be same as those set for Annett's ferry.

There is no evidence that any of these lines ever operated. The earliest known service was operated by the steamboat *Thomas Hulse*, built in 1851. Excursion ads of 1853 show the boat running up the Hudson. A July 1863 real estate ad is the earliest showing it running to Edgewater. The 30 May 1867 issue of Jersey City's *American Standard* advertised three round trips daily between Fort Lee, Pleasant Valley, Shady-side, and Christopher Street, Manhattan. It left Fort Lee at 7:30 am, 12 noon, and 3:45 pm, and Christopher Street at 10 am, and 2 and 3:45 pm. Captain G. W. Annet was at the helm. An oil painting by J.G. Brown (1832-1893) in the collection of John D. Rockefeller 3rd shows the *Thomas Hulse*. The boat is approaching Sneads Landing, later the site of the Fort Lee Park boat landing.

The Fort Lee, Edgewater, Bull's Ferry and New York Peoples' Ferry Co. was incorporated on 31 March 1865 in New York and on 17 April 1866 in New Jersey. The New York charter also bore the name of The Palisades Ferry Co. With two corporate names, the ferry was referred to either as Peoples' or Palisade Ferry. The company bought the wooden, 196-ton, side-wheel steamboat *Island City* which had been built in New York in 1850 by Thomas Collyer. It was renamed *Palisade* in 1867 and put under the com-

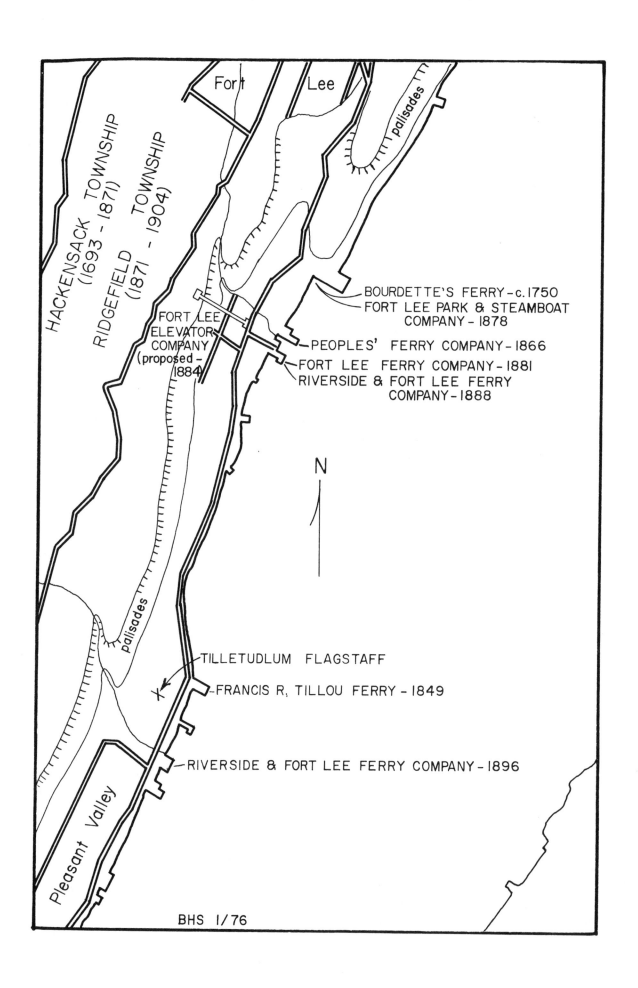

Fort Lee

HACKENSACK TOWNSHIP
(1693 - 1871)

RIDGEFIELD TOWNSHIP
(1871 - 1904)

palisades

FORT LEE
ELEVATOR
COMPANY
(proposed -
1884)

BOURDETTE'S FERRY - c. 1750
FORT LEE PARK & STEAMBOAT
    COMPANY - 1878

PEOPLES' FERRY COMPANY - 1866
FORT LEE FERRY COMPANY - 1881
RIVERSIDE & FORT LEE FERRY
    COMPANY - 1888

N

palisades

TILLETUDLUM FLAGSTAFF

FRANCIS R, TILLOU FERRY - 1849

RIVERSIDE & FORT LEE FERRY COMPANY - 1896

Pleasant Valley

BHS 1/76

View of the Palisades, Hudson River, 1867, with the *Thomas Hulse* approaching Snead's Landing. Painted by J. G. Brown. From the collection of Mr. and Mrs. John D. Rockefeller 3rd.

mand of Captain Patrick O'Leary of Fort Lee. The *Palisade* was sold in 1870 to a line operating on the James and Potomac rivers in Virginia. The Palisade Ferry Company purchased a new side-wheel steamboat *Pleasant Valley* which was built at the Terry yard in Keyport, N. J. in 1870. The *Pleasant Valley* operated between Fort Lee, Pleasant Valley, Shadyside and Christopher Street, Manhattan. A competing service, owner unknown, was offered from Fort Lee to Spring Street, Manhattan. In 1871 Thomas Dunn English wrote that there were bitter feelings and rivalry between the two boats. On summer weekends each line carried about 3000 passengers who escaped the heat and smells of the city by a visit to Fort Lee.

The Peoples' Ferry was succeeded on 22 September 1878 by the Fort Lee Park and Steamboat Co. which was chartered on 15 November 1878 and which built the Fort Lee Park and Pavilion, a summer hotel and amusement park on the site of the Bourdette homestead in Fort Lee (Ridgefield Township). In order to draw business, the company contracted with the Brooklyn Annex ferry early in 1880 to operate its *Annex No. 2* between West 129th Street and Fort Lee Park. Revenue trips commenced on 23 May 1880 and about 1600 passengers were carried each way. This was probably the first scheduled ferry crossing to Upper Manhattan.

Fort Lee Ferry Company

The first franchise for a ferry to Fort Lee based in New York was auctioned by the New York Sinking Fund Commission to one Edward H. Coffin who was to pay eight percent of the gross receipts on the New York side. The franchise, to run ten years from 1 May 1881, was granted on 30 April 1881. All-year service was to be provided and the passenger fare was set at ten cents. Coffin assigned the franchise and a lease of New York City waterfront facilities to the Fort Lee Ferry Co.

The Fort Lee Ferry chartered the double-end side-wheel ferryboat *George Mark* from the West Troy Ferry Company. The Fort Lee Park and Pavilion Co. would not permit the *George Mark* to use its dock and the Fort Lee Ferry was forced to a build a new dock further south at Orchard Street adjacent to the Peoples' Ferry Company property. The new ferry commenced service on Sunday, 5 June 1881. In the meantime the Fort Lee Park and Pavilion owners chartered the steamboat *Osseo* and began sailing between West 139th Street, Manhattan and the Fort Lee Park dock, advertising the service in New York papers. The Fort Lee Ferry obtained an injunction against the Fort Lee Park and Pavilion's line and on 18 June 1881, the *Osseo* discontinued service.

The *Englewood Standard* reported that on Sunday, 19 June 1881, an estimated 6000 people visited Fort Lee. At the departure of the 8 pm trip of the *George Mark* the crowd forced down the gates and rushed frantically for the boat. The newspaper stated, "This was simply the result of overcrowding the boats and if people were assured of seats there would be no such rushes for the boat." The Fort Lee Ferry crossed the Hudson every half hour from 6 am to 7:30 pm.

From the *American Standard*, Jersey City.

On 25 January 1882, the Fort Lee Ferry purchased the *Maspeth*, a double-end wooden boat of 430 gross tons built in 1866 at New York, from the Nassau Ferry Company which operated on the East River. The boat was overhauled at a Jersey City shipyard and renamed *Fort Lee* on 22 May 1882. Until the *Fort Lee* was ready for service the *Midland* of the New York Midland Railroad (a predecessor of the New York, Ontario and Western R. R.) was chartered. The *Midland* was built in 1872 at Greenpoint, Brooklyn, N. Y. for service between Weehawken and Manhattan. A timetable in a September,1882 issue of the *Englewood Standard* showed the first trip from Fort Lee at 5:45 am and the last at 8:50 pm with one boat in service. During the summer of 1882 stages ran from Pleasant Valley and Fort Lee connecting with the ferries and to the Palisade Mountain House located on the Palisades crest overlooking Englewood and the Northern Valley. The Palisade Mountain House, opened on 7 June 1860 and burned in 1884, had been owned by Senator Cornelius Lydecker and William B. Banta.

The Fort Lee Ferry was incorporated in New York on 7 February 1884 with Edward H. Coffin as president and Hiram R. Dixon as secretary. The deed to the Orchard St. property was obtained by Coffin for the ferry company on 12 April 1882. Coffin leased the land underwater at the Orchard St. landing from the State of New Jersey on 20 May 1882. On 6 March 1886 the directors of the Fort Lee Ferry Company passed a resolution to borrow money to purchase certain rights, titles and interests held by Coffin. The proceeds of a $50,000 mortgage secured from the Union Trust Company of New York in January 1887 was used for this purpose. The waterfront property (wharfage and bulkheads) from 130th to 131st Street at Manhattanville was leased by the ferry company from the City of New York on 29 April 1887.

Riverside and Fort Lee Ferry Co.

Coffin withdrew from the ferry management in early 1888. He transferred the Orchard Street property, the New York franchise and the underwater rights at Edgewater to Edward P. Steers in early April. Steers, James P. Pauling, Elisha Wells Sackett, Antonio Rasines and William Moores filed for incorporation on 28 June 1888 for the Riverside and Fort Lee Ferry Company. John S.

The *Pleasant Valley* operated between Fort Lee and Christopher St., Manhattan, from 1870 to 1896.

Williams was president of the new company; William Moores, secretary; and Edward Lawson, general manager. The *Fort Lee* was sold to the new company by Coffin.

Steers deeded the Orchard Street property to the Riverside and Fort Lee Ferry Co. on 23 March 1889. In April 1889 the company purchased the *George Washington* from the Williamsburgh Ferries on the East River, New York City. The boat, which was not renamed, was a wooden side-wheeler measuring 414 gross tons built at Brooklyn in 1856. The wharfage and bulkheads between 130th and 131st streets was leased to the Riverside and Fort Lee on 1 June 1889 by the City of New York. The 1881 franchise was assigned by Steers to the Riverside and Fort Lee Ferry Company on 30 December 1889. The lease and franchise both expired on 1 May 1891 but were renewed on 20 April 1891 in the names of Edward P. Steers and Edward W. Lawson, who assigned lease and franchise to the ferry company on 11 July 1892. The underwater lease at Edgewater had been

A builder's photo of the *City of Englewood* taken at Wilmington, Delaware in 1896.

assigned in March 1890. The Ferry Company obtained a $100,000 mortgage from the State Trust Company of New York on 19 April 1890.

New officers elected on 22 July 1892 were Alven Beveridge, president and Edward W. Lawson, secretary.

The construction of Bergen County Traction's railway caused drastic changes for the ferry operation. The BCT acquired control of the ferry in order to control access to upper Manhattan. The ferry company secured a new franchise from New York City on 1 June 1895 and became lessee of the Manhattan ferry and wharf property on 26 June, eliminating the former interested parties. The traction company decided to establish a more direct route to Manhattan and relocated the New Jersey ferry landing from Fort Lee to a riverfront property in Edgewater lying between River Road and the Hudson River at the foot of Dempsey Avenue, a

location known as Pleasant Valley. This was acquired by the Highland Improvement Co., a land development company owned by Bergen County Traction, and deeded to the Riverside and Fort Lee Ferry on 1 November 1895. Close cooperation enabled the transfer of the Edgewater landing from Orchard Street to Dempsey Avenue during 1896. The ferry company leased the riparian rights for the new ferry landing from the State of New Jersey on 4 April 1896 for an annual fee of $637.

Bergen County Traction began operation on 20 April 1896 and ferries began landing at Dempsey Avenue. Thereafter the Orchard Street landing was used only as a mooring for out-of-service boats. Fort Lee had already lost direct ferry service to lower Manhattan when the Fort Lee Park and Steamboat Company found business unprofitable and in November,1895 discontinued service. The *Pleasant Valley* was sold in 1896 to the Delaware River Rapid Transit Company and operated from Philadelphia to Gloucester City and Washington Park, New Jersey until 1912. The Fort Lee Park

and Steamboat Company was dissolved on 8 November 1900.

The Riverside and Fort Lee Ferry acquired a new ferry boat, *the City of Englewood*, which was commissioned on 27 April 1897. This and subsequent purchases are discussed at the end of this chapter.

New Jersey and Hudson River Railway and Ferry Co.

Ford, Bacon and Davis, consulting engineers, and A. Merritt Taylor, of Philadelphia, purchased all of the stock,rights, titles, deeds and interests of the Riverside and Fort Lee Ferry company on 20 February 1900. On 23 February an agreement was made to form a corporation consolidating the Bergen County Traction Company, Ridgefield and Teaneck Railway Company, Riverside and Fort Lee Ferry Company, and the Highland Improvement Company. The New Jersey and Hudson River Railway and Ferry Company was incorporated on 27 February. The ferry and real estate companies continued to exist. The ferry company was not dissolved until 1949

The *Edgewater* approaching the Edgewater Terminal on 23 June 1922. It was later rebuilt as single deck.

and the Highland Improvement Company was merged into Public Service Coordinated Transport on 30 November 1940.

The first improvements made by the new company were a new ferry building and two ferry slips in Manhattan. Construction was delayed pending construction of a new bulkhead 150 feet further out into the river by the City of New York. The contract for the new ferry house was awarded to John Monk and Son of New York. The dock work on both sides of the river was awarded to P. Sanford Ross, Inc. of Jersey City. A new ferry, the *Edgewater,* was launched in Jaunary 1902, replacing the *George Washington.* The *Easton* was acquired second-hand in 1906 and renamed as the *Leonia.*

The new ferry house at the foot of 130th Street, Manhattan, was opened on 2 July 1903. The building had a steel frame with copper front and clock tower. The interior was similar to the Desbrosses Street ferry house of the Pennsylvania R. R. Because of the configuration of New York streets, 125th and 130th streets both reached the river at the same point. Street cars were signed for "130th St. Ferry" but in the late 1930s PSCT buses advertised the ferry as "125th St. Ferry."

The company was reorganized in early 1909 to increase the authorized capital stock to $1 million for construction of new facilities including a second ferry slip on the south side of the slip at New York. The name was changed on 14 April from Riverside and Fort Lee Ferry Company to The Riverside and Fort Lee

Ferry Company.

The New Jersey and Hudson River Railway also incorporated the Alpine Navigation Company on 10 May 1910 for navigation on the Hudson River. The company never operated and was dissolved on 5 July 1911.

Public Service Corporation

Public Service Corporation of New Jersey took control of the New Jersey and Hudson River Railway on 1 July 1910 after purchasing 97.79% of the company's stock. The takeover included The Riverside and Fort Lee Ferry which continued as a New York corporation wholly owned by Public Service. Public Service Corporation leased the NJ&HR and The Riverside and Fort Lee Ferry Co. to Public Service Railway on 1 May 1911.

Two views of the 130th St. Ferry in Manhattan as it was in 1912. The *Englewood* is at the dock.

The new management installed turnstiles for fare payment in January, 1911. Two were put in use at Edgewater and one in Manhattan. As a result of the money-saving devices many passengers missed the boats and reached their homes or place of business late.

During 1912 the Bergen County Freeholders brought legal action to force a fare reduction from five to three cents. The plaintiff traced the lineage of The Riverside and Fort Lee Ferry Company back to Francis R. Tillou's 1849 ferry charter in which the State of New Jersey authorized Bergen County to establish fares. The corporate lineage to Tillou's ferry was not proven but the Freeholders adopted a resolution on 21 October 1912 ordering the reduction. Another resolution was passed on 15 June 1914, ordering the 3-cent fare to go into effect on 25 June. Public Service Corporation secured a temporary injunction in the Federal District Court on 23 June 1914 blocking the reduction. The ferry passenger fare nagged into 1915 and on 29 October 1915 Public Service Corporation of New Jersey offered a 50-trip ticket for $2.00 which was good anytime during the year issued.

A new ferryboat was built in 1915. The contract was awarded to W. and A. Fletcher of Hoboken. The construction of the hull was sublet to Harlan and Hollingsworth at Wilmington, Delaware. The hull was launched on 29 June 1915 and christened *Fort Lee* by Miss Ellen G. McCarter, daughter of Thomas N. McCarter, president of both Public Service Corporation and the ferry company. The hull was towed to the Fletcher yard where the machinery was installed and the boat completed. The *Fort Lee*, which cost $196,000, was commissioned on 23 October 1915.

"Clang! Clang! booms the bell. Ting-a-ling goes the jingle bell down in the engine room, one blast of the big whistle and we are off....." so goes the description of a sail across the Hudson on board the 125th Street ferry presented in the August, 1917 issue of *The Trolley Wheel*, a monthly publication devoted to the interests of employees of Public Service Railway Company. "Go up on the deck of the *Edgewater* as she moves out of the slip on the Jersey side and see the beautiful view spread out before you. The majestic Hudson is dotted with craft of all kinds from big ocean going vessels to tiny launches, while directly ahead is New York with its millions of people and to the west stand the Palisades keeping guard over the Jersey shore.

"Clang! goes the engine room gong, and the engines slow down; Another stroke on the gong and they stop. Clang! Clang! again the reverse; Once again the gong rings and the engine stops, there is a slight jar as the boat touches the bridge, the cables are made fast, the ratchets sing their metallic tune, up go the gates and the crowds pour ashore at 130th Street, New York..." The article provided the names of some of the ferry employees during 1917: Captain Edgar Van Name, who was in charge of Public Service's two ferry routes; Captains Tracy, Brannigan, Herring, Holzwarth, Mc Cabe, Logan and Hasbrouck. The mechanical department of the ferries was presided over by Chief Engineer Van Woert who used a tallow cup as a rattle when he was a baby

and grew up with a monkey wrench in his hand. Below decks on the ferries were Engineers Morris Kinhoeffer, Louie Larson, Fred Swanson, William Dick, and John Seeker.

In 1917 The Riverside and Fort Lee Ferry maintained its schedule with two boats on weekdays and three on weekends. At this time there were four ferryboats on the roster: *Leonia* (built 1893), *Englewood* (1897), *Edgewater* (1902), and *Fort Lee* (1915).

During World War I the ferry and the Englewood car line had heavy traffic transporting soldiers and civilians to and from Camp Merritt at Bergenfield. Postwar labor strife disrupted ferry service from 9 to 12 January and from 3 to 8 March 1919. During the March strike limited service was provided with one boat with ferry superintendent Captain Van Name at the wheel; engineer and fireman from Public Service Electric Company; and deckhands from Public Service Railway

During the 1920s service was increased and additional ferry boats ac-

quired. Two second-hand Long Island Railroad boats were purchased on 8 June 1921, one from the City of Boston on 25 February 1927, and one from the state of Mainein 1928. The company owned six boats in 1928: *Leonia* (built 1893), *Edgewater*(1902), *Ridgefield* (1901), *Hackensack* (1906), *Tenafly* (1906), and *Fort Lee* (1915). In 1928 the 130th St. Ferry operated four boats on weekdays and six boats on weekends.

The City of New York built a third slip at 130th Street which opened on 15 April 1925. The city also enlarged the ferry house and leased both to The Riverside and Fort Lee Ferry for a term of 25 years. The addition had a frontage of 110 feet and, with the older building, gave a total of 260 feet frontage on the ferry plaza.

With the formation of Public Service Coordinated Transport Company on 31 January 1928, The Riverside and Fort Lee Ferry Company became a subsidiary of the new company.

The ultimate demise of the Fort Lee ferry became inevitable with construc-

The 130th St. Terminal was expanded in 1925. The *Leonia* (ex-*Easton*) is at the slip. New York Central R. R. freight trains sometimes blocked the ferry entrance.

tion of the George Washington Bridge between Fort Lee and West 176th Street, Manhattan beginning in 1927. The bridge was opened on 25 October 1931. State highways 1, 4, and 6 (now 46), were immediately opened connecting inland New Jersey to the bridge. Motorists found the new highways to be faster and more convenient than old state highway 5, which connected with the Edgewater ferry. Route 5 was serpentine and required a hard climb up the Palisades with several traffic lights. Motorists waiting for the ferries generated long lines of automobiles often backing up the hill. Still the ferry had some years remaining. In 1931, the boats carried 2,636,000 vehicles. Traffic declined in 1932 and 1933 but began to climb annually to a peak of 3,491,200 vehicles. The increase was

The Englewood ferry terminal from the Hudson River showing the Palisades Amusement Park atop the cliffs in the rear. The *Leonia* is in the ferry slip.

caused in part by gradual economic recovery during the New Deal, plus a 25-cent fare for car and passengers versus a 50-cent toll on the bridge. During the 1930s Public Service buses advertised the cheap ferry fare on their rear windows

Public Service renewed the ferry line's lease of the ferryhouse and property in New York during 1936.

The Public Service Bayonne ferry (Port Richmond and Bergen Point Ferry Company) lost traffic to the Kill von Kull Bridge and, on 21 May 1937, the ferry rights and necessary real estate were sold to Electric Ferries, Incorporated who replaced the Public Service steamboats with diesel-electric vessels. The first boat in service was the *Westchester* (ex-*Frederick Pierce*) built in 1926 for the original Electric Ferries operation from Weehawken to West 23rd Street, New York. The *Paterson* and *Englewood* were tied up at Edgewater, the *Paterson* being scrapped in 1939 and the *Englewood* sold to the New York and Englewood Ferry Company in the same year.

During 1940 alterations were made to the Edgewater ferry building following discontinuance of the Hudson River trolley in 1938. A new bus terminal was provided and the ferry house exterior and interior was painted.

Public Service Coordinated Transport discontinued the Riverside and Fort Lee Ferry on 31 July 1943. The Edgewater terminal property and ferry rights, ferryboats excluded, were leased to Electric Ferries, Incorporated for ten years from 1 August 1943. Public Service said that this action was brought about because of the wartime conditions which reduced automobile traffic due to gasoline rationing and the conservation of rubber for automobile tires. Public Service Coordinated Transport filed a certificate of dissolution for The Riverside and Fort Lee Ferry Company on 15 November 1949.

The Electric Ferries advertised modern diesel-electric ferryboats with open decks and six lanes having a capacity of 50 automobiles. Their fleet at Edgewater included the *Palisades*, *Hudson*, *North Jersey*, and *E. G. Diefenbach*. An observation made by the authors was that the diesel-electric boats were slower and noisier than the Public Service's steam ferryboats.

In Manhattan the Third Avenue Ry. (Third Avenue Transit System) operated three trolley car lines to 125th St. ferry terminal until 1946; X — 125th St. Cross Town; 10th Ave. — Tenth Avenue to the 42nd St. West Shore ferry terminal; and W — Willis Avenue to Third Avenue and Fordham Road in the Bronx. Also about two blocks up 125th St., the IRT Seventh Avenue-Broadway subway line was available.

By this time, Amsterdam Ave. had been renamed W. 125th St. and old 125th St. was renamed LaSalle St. Electric Ferries discontinued service on the 125th Street ferry on 16 December 1950. Signs notifying the public had been posted as early as 27 September. The *Palisades* made the last crossing, leaving the 125th Street terminal at midnight. The franchise granted by the City of New York to the ferry expired with the last sailing.

The Public Service car houses on Dempsey Avenue were sold in 1959 to the Excel Pharmacal Company, a New York business. The ferry plaza property and waterfront riparian rights were sold to Mid-Em-Cee of Iselin, New Jersey and to Mid-Em-Ess Corporation of Brooklyn, New York. Both companies were subsidiaries of Summer Brothers Construction Company of Iselin, New Jersey. In 1961 a $1.3 million apartment building, The Caribbean House, was constructed on two acres at the site of the original Orchard Street ferry landing of the old Fort Lee Ferry Co. Today little remains as a reminder of crossings from Fort Lee and Edgewater. Older Edgewater residents still refer to the ferry plaza area as the center of town; their mourning of the passing of the ferry continues.

RIVERSIDE AND FORT LEE FERRY BOATS

Fort Lee (1st). The *Fort Lee* was acquired from the Fort Lee Ferry Co. in 1888 and is discussed on page 88. It was replaced by the *City of Englewood* and abandoned on the mud flats at Orchard Street during 1897.

George Washington. This boat was built at Brooklyn in 1856 and was a wooden side-wheeler of 414 gross tons. It was purchased in April 1889 from the Williamsburgh Ferries on the East River, New York City. It was not renamed. In 1902, the *Edgewater* supplanted the *George Washington* which was chartered by the Washington and Alexandria Ferry for Potomac River service from July, 1903 until May, 1905 to replace a boat destroyed by fire. The *George Washington* made her last trip on 7 May 1908. She was later towed by two tugs from her mooring at Edgewater to the Orchard Street

slip. She was converted into a house by Captain George White who was in charge of the craft moored below the old ferry slip during the winter. He leased it for $250 annually until 1918.

Englewood. This boat was ordered from the Jackson and Sharp Company of Wilmington, Delaware and launched on 16 November 1896. It was christened *City of Englewood.* After being outfitted with machinery and trials on the Delaware River it arrived at Edgewater on 14 January 1897 and was commissioned on 27 April. The new boat had an iron hull, vertical-beam engine with paddle wheels, measured 484 gross tons, and cost $38,000. The boat was renamed *Englewood* on 23 March 1901.

The *Englewood* was transferred to the Port Richmond & Bergen Point Ferry in 1921 and replaced in 1937. It was tied up at Edgewater and in 1939 was sold to the New York and Englewood Ferry Co. and operated as the Dyckman Street ferry. It was scrapped at Passaic Wharf, Newark, in March 1940.

Edgewater. The *Edgewater* was launched on 9 January 1902 at the Harlan and Hollingsworth Company yard in Wilmington, Delaware. It was reported to be one of the swiftest ferryboats in the harbor. Its hull was constructed as a powerful ice breaker to force its way through the large ice floes encountered in this part of the Hudson River. The boat was commissioned on 3 July 1902 and its maiden voyage left Edgewater at 3:00 pm. It ran to 130th Street where additional guests boarded, then steamed up the Hudson to Yonkers and return.

The boat was sold to Pearsall Equipment Co., Brooklyn, N.Y. and chartered by Kass Ferries, Inc. of Camden, N.J. It operated from Kaighn Ave., Camden, to South Street, Philadelphia. Service ended 31 December 1945 and the boat was laid up at Philadelphia and was scrapped at Tacony, PA in 1948. When at Camden the smokestack still carried the Public Service circle and triangle logo

Leonia. The *Easton* of the Central R.R. of New Jersey was purchased on 10 Feb-

The second *Fort Lee* approaches the Edgewater ferry terminal with a full load in July 1925. Note the separate entryways for men and women. Men/women cabins actually indicated smoking/no smoking. Non-smoking men were welcome in the Ladies' cabin on a ferry boat.

ruary 1906 for $50,000. The *Easton* (and sister boat *Mauch Chunk*) had been built in 1893 by Harlan and Hollingsworth and ran on the Royal Blue ferry from Jersey City to the Battery, which ended service in 1905. The *Easton* was a commodious double-deck boat and could attain a speed of 15 knots. Painted white by the Central R. R., it was repainted brown by the Riverside and Fort Lee Ferry and was commissioned as the *Leonia* on 24 April 1906. It was sold on 14 February 1945 to the Westchester Ferry Corp. and was scrapped at Newburgh, N.Y. in 1947.

Fort Lee (2nd). This ferryboat was built in 1915. The contract was awarded to W.

A gallery of Riverside & Fort Lee ferryboats in service during the 1930s. From the top, they are:

the *Hackensack* in a view taken on 14 August 1937,

the *Leonia,* taken on 15 May 1938 with the New Jersey shore in the background,

the *Edgewater,* photographed on 7 June 1936, and

the *Tenafly,* shown entering the 130th Street ferry slip in Manhattan, date unknown.

The City of New York's ferryboat *Bay Ridge* and the Riverside & Fort Lee's *Englewood* await scrapping at Passaic Wharf, Newark, on 23 March 1940.

and A. Fletcher of Hoboken. The construction of the hull was sublet to Harlan and Hollingsworth at Wilmington, Delaware. The hull was launched on 29 June 1915 and christened *Fort Lee* by Miss Ellen G. McCarter, daughter of Thomas N. McCarter, president of both Public Service Corporation and the ferry company. The hull was towed to the Fletcher yard where the machinery was installed and the boat completed. The *Fort Lee*, which cost $196,000, was commissioned on 23 October 1915.

The boat was sold to Norfolk County Ferries in October 1943 for the Norfolk to Portsmouth ferry (Virginia). It was sent to Colounas Shipyard, Berkley, Virginia in August 1949. and was broken up in September 1950.

Hackensack and
Tenafly. The ferry fleet was increased by the purchase on 8 June 1921 of two second-hand Long Island Railroad boats, the *Hempstead* and *Babylon*. Ownership was vested in the Holland Company which was organized on 27 July 1892 to conduct a real estate business in New York and New Jersey. Its stock was held by Public Service Corporation. The *Hempstead* was renamed *Hackensack*, and the *Babylon* was renamed *Tenafly*. When the *Hackensack* and *Tenafly* went into service the *Englewood* were transferred to Public Service's Port Richmond and Bergen Point ferry (Bayonne). In 1924 the *Hackensack* and *Tenafly* was altered at the Todd Shipyard in Hoboken, getting four teamways instead of two by narrowing each passenger cabin by eight feet. The upper-deck passenger cabins were removed.

The *Hackensack* was laid up at Passaic Wharf, Newark, in August 1943. It was sold on December 1945 to the Massachusetts Steamship Company and renamed *Islander*. On 28 April 1949 the *Islander* was acquired by the New Bedford, Woods Hole, Marthas Vineyard and Nantucket Steamship Authority. Sold to the Whale City Dredging and Dock Co. of New Bedford in May 1950, and on 6 June 1951 was towed to Baltimore where it was scrapped in October 1951.

The *Tenafly* was sold and stripped down to a contractor's work float and was used in the construction of the Brooklyn-Battery Tunnel in 1947. In 1949 it was seen at Shooters Island at the entrance to Newark Bay.

Paterson. The *Governor Russell* was purchased from the City of Boston on 25 February 1927 and brought to the Tietjen and Lang yard at Hoboken for refurbishing. It was renamed *Paterson*. and went into service on 26 April 1927. On 2 January 1928 it was transferred to the Port Richmond and Bergen Point Ferry to supplement the *Englewood*. Replaced in 1937, it was chartered to the North River Ferry Co, for the Nyack-Tarrytown ferry in 1938 and was scrapped at Passaic Wharf, Newark in the summer of 1939.

Ridgefield. The *Governor King* was purchased from the State of Maine in 1928. It was renamed *Ridgefield*; altered to provide four teamways; and placed in service on 16 June 1928. It was scrapped at Passaic Wharf, Newark in 1935.
Thomas N. McCarter. The last ferryboat purchase was made in April 1938 when the *Philadelphia* was purchased from the Reading Co., owner of the Delaware River Ferry Co., operating between Kaighns Point, Camden and Philadelphia, which had been recently abandoned. The vessel, built in 1926, was a welcome addition to the Public Service fleet and was renamed *Thomas N. McCarter*, chairman of the board of the Public Service companies since their founding in 1903. The *Thomas N. McCarter* was placed in service on 12 July 1938.

The boat was sold to the Chesapeake Ferry Co. on 29 July 1943. and was renamed *Newport News* in September 1943. The company and boats were sold to the Commonwealth of Virginia in 1948. The *Newport News* returned to Camden, N. J.. and was rebuilt as a diesel-powered boat in October 1951 at the John H. Mathis yard. It was sold in January 1958 and the engines removed for use in tug boats. The hull became a barracks boat at Electric Boat Company, Groton, Connecticut. It was again sold in 1980 to Sam Sardinia of Miami, Florida. It was rebuilt as a giant house boat which was completed in 1988 and towed to Annapolis, Maryland and on to Florida.

6

THE BERGEN TURNPIKE LINE

The Bergen Turnpike

During the closing years of the 1700s, the sticky, clay-like mud and uncertain bottoms of the mire on New Jersey's roads every spring made them scarcely passable and often were worse than the year before. The roads had largely been constructed by local farmers and were not intended for use as trunk or through routes and their heavy traffic. Thus, the sentiment for turnpikes and the improved roads they would bring soared after the arrival of the new century. The New Jersey State Legislature was besieged with turnpike bills and dozens of turnpike charters were granted during the first decade of the nineteenth century.

Bergen County shared in the sentiment and plans for a turnpike connecting the Hoboken ferry landing with a little village on the west bank of the Hackensack River in New Barbadoes were brought to reality on 30 November 1802 when the state legislature granted a charter to the Bergen Turnpike Co. The incorporators were John Stevens, Lewis Moore, Robert Campbell, Nehemiah Wade, Garret G. Lansing and Adam Boyd. The company was granted the authority to construct, maintain and operate a toll road between Hoboken in Bergen Township and Hackensack in New Barbadoes Township. This became one of the longest-lived transportation companies in New Jersey — 135 years (1802-1937).

Colonel John Stevens of Hoboken is better known for his accomplishments with steamboats and the first American-built steam locomotive than for his association with the Bergen Turnpike. Stevens was the first president of the company. In an 1804 letter inviting the New Jersey Secretary of State to inspect the pike on its opening day, he spelled the

company's name with a hyphen in turnpike. The hyphenated spelling was used until the 1850s.

The original turnpike was a dirt road covered with gravel or broken stone. During rainy seasons, deep ruts appeared which interrrupted travel. Three foot by eight foot planks were added to the roadbed in the 1850s which led to naming present-day 32nd Street, Union City, as the Hackensack Plank Road. Prior to the coming of the turnpike, Hackensack Plank Road was a trail dating back to 1718.

The northern terminus of the turnpike was described in an 1855 survey as"beginning in the upper part of the village of Hackensack in the county of Bergen in line or range of the southside of the Road to Paramus in the road leading to New Bridge..." The survey noted two stores at the Hackensack terminus: Banta Anderson & Co. and Henry Berry & Co.

About 1783 the first stage coach line was established between Hoboken and Hackensack. For several years prior to the opening of the Bergen Turnpike, a stage coach operated by Adam Boyd linked Hackensack with West Hoboken. Boyd advertised that he owned first-class equipment with horses and wagons in prime condition. Boyd was also proprietor of a tavern in Hackensack, had served as a lieutenant in the Revolution, was a county sheriff, and an incorporator of the Bergen Turnpike Co. Other stage lines continued operation over the years; in 1836 the through fare by stage coach between Hoboken and Hackensack was 37 1/2 cents.

Steam Railway Competition

The turnpike was subjected to competition from steam railroads during much of the 19th century. The first

threat appeared during 1832 when the newly-formed Paterson and Hudson River Rail Road Co. made overtures to the stage lines running from New York City through Hoboken, Hackensack, Hoppertown and Ramapo to Albany to abandon the Bergen Turnpike and connect with the railroad in Paterson. The railroad's proposal was presented as follows:

"...from Hoppertown it is about 7 1/4 miles to Paterson, and thence by the Rail Road to Jersey City it is 16 1/8 miles, and from Hoppertown through Hackensack to Hoboken it is about 21 miles, which is but 2 7/8 miles less than through Paterson to Jersey City. If we suppose the rate of travelling on the common or turnpike road to be six miles an hour, the route through Paterson will be passed over in 1 hour and 17 minutes less time than through Hackensack; and this difference in favor of the Rail Road route will be increased in the season of bad roads."

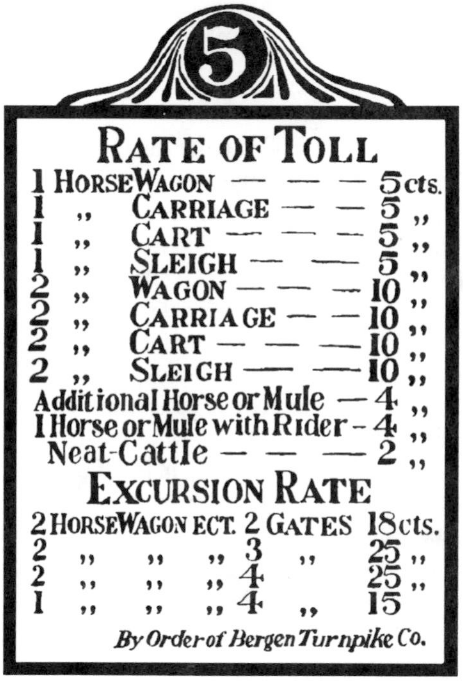

RATE OF TOLL

1 Horse Wagon	— — —	5	cts.
1 „ Carriage	— —	5	„
1 „ Cart	— — —	5	„
1 „ Sleigh	— —	5	„
2 „ Wagon	— — —	10	„
2 „ Carriage	— —	10	„
2 „ Cart	— — —	10	„
2 „ Sleigh	— — —	10	„
Additional Horse or Mule	—	4	„
1 Horse or Mule with Rider	—	4	„
Neat-Cattle	— — —	2	„

EXCURSION RATE

2 Horse Wagon ect. 2 Gates			18	cts.
2 „ „ „ 3 „				25	„
2 „ „ „ 4 „				25	„
1 „ „ „ 4 „				15	

By Order of Bergen Turnpike Co.

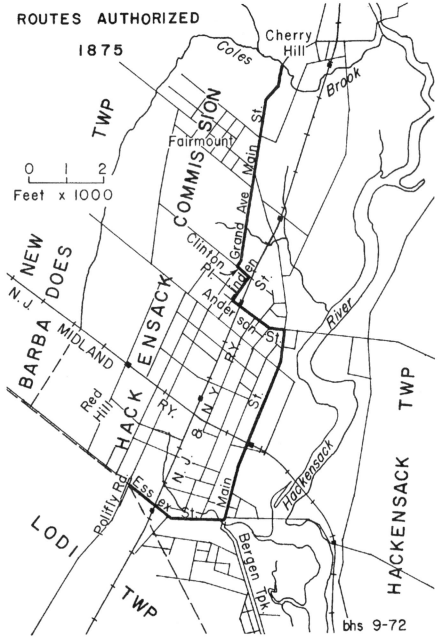

ROUTES AUTHORIZED

1875

0   1   2
Feet x 1000

bhs 9-72

The turnpike first responded with a charter amendment approved on 15 March 1858 allowing it to lay iron tracks on the toll road and to purchase cars, horses and mules, and any other equipment necessary. A prohibition on the use of steam locomotives was repealed on 2 April 1869. The lingering depression following the financial panic of 1857 and the exigencies of the Civil War contributed to the failure of the project, even though the turnpike was profitable during the war. Between November 1861 and November 1863, revenues were $21,634.17 and expenses were $10,066.13, for a net income of $11,568.04.

The panic of 1873 and the five-year depression that followed did not deter the turnpike from trying again. A charter amendment granted on 25 February 1875, authorized construction of a horse railway on two routes in the Hackensack Commission, including connections between the several steam railroad depots in Hackensack. The track gauge was to be equal to the standard wagon gauge and the company was authorized to purchase machinery, horses and mules, cars and other necessary equipment.

The turnpike again failed to build a line. After nearly two more decades of inaction, the state legislature's Committee on Railroads and Canals held a hearing during February 1892 offering the turnpike's 1875 franchise to any interested group. There appears to have been no takers.

Electric Railway Proposals

The 1892 hearings and the development of electric railways may have been the incentive for a reorganization of the company directorate in May 1893 in which Captain Andrew Zabriskie was elected President. The new directors announced a plan to build an electric railway from Hoboken to Hackensack.

Zabriskie met with the Hackensack Commission in May 1894 and asked permission to operate an electric railway on Main St. The Commission refused but asked Zabriskie to return with more detailed information. Messrs. George W. Wheeler and David A. Pell, represented the company at a meeting in August and expressed the desire to proceed at once with construction. The line was to start in

The railroad evaluated the freight business it could attract thusly:

"...there are six regular boats on the Hackensack River, plying between Hackensack and the city of New York, and it is stated by one of the principal merchants of Hackensack, that the business direct from there to Paterson employs at least one of those boats; and the others, besides supplying the town of Hackensack and its vicinity, are also employed in freighting the goods for fourteen manufacturing establishments, besides stores, situated in the vicinity of Hoppertown, Godwinville and Paramus, which establishments are nearer by some miles to Paterson than to Hackensack."

"The price of the freight of goods from New York to...Hackensack...is $1.25 per ton, and the transportation from...[Hackensack]...by the common or turnpike road, is also $1.25 per ton..."

After the Paterson and Hudson River RR was completed, other steam and horse railroad proposals appeared. These included the Northern Railroad of New Jersey in 1854, the Hackensack & New York RR in 1856, the Westfield & Hackensack Horse RR in 1860, the New Jersey Midland Railway in 1870, the Hackensack & Englewood Horse Railway in 1872, and the New York West Shore & Buffalo Railway in 1881. These companies were discussed in chapter one.

106

The Sand Hill substation on South Hudson St., Hackensack, also served as Bergen County Tollgate No. 5. Cars used on the northern section of the Bergen Pike line were stored on the wye north of the building. Picture taken on 22 March 1917.

The New Durham Substation, located at Fisher St. on the Bergen Turnpike in North Bergen Township, also housed Tollgate No. 1 for the turnpike was built from the same blueprints and was identical in every detail.

Little Ferry and follow the turnpike through New Barbadoes Township, and run on Hudson and Main streets in Hackensack to Anderson St. Turning west it followed the route to Cherry Hill which had been granted to the turnpike in 1875. The power house was to be at Little Ferry.

Once again, the Commission refused permission but the company was not deterred. During the latter part of October 1894 track laying commenced on the east side of Bergen Turnpike in Little Ferry. When the construction forces crossed the New Barbadoes Township line, they were arrested by local authorities. Work was halted on the premise that fifty percent of the abutting property owners along Hudson St. had to give their consent and that plans for the railway had to be approved by the township committee before construction would be permitted to resume. The company failed to obtain the necessary consents and approvals and construction was not resumed.

During the period from November 1894 to November 1896, the turnpike's revenues were $25,328.17 and expenses were $17,494.65. Compared with the 1861-1863 report period, net income was down 32 percent with expenses increas-

ing 74 percent while revenues increased only 17 percent. According to a report filed with the New Jersey Secretary of State on 15 January 1897, the construction and reconstruction of the road had cost $91,475. The portion from the east side of Weehawken Hill to the Hoboken Ferry had been sold in 1869 for $19,964.15, leaving the net capital expenditures at $71,510.85.

Jersey City, Hoboken & Paterson St. Ry. Co.

A commanding transportation development figure in northern New Jersey during the 1890s, B. M. Shanley consolidated most of the traction companies in Northern Hudson and Passaic counties and created the Jersey City, Hoboken and Paterson Street Ry. Co. on 1 November 1899. Three more traction companies were absorbed by the JCH&P in 1901.

The JCH&P acquired a majority of the capital stock of the Bergen Turnpike Co. during May 1900. The turnpike company was reorganized at Jersey City on 11 June 1900 with David Young as president, George W. Wheeler, vice president; Nathaniel B. Zabriskie, secretary; and James E. Hulshizer of the New Jersey

Title and Guarantee Trust Co., treasurer. Young was also president of the JCH&P and general manager of the North Jersey St. Ry. Co. The effective date of the acquisition of the Bergen Turnpike Co. was 12 June 1900 and the office was established at 83 Montgomery St., Jersey City.

During August 1900 the turnpike company petitioned for franchises for a trolley line between Hoboken and Hackensack. Messrs. Ralph Earle, an engineer, and Howard Griffiths, an attorney, were engaged to secure the franchises. Perpetual franchises were secured in each municipality on its route except Hackensack where the Improvement Commission on 7 October 1901 granted a perpetual franchise subject to an approval referendum at the end of 99 years.

While franchises were being sought, a $1 million mortgage secured by collateral bonds was obtained from the New Jersey Title and Guarantee Trust Co. on 16 April 1901. JCH&P stockholders approved the bond issue on 31 April 1901. Principal stockholders were Edward F. C. Young, David Young, Edward L. Young, John P. Feeney, James E. Hulshizer and Dennis McLaughlin of

Two Bergen Turnpike Co. cars (car 121 in the front) at the NYS&W RR grade crossing across Bergen Turnpike at Fairview in 1903 or 1904.

Hudson County and David A. Pell, Samuel Taylor and Andrew Zabriskie of Hackensack.

After the JCH&P acquired the Saddle River Traction Co. in 1899, David Young began an effort to obtain a franchise to enter Hackensack from Lodi. Young was continually thwarted by William C. Giles whose Newark & Hackensack Traction Co. was seeking a franchise to enter Hackensack from Hasbrouck Heights. To break the stalemate, Young proposed a connection between the Saddle River Traction line in Lodi and the Bergen Turnpike line in Little Ferry. This connection, which was never built, would have provided trolley service between Hackensack, Little Ferry, Lodi, Garfield and Passaic.

Rail Construction Commences

Construction of the Bergen Pike line started in North Bergen Township at the intersection of Summit Ave. and 32nd St. (Hackensack Plank Road) in April 1901. By the end of May track had been extended to the bridge spanning the West Shore RR at New Durham where construction was halted by an injunction obtained by the New York Central RR. The West Shore tracks were 20 feet below the grade of the toll road and were spanned by an iron bridge built under a contract dated 18 March 1881, under which the turnpike agreed to allow the railroad to build and maintain the bridge. A court decision on 3 September 1901 upheld the

railroad's objection to trolleys using the bridge because it was deemed too weak to support their weight. The court ruled that the Bergen Turnpike must rebuild the bridge, making it strong enough to support the trolleys.

Track was completed to Granton, a place in North Bergen Township near the West Shore RR locomotive terminal, roundhouse and shop, on 3 June 1901 and to Little Ferry during September. As construction progressed towards Hackensack during October, reconstruction of the aged wooden toll road bridges spanning Overpeck Creek and the Hackensack River was started. The bridges, built in 1828, were replaced by steel truss structures carrying a double-track railway.

The Hoboken terminal was established at the foot of 14th St. on the Hudson River. The Hoboken Ferry Co. which was operated by the DL&W RR and called the 14th St. Lackawanna Ferry, furnished connecting service to Manhattan. The ferry had commenced operations between 14th St., Hoboken, and West 14th St., Manhattan, on 1 May 1886. On 1 November 1904 the Manhattan landing was changed to West 23rd St.

The Bergen Pike Line Opens

The first trolley car to operate over the Bergen Pike line ran on 17 April 1902. It carried David Young and other JCH&P officials from the Hoboken Terminal to the West Shore RR at New Durham where

the bridge over the railroad was being rebuilt with a single track laid on the east side of the bridge's center line. The Bergen Pike line operated over JCH&P tracks in Hoboken and the West Hoboken and Union Hill areas of Union Township. The line ascended the Palisades via a horseshoe curved route named Hillside Road. The North Hudson County Ry. Co. had built the Hillside Road and opened it on 19 November 1893.

By July 1902 the line was completed between Hoboken and Little Ferry. Construction was delayed in Hackensack by a dispute over the type of brick paving used between the rails on Main St. On 23 July 1902 it was resolved that Mack brick would be used and construction resumed. On 15 August 1902 part of the construction force was shifted farther north to lay track on Main St. between Anderson St. and Cherry Hill. A crossing with the NJ&HR line at Main and Mercer streets in Hackensack was completed on 14 November.

A second location where the New York Central RR blocked a grade crossing was in Ridgefield Park by the Little Ferry depot. The turnpike and the New York, West Shore & Buffalo Ry. had made an agreement on 8 December 1881 permitting the railroad to cross the toll road at grade but no provision had been made for the turnpike to build a railway. The railroad obtained a restraining injunction in 1902. Prior to the injunction

Toll house No. 2 was an unprepossessing building located at Wolf's Creek, Ridgefield. This view, taken on 16 May 1906, shows a work crew cleaning up the property and burning the debris. The muddy, rutted condition of the road, which was paved only between the rails was the cause of much dissatisfaction by residents.

Toll house No. 3 predated the construction of the Bergen Turnpike car line. It was located at the north end of Overpeck Creek drawbridge. The sign on the side of the house announced a $50 fine for automobiles operating over the bridge at more than eight miles an hour. Picture taken in early 1916.

View east along the Bergen Turnpike from the Hackensack River drawbridge. The Little Ferry railroad grade crossings are in the distance. A car bound for Hackensack stands at the crossing. The track break at this point was never filled and the line ran in two sections until the end of service. The sign at the end of the bridge directs passersby to the Little Ferry Paper Co., off the photo to the left.

the West Shore RR ran a steam locomotive to and fro over the crossing at night to block any attempt to construct a crossing. A 31 August 1902 newspaper account stated that "detectives attired as hoboes, a monster wrecker on one side of the crossing and a locomotive and six box cars on the other, and two section gangs of laborers constitute the defence of the West Shore RR Co. against the efforts of the Bergen Turnpike Co. to lay frogs on the

crossing at Little Ferry. . . It was said yesterday that a scheme was underway by the trolley people to send a scow through the drawbridge. . . then block the bridge so as to keep the wrecker from the north side of the bridge. . . It was this rumor that caused the presence yesterday of an engine on the north side of the crossing."

The First Cars

During November 1901 the Bergen Turnpike received fifteen double-end double-truck closed cars numbered 111 to 125 from Laclede Car Co. of St. Louis. The cars were 25 feet long over the body, 38 feet 4 inches overall, and had ten windows on each side and longitudinal seating. Ten identical ten cars, numbered 101 to 110, were delivered to the JCH&P at the same time, of which 109 and 110 were assigned to the Turnpike. Two more cars (126 and 127) arrived in August 1902. The Bergen Turnpike color scheme was carmine red with light cream

lettering and striping. The cars were lettered "B. T. Co." in extra extended Gothic type which strongly resembled Pennsylvania RR type style. Eleven of the cars were assigned to the West Hoboken car house and eight to the Sand Hill substation wye at Toll Gate No. 5 in lower Hackensack.

By 1 January 1903, the line had been completed between Hoboken and the NJ&NYRR Main St. crossing in Hackensack. It was a single-track line with nineteen turnouts and was punctuated with track breaks at five railroad crossings. Because of the grade crossing disputes, no scheduled cars were operated north of New Durham during 1902. The West Shore RR claimed it would cost more than $30,000 for interlocking signals and safety devices to protect the Little Ferry crossing. A bill introduced into the state legislature in March 1903 which would have amended the Bergen Turnpike charter to allow an electric railway on the road was defeated.

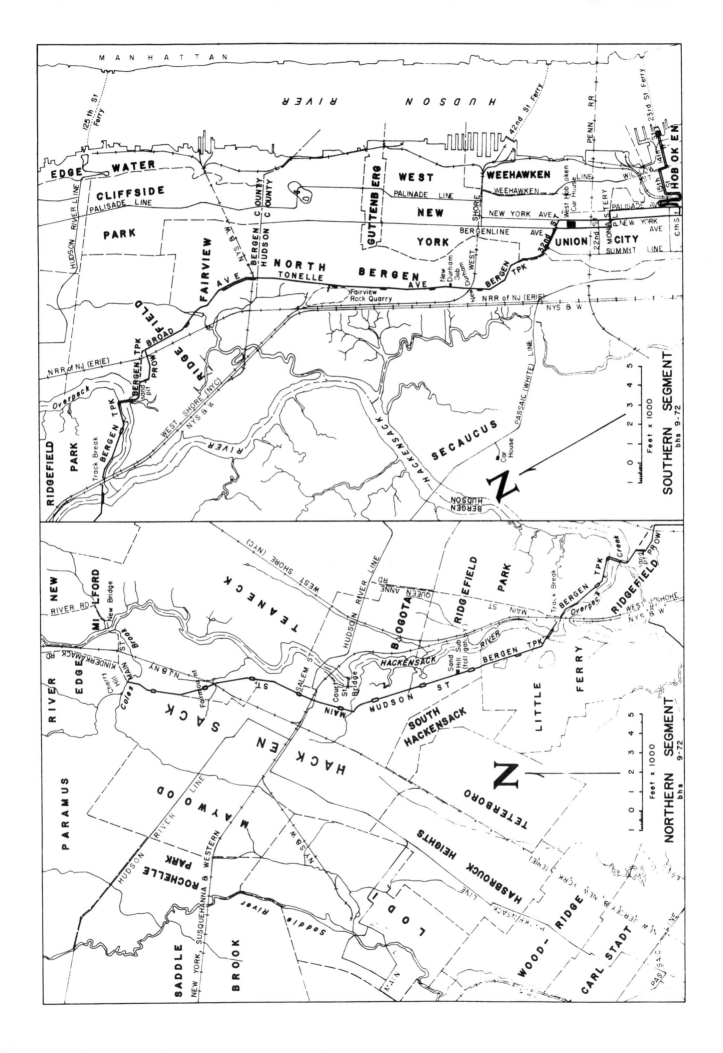

Toll gate No. 4 was located at the west end of the Hackensack River draw bridge in the Little River section of Lodi Township. The billboard at the bend in the road adversiting Texaco gasoline and motor oil was a harbinger of things to come.

Service Opened to Hackensack

The line was finally extended north of New Durham on 3 April 1903 when the first car reached Mercer St., Hackensack about 3 p.m. "The car was crowded with men and boys; a free ride was given to everybody who jumped aboard. During the morning, two cars were drawn across the Northern RR of New Jersey at Ridgefield and it was possible to run them between that point and Collins Hotel at the Little Ferry depot. One of the cars was hauled over the West Shore and Susquehanna RR tracks in Ridgefield Park and then headed towards Hackensack. The car stayed at Mercer St. for only a minute, then returned to Little Ferry."

During the early months of service through Hackensack, citizens living along the route seemed unhappy about their new public conveyance. They protested to the city commission that cars on Main St. were operating at 15 mph in defiance of an 8 mph speed limit. Car 121 was attacked for noise that "sounds as though the car has flat wheels and is shaking to pieces. It's ruining the nerves of the people who live along the route." In

North Bergen Township, the trolleys struggled up the steep hill as they passed Schuetzen Park. On 25 October 1903, car 124 stopped for a passenger halfway up the hill. When the current was turned on to move the car again, a fire was discovered. The trolley pole was removed from the overhead wire but the fire continued to burn and the damaged car had to be towed to the West Hoboken car house.

PUBLIC SERVICE CORP. OF NEW JERSEY

Public Service Corporation received its certificate of incorporation on 6 May 1903. As described in chapter 4, on 16 May, David Young sold his controlling interest in the JCH&P and its subsidiaries, including the Bergen Turnpike, to Public Service.

During 1904 Public Service sorted out and renumbered the trolley cars it had acquired, renumbering them according to body design. The Bergen Turnpike cars were renumbered 904 to 918 and the route was designated as the Bergen Pike line. The cars were repainted into the standard Public Service color scheme of chrome yellow with light cream trim and

black lettering and maroon striping. No corporate identity was lettered on the cars prior to 1907, except in South Jersey where some cars operating in the Camden area were lettered P.S.C.

The Track Gaps Closed

A solution to the grade crossing problem in Hackensack was sought in 1904 when Public Service asked the Hackensack Improvement Commission for a franchise bypassing the NYS&W Main St. crossing. The proposed route ran east from Main St. over the NJ&HR tracks on Mercer St. to River St., then north, leaving the NJ&HR and continuing to Salem St., then west to Main St. rejoining the Bergen Pike track. The cars would have passed under the NYS&W at River St. but the franchise request was rejected on 17 October 1904.

Until June 1904, the Bergen Pike line terminated in Hackensack at the NJ&NYRR Main St. crossing near the Fairmount depot. On 30 June the overhead wire was completed and energized to the Cherry Hill terminus at Coles Brook and a trolley car was hauled across the railroad to operate as a shuttle over this

Bergen Turnpike Company Car Series 111-125, later Public Service Railway 904 to 918. Built by Laclede in 1901. These cars were identical with Jersey City Hoboken and Paterson Cars 101 to 110 and 126 to 127.

Bergen Turnpike Sprinklers, Series 33 and 34, later Public Service Railway 5017 and 5018. Built by Brill in 1902.

The track gap over the NYS&W RR's Edgewater branch was eliminated by this bridge. The picture was taken on 23 November 1905, three days after the bridge girders were set in place.

0.9-mile section of track. The first car ran on 1 July, marking the opening of the line for its full 13.7 mile length.

As patronage increased, the track breaks became bigger inconveniences, especially in bad weather. The line was referred to as the "Kangaroo Line" by passengers and local newspapers because of the need to "hop" from car to car. On 13 July 1904 Fairview Township granted permission for a viaduct over the NYS&W's Edgewater tunnel branch. This was built under contract by the Hudson River RR and Terminal Co. which was responsible for its maintenance. Since midnight on 28 August 1902 when a NYS&W locomotive and officials blocked attempts to lay frogs across the Edgewater branch, detectives had remained on duty at all times to prevent the trolley company from stealing a crossing.

Public Service requested permission to build a viaduct over the Northern RR at Edgewater Ave. in Ridgefield but abutting property owners protested strongly. Instead, on 14 February 1905 the Public Utility Commission granted permission to reroute over a private right-of-way south of the Ridgefield depot, crossing over the railroad on a plate girder trough

bridge and descending to the turnpike road via an earth fill around the old church yard. On 20 November 1905 the Erie RR assisted by having one its cranes set the bridge girders in place. The bypass was opened for service on 15 December. Part of the right-of-way and the bridge, which was rebuilt in 1931, are now a public street named Hendricks Causeway.

The Bergen Pike and Hudson River (NJ&HR) lines were joined by a portable switch at Mercer and Main streets, Hackensack, in the early morning hours of 17 September 1904. This aroused the interest of city officials who had never granted permission for a connection. It was explained that a temporary track was laid on the brick pavement in order to transfer three cars from the Paterson shops over the Hudson River line.

The first notable collision between trolleys in Hackensack on the Bergen Pike line also involved a Hudson River car. Bergen Pike car 918 and Hudson River open car 53 collided at Main and Mercer streets on 3 June 1905. Car 918 was standing at the NYS&WRR crossing on Main St., while car 53, bound for Paterson, was discharging passengers at the railroad depot on Mercer St. Both

cars apparently started simultaneously with 918 reaching the intersection first. Car 53 knocked 918 off the track. Luckily both cars were moving slowly so that no one was injured, but the headlight on 53 was smashed.

With a continuous line now running between Hoboken and Ridgefield Park, Public Service increased its efforts to eliminate the remaining track breaks. Success was attained in Hackensack on 20 March 1906 when permission was given to cross the NYS&W and NJ&NY railroads at grade on Main St. Public Service was required to install derailing devices on each side of the grade crossings which were operated by an employee stationed at the crossings. When a car came along, the conductor would alight and proceed to the crossing, giving the signal that all was right to the switchman who turned the derail switch allowing the car to proceed. Work on the crossings began on 15 April 1906 and they were completed 58 days later. Through service from Cherry Hill to Little Ferry began on 11 June.

The company was still unable to gain approval to cross the two railroads at the Little Ferry depot in Ridgefield Park.

The 14th St. (Hoboken) ferry terminal served boats running to 14th St., Manhattan from 1 May 1886 to 1 November 1904, when service was shifted to 23rd St., Manhattan. Service ended on 27 April 1942 when the Hoboken slips were requisitioned for war production. The terminal was served by the Bergen Pike line and several Hudson division lines. The car on the left is signed for Washington St., Hoboken; that on the right for Bergenline Ave.

During 1906, Public Service announced a plan to reroute the line through Ridgefield Park and Bogota to the Court St. bridge in Hackensack. The village trustees favored the plan, thinking it would increase Ridgefield Park's population by 50 percent. However, no agreement was reached and the plan was shelved.

On 11 June 1906, the 11:30 p.m. car No. 530, from Cherry Hill, ran through an open switch at the Sand Hill substation toll gate wye, bounded into the wye and struck car 911 which was stored there. The speed of car 530 was sufficient to wreck the platforms of both cars but, fortunately there were no injuries.

Public Service Railway

The formation of the Public Service Ry. Co., took effect on 30 July 1907 and was approved at the Public Service Corporation annual stockholders' meeting on 20 August. Public Service Ry. leased the Bergen Turnpike Co. from the Public Service Corporation on 2 January 1908 for 999 years. The railway continued to operate the turnpike although forces working for the abolition of the tolls were growing stronger. The Bergen Pike line was assigned to Public Service Railway's Hudson Division and operated from the West Hoboken car house.

A near tragedy was averted on 26 December 1907 at Ridgefield when the motorman on a northbound car fell headfirst to the trestle spanning the Northern RR. None of the passengers had seen the motorman fall and at first no one perceived the danger. As the car dashed forward with increasing speed across the 30-foot structure and began rocking violently from side to side, fear seized the occupants. A male passenger rushed to the front platform to stop the car and grabbed the controller but, instead of shutting off the power, he unintentionally turned on more power. The car darted ahead with greater speed although several other passengers had succeeded in applying the brakes and it seemed certain that the car would jump from the track. Finally the conductor succeeded in stopping the car and a search was made for the missing motorman who was found lying unconscious on the Northern RR. tracks under the trestle. He had fallen through the trestle and struck his head on the beams, then fell to the tracks. He was rushed to a hospital and recovered from his injuries.

Public Service Ry. rebuilt the platforms on its cars to "pay-on-platform" type between 1908 and 1910. Much of the work was done by the John Stephenson Co. at Elizabeth, N.J., including Bergen Pike cars 904 to 918 which were converted in August and September 1910. The cars never returned to the Bergen Pike line and were reassigned to lines in Passaic, Hudson and Essex counties, and Trenton. Nine pay-on-platform 1100-series cars were assigned to the Hoboken-Little Ferry segment of the Bergen Pike line on 20 November 1910. They had been built for the North Jersey St. Ry. by Laclede in 1898. The Little Ferry-Hackensack segment was assigned eight high-numbered 900-series cars built for the Elizabeth, Plainfield and Central Jersey by Jackson and Sharp Co. of Wilmington, Delaware in 1900.

During 1910 Public Service Corporation formed the Public Service Electric Co. On 1 July 1910 all of the railway company's power generating stations and substations were leased to the electric company. The Bergen Pike's Sand Hill and New Durham substations were included in the lease.

Public Service Ry. again surveyed an alternate route to close the remaining gap at the West Shore and Susquehanna railroads in Ridgefield Park in 1911. On 11 March, it asked Bogota's borough council for a fifty-year franchise over Queen Anne Road from the Hudson River line on Main St. south to the Ridgefield Park boundary. In Ridgefield Park, a franchise was requested over Main St. from the Bogota boundary to the existing track on Bergen Turnpike. The route was identical to that surveyed by the Ridgefield &

115

Bergen Turnpike trolley service was always hampered by the track breaks at railroad crossings as can be seen in these pictures. Above: Bergen Pike car 915 pauses at the NJ&NYRR crossing of Main St., Hackensack on 16 February 1906.

At right: The track break at the NYS&WRR on Main St., Hackensack, shows clearly in this picture taken from the roof of the Hackensack Trust Building.

Below: A view northward on Main St. from the NJ&NYRR grade crossing. The trolley wire continued over the railroad tracks.

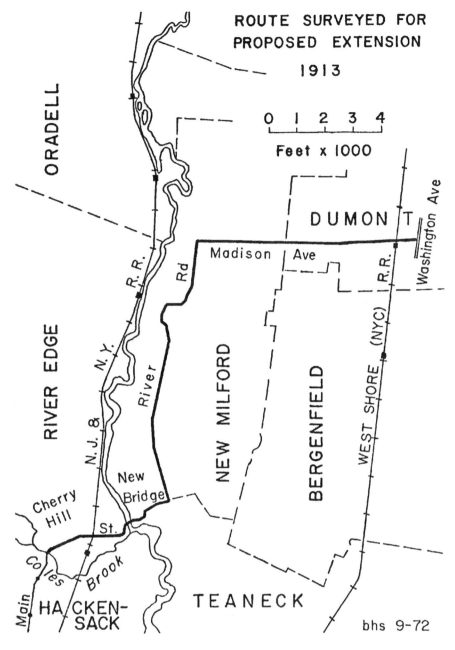

ROUTE SURVEYED FOR
PROPOSED EXTENSION
1913

0 1 2 3 4

Feet x 1000

bhs 9-72

Teaneck Ry. in January 1900. The franchises were granted by Ridgefield Park on 14 November 1911 and by Bogota on 25 June 1912. Both included terms unacceptable to the company, which allowed them to expire.

During June 1911, Public Service Ry. began erecting apparatus for construction of a viaduct over the two railroads along the south side of the turnpike. Abutting property owners refused to give consents and during July, the railway removed its pile drivers and shelved its plans. The 110-feet gap at the Little Ferry depot remained unfilled until buses replaced trolleys.

During the winter of 1912-1913 Public Service Ry. made a study to extend the Bergen Pike line beyond North Hackensack to Dumont via New Milford. The route was surveyed via River Road and Madison Ave. during April 1913 but it was never constructed.

A severe snowstorm resembling the blizzard of 1888 hit the New York metropolitan area during the evening of 1 March 1914. Winds reached a velocity of 75 mph during the night and by next morning all forms of transportation were at a standstill. A Bergen Pike trolley became marooned on North Main St. in Hackensack and the crew slept in the car all

night. Normal service on the Bergen Pike line was not restored until the afternoon of 3 March.

On 3 January 1916, the Bergen Pike line was renamed as the Bergen line. The old name continued in common usage long after the change and in Hackensack it was most often called the "Main St. trolley." The Main St. line, which had been operating between Hackensack, Lodi, Passaic and Paterson since 1904, was most often called the "Lodi trolley."

Bergen Turnpike Deeded to Bergen County

Turnpike toll collection in Hudson County had been discontinued about 1895. For many years, maintenance had been inadequate and when the turnpike company was urged by municipal officials to repair or improve the surface it had invariably replied that toll revenues were sufficient only to pay taxes and make minor repairs.

The Bergen County Board of Chosen Freeholders formed a committee on 2 January 1912 to confer with Public Service about acquisition of the Bergen Turnpike toll road. Company proposals were unsatisfactory to the county and the deal was called off on 17 June, another failure in the twenty-five years of agitation for the abolition of the tolls. Three years later, on 1 November 1915, that portion of the turnpike in Bergen County was deeded to the county for $1.00. Public Service Corporation agreed to assume payment of $1 million in outstanding bonds with interest. A freeholders' resolution on 22 November accepted the turnpike as a county road.

Title to the turnpike was conveyed by Bergen County to the N. J. Highway Department on 17 January 1920. The portion in Hackensack was excluded and the remainder became part of State Highway 10. The portion of the turnpike in Hudson County was conveyed by Public Service Corporation to the county on 28 July 1921.

The Fairview Quarry

Public Service Ry. operated a trap rock quarry in the Granton area of North Bergen Township, west of the Bergen Turnpike opposite 80th St. It was purchased on 26 April 1906 from the Fairview

117

The Fairview quarry provided crushed rock for Public Service Railway operations and for sale for area construction projects. At the top, car 908, formerly Bergen Pike 115, is serving ignominiously as motive power for car 5640, a wooden center-dump car. The lower view shows 5622, a rail car purchased from Smith & Wallace in 1906, and 5604, an open work car built by Cincinnati Car Co. in 1904. The cars carried stone from the quarry and distributed supplies from Passaic Wharf when returning empty.

Stone Crushing Co. to supply track ballast. The company was dissolved in early 1907. The quarry was enlarged during 1910 from 10 to 25 acres which gave it a visible supply of 1.5 million cubic yards of trap rock. The rock was taken from a 1400-foot-wide knoll which formed a geological connection with the Palisades igneous rock system and was about 100 feet high at its highest point. In 1911, the quarry operated three Allis-Chalmers crushers with a combined capacity of 600 cubic yards a day. The blasted rock was brought to the crushers in narrow-gauge railway cars instead of by horse teams which had been the former method. All of the apparatus, except the pneumatic drills, were electrically operated. The combined motor capacity of the crushers and air compressors was about 500 horsepower. The cost of delivering crushed stone in 1911 to any job within a 20-mile radius averaged 47 cents a cubic yard but was reduced to 38 cents by using trail cars. Another economy was effected by returning empty cars to Passaic Wharf for the distribution of supplies. About 85 men were employed at the quarry during its busy season. By 1925 there were four crushers but peak capacity had been reduced to 300 yards per day. The quarry was sold during 1926 to the Belmont-Gurnee Stone Co. of North Bergen, N.J.

The Bergen Turnpike, being unpaved and rural, required dust control. This was provided by two 4000-gallon sprinklers, numbered 33 and 34, which were built by Brill in 1902. They became Public Service 5017 and 5018. Car 34 was photographed at Secaucus car house between 1902 and 1907. The dummy body was designed to reduce the danger of scaring horses.

DECLINE AND ABANDONMENT

Post World War I Years

During the autumn of 1920, Public Service announced that it would discontinue service on the two-mile section of the Bergen line north of the NYS&WRR in Hackensack because of low revenues, poor track conditions and a plan to widen Main St. to 30 feet, which would have required major track work. This caused quite an uproar, especially in Fairmount's fifth ward. The Fifth Ward Improvement Association complained about the Bergen line cars dumping passengers some distance short of the Coles Brook terminus and being told the car would go no further. This was done because of traffic delays on Main St. which made it impossible to follow the schedule if they continued all the way to North Hackensack. Bus substitution was considered unsatisfactory because many people were afraid to ride in the primitve buses of that time. One spokesman, J. Pell Zabriskie, said, "If the trolley was abandoned it would deter the growth of the Fairmount section and it would also erase the hopes for a proposed extension of the Bergen line to Westwood upon Kinderkamack Road."

Hackensack Traffic Jams

Bergen line cars caused many traffic jams on Main St., Hackensack. The passing turnout at Salem St. was the scene for most of the tie-ups because the first car arriving had to wait for the car coming from the opposite direction in order to pass and there was insufficient room to pass between the street car and parked automobiles.

A humorous snarl occurred on a June 1921 Saturday night when a Ridgewood bus heading south on Main St. was riding the rails to avoid bumping its occupants' heads on the ceiling and met a northbound trolley. The car couldn't turn off the track, nor could the bus because of parked automobiles on both sides of the street. The din of auto horns and klaxons drowned out the trolley car crew and bus driver as they began to argue. Behind the bus and trolley were lines of automobiles making it impossible for either to back up and there they stood glaring at each other. A policeman finally straightened out the mess and the event generated additional pressure for the complete removal of the cars from Main St.

The Hackensack Commission also complained about Main St. track conditions. It noted that rails in some places were 4 1/2 inches below the surface of the street, that there was substantial deflection of the rails by passing trolleys which

caused the pavement to break up, that the derail devices on each side of the NYS&WRR crossing were inoperative, and that plugged drains caused floods during rainfalls. Hackensack Mayor Baldwin said, "The condition of the Bergen car line's tracks on Hudson St. is such that sooner or later the trolley cars will land in sombody's home, as the tracks are in terrible condition." The railway replied that necessary repairs would be made, except for the track drains and that plans were underway to abandon the entire Bergen line since the route had been a failure from the start. Repairs were carried out during the widening of Main St. between July and September 1921.

Birney Cars Arrive

The eight old double-truck cars which had been running between Hackensack and Little Ferry since 1910 were replaced without fanfare by new Birney single-truck safety cars on 10 October 1921. The cars were named for Charles O. Birney of Stone & Webster Engineering Corporation who designed the car in 1915. The one-man cars cut platform wages in half, were 27 feet 10 inches long and weighed about eight tons. Lighter than the old cars, they reduced track maintenance costs and made it possible to continue using badly worn tracks. The controllers and brakes were designed so that

Birney car 7190 was the last car to operate on the northern section of the Bergen Pike line on 26 April 1926. It is shown here at North Hackensack with J. Pell Zabriski on the step. The Zabriskie family had controlled the turnpike from about 1882 until it was acquired by the JCH&P and several of its members remained in the employ of Public Service in later years.

all power would be shut off and the brakes applied if the motorman released the controller handle while the car was in motion. An interlocking door switch made it impossible to start the car until the door was closed. The cars were slow mainly because of their 26-inch diameter wheels but were able to accelerate and decelerate more rapidly than the older heavier cars. The Birney's small, squat, squarish appearance did not compare favorably with the more pleasing lines of the larger cars. Their wooden slat seats were very uncomfortable and their tendency to gallop and nose made their riding qualities unpleasant.

Public Service Ry. ordered 200 Birneys (Nos. 7000-7199) from the Osgood Bradley Car Co. of Worcester, Massachusetts on 1 July 1920. Delivery began in the late summer and on 5 September 1920 the first Public Service Birneys began regular service on the Riverside line in Paterson. By the close of 1920, seventeen lines in the Passaic, Hudson and Central divisions had been equipped with Birneys. Their service life on Public Service lines was comparatively short. Birneys last operated on the Easton car line in New Brunswick when 7059, 7095 and 7197 were withdrawn from service on 2 August 1931.

Bus Competition

The Bergen line was affected by the 1923 decision of Public Service to buy up independent bus permits and to operate bus lines. The Hackensack-Little Ferry trolleys had been competing with the Inter-Boro Bus Line, owned by Richard Dreyfuss of Hackensack. Inter-Boro operated two Garford buses on a half-hour headway between the two points (3.1 miles) and also operated a 3.5-mile route between Hackensack and Ridgefield Park via Bogota with three Garford buses. This later became Public Service Coordinated Transport route 4 and continued to operate until 1952.

During the 1923 strike, discussed in chapter 4, Inter-Boro increased its Hackensack-Little Ferry service to a 20-minute headway with three buses. The Bergen line restored service on the afternoon of 21 September. The union had agreed to one-man operation of all trolleys and one-man cars began serving the southern (Hoboken-Little Ferry) segment of the Bergen line on 16 December 1923.

Public Service Electric Co.'s Sand Hill substation on Hudson St., Hackensack, was converted to a bus garage during July 1924. Bergen line trolleys continued using the storage track adjacent to the north side of the building. All five buses of the Inter-Boro Bus Lines, Inc., which had been incorporated on 4 December 1923 and sold to Public Service Transportation on 10 May 1924, were housed in the old substation. A large entrance was cut through a brick wall and a bus repair shop established inside the building.

Abandonment North of Fairview

Public Service Corporation, realizing the superiority of buses over Birney cars began an extensive conversion program in the mid-1920s. The purchase of new buses increased from 41 in 1923 to 407 in 1926. The low quantity of new buses purchased in 1923 was mainly due to the large number of second-hand buses acquired through purchases of the competing bus routes. Due to the redundancy of bus and trolley services in urban areas, Public Service began including in its route names the type of conveyance, such as "car line" and "bus line."

On 31 July 1924, Public Service Ry. revealed a plan to replace the northern segment of the Bergen car line with buses as they became available. However, it was not until March 1926 that application was made to the New Jersey PUC for a new bus line, using 12 buses, between North Hackensack and Weehawken, replacing the Bergen car line north of Fairview.

The last Bergen Birney galloped and bumped its way over the northern segment late on Sunday night, 25 April 1926. The next morning, 12 new 2100-series chrome-yellow gas-electric buses began running between North Hackensack and the West Shore RR Ferry terminal in Weehawken. The buses seated 31, had arch-roof Yellow Truck & Coach bodies and were mounted on YT&C model Z-AL-265 gas-electric chassis. A six-cylinder gasoline engine was directly connected to a General Electric generator which produce electric current to drive two motors — one for each rear wheel. The gas-electric bus was designed to eliminate gear shifting and clutches to

Bus 2154 is shown on Pershing Hill Road, Weehawken, on 12 August 1926, on the 34 — Bergen line, signed for North Hackensack. It was one of the group of Yellow Coach buses which replaced the Birney cars.

provide smoother acceleration and eliminate sudden jolts

The new bus route was designated as the 34—Bergen bus line and operated from the Union City car house. It was actually an extension of the Eastern Boulevard bus line which had been purchased by Public Service in 1924. The Bergen car line had been designated as route 33—Bergen in 1925, but the cars never carried route number signs.

In 1927 Public Service Transportation purchased the Hackensack-Westwood franchise of the Westwood Transportation Co. and on 4 June 1927 began operating the 46—Hackensack-Westwood bus line via Kinderkamack Road. On 1 January 1933 the 46 bus was absorbed into the 34—Bergen bus line and through service operated between Westwood and Weehawken.

Hackensack officials were jubilant over the removal of the Bergen trolleys from Main St. In contrast to the trolley blockades, the new 34—Bergen buses were praised for their swiftness and ability to pull to the curb for passengers. The through service from Hackensack to the West Shore Ferry eliminated the need to transfer trolleys at the track gap in Ridgefield Park. Also, the West Shore ferries delivered passengers to 42nd St. and Cortlandt St. in Manhattan which was more convenient for commuters than the 23rd St. ferry landing.

Final Abandonment and Dissolution

During 1926 the Bergen car line continued to operate south of Fairview Ave. with ten cars. The New Jersey State Highway Department began reconstructing Bergen Turnpike between Ridgefield and New Durham in June 1927. The road was widened to 43 feet and renamed Tonnelle Ave. Before reconstruction started, the car line was cut back to Hudson County Blvd. on 18 March 1927 and the schedule maintained with three cars. About the same time Public Service opened a new bus line to replace the Bergen car line south of Fairview. The 36—Fairview bus line operated between the Union City car house and Fairview. It was extended in 1928 over Shaler Boulevard in Ridgefield to Maple Ave. and was discontinued in 1952.

The Bergen car line was cut back to Union City car house on 26 March 1927 and continued operating between the car house and the 14th St. Ferry in Hoboken. Operation finally ceased on 3 January 1928. Replacement service was provided during rush hours by an extension of the Union City car line and at all times by the Crosstown car line, which operated over the same route to 32nd St., Union City. The Union City car line rush-hour service dwindled away and the Crosstown line was discontinued on 2 September 1928, ending all trolley service over the Hillside Road to Hoboken. Crosstown cars were replaced by the 20—48th St. bus line. This was renamed as the 20—Union City bus line in 1929 and discontinued in 1952.

The Hackensack River draw bridge at Little Ferry was removed following the opening in September 1934 of a new state highway bridge located 800 feet upstream. The draw bridge spanning Overpeck Creek located east of the New Jersey Turnpike was replaced in 1971 by a new reinforced-concrete trestle.

Public Service started the 18—Fairmount bus line on 5 July 1928 between downtown Hackensack and the Fairmount section, terminating at Catalpa Ave. It was combined with the 34—Bergen bus on 6 May 1932 then separated again on 23 September 1935 as the new 18—Fairmount-Little Ferry line. On 25 August 1954 this line was merged into the 72—Dumont-Hackensack line. The 34—Bergen bus line made its last runs on 31 October 1956, about three years before the New York Central RR discontinued the West Shore Ferry.

The Lincoln Tunnel opened in December 1937 but it wasn't until 1939 that the ICC permitted suburban bus routes to use the tunnel. On 17 May 1939 Public Service Interstate Transportation Co. began service over the 165—Westwood-New York bus line, via the Lincoln Tunnel to Times Square. It duplicated the 34—Bergen bus line north of Pershing Ave., Weehawken.

Public Service Ry. and Public Service Transportation merged on 31 January 1928 to form Public Service Coordinated Transport Co. Public Service Corporation began simplifying its corporate structure during the 1930s by merging and consolidating its many subsidiary companies. The Bergen Turnpike Co. was merged into Public Service Coordinated Transport on 6 July 1937. The merger ended 135 years of shaky survival first as a toll road and later as an electric railway. In both cases the corporation was not a financial success. The Public Service Interstate Transportation Co. was merged into Public Service Coordinated Transport Co. on 31 March 1953. In order to separate its identity from the Public Service Electric & Gas Co., the bus company changed its name on 23 August 1971 to Transport of New Jersey.

OPERATIONS
Operating Practices

While Bergen Pike line cars could not operate through because of track breaks at railroad crossings, when a scheduled car arrived at the break, the crews simply changed to the car ahead until they completed the entire 13.7 route miles. Bergen Pike cars operated on a half-hour headway and it required approximately 90 minutes for a one-way trip. Crews began and ended all runs at the West Hoboken car house. The northern segment of the line, isolated by the track break at Ridge-

field Park, stored its cars adjacent to the north side of the Sand Hill substation in Hackensack. When a crew made the last trip of the day from Cherry Hill to Hoboken, they would pick up the watchman at the toll gate "Y" (Sand Hill substation) and take him to Ridgefield Park. Then the watchman dead-headed the car back to Sand Hill. The procedure was reversed in the morning to meet the first car from Hoboken.

No maintenance was done at Sand Hill. Instead, cars were dead-headed to the West Hoboken car house. It was possible to operate cars under their own power across the railroad grade crossings at Ridgefield Park on a portable track jumper since the overhead trolley wire was continuous across the railroads.

Electric Power

The original power sources for the Bergen Pike line were the 550-volt dc circuits from the Hoboken, Grand St.,

Palisade Ave., Secaucus and Coal St. generating station group. It was possible to transfer load from one station to another according to needs, which was done almost every evening. In addition, several 13,200-volt 25-hertz circuits were placed in service in 1902 when Secaucus generating station was tied to Palisade Ave., Passaic, New Durham and Sand Hill substations. In 1904 Coal St. generating station was tied to Palisade Ave. substation through a 13,200-volt, 25 hertz AC circuit. The Bergen Pike line substations at New Durham and Sand Hill were each equipped with a 300-kw rotary converter. The New Durham and Sand Hill substations were designed by Thomas Cressey, architect, of Newark for the JCH&P St. Ry. in 1902.

With the opening of the Marion generating station in December 1905, additional 13,200-volt, 25 hertz AC circuits tied Marion to Secaucus, Hoboken, Hackensack, and Passaic.

PUBLIC SERVICE STREET RAILWAY POWER STATIONS IN NORTH JERSEY

Coal St. (Newark)	1894 to 6-5-1928	14,800 kw
East Rutherford	1897 to March 1913	600 kw
Edgewater	1895 to 3-10-1926	2,100 kw
Grand St. (Jersey City)	1893 to August 1909	2,325 kw
Hoboken (14th St.)	1892 to April 1924	3,000 kw
Marion (Jers. C. - Ry. only)	1905 to 1-10-1974	28,000 kw
Palisade Ave. (Jersey City)	1892 to March 1905	
Passaic	1899 to July 1910	1,550 kw
Paterson	1896 to Nov 1927	2,800 kw
Secaucus	1895 to Nov 1920	3,550 kw

BUSES
Inter-Boro Bus Line

The Inter-Boro Bus Line was acquired on 1 February 1925 together with five buses bearing Hackensack permits, 38, 39, 40, X and X, the X denoting extra or substitute vehicles. They were renumbered 678-682. They were built by Garford Motor Truck Co. of Lima, Ohio, in 1922 (678,681,682) and 1923 (679-680). Buses 679-681 were sent to Passaic Wharf for scrapping in the summer of 1926. Buses 678 and 682 were traded to Yellow Coach in early 1927 as part of a deal for new buses.

34—Bergen Bus Line

This line, when started by Public Service Transportation Co. was assigned buses 2136-2137, 2139-2140, 2147-2148, 2150-2151, 2154-2156, and 2159. These buses were built by Yellow Truck and Coach Co. in 1926 and were gas-electric model Z-AL-265 buses with Yellow Coach bodies, except 2155 which had a body built by Public Service in its own shops.

JCH&P BERGEN TURNPIKE CO. — ROLLING STOCK

BTCo Numbers	Body Length	Overall Length	Windows	Trucks	Motors	Builder/Date	PSNJ Numbers	Notes
111-125	25' 0"	38' 4"	10	Peckham 14B3	GE 67	Laclede, 1901	904-918	
30-32		27' 6"	Sweeper	Pedestal		J. G. Brill, 1902	5158-5160	
33-34	24' 6"	32' 6"	Sprinkler			J. G. Brill, 1902	5017-5018	

PUBLIC SERVICE BERGEN TURNPIKE CO. — ROLLING STOCK

PSNJ Nos.			Windows	Trucks	Motors	Builder/Date	Former.Nos.	
526,530	24' 8"	33' 10"	7			Gilbert, 1892	188, 192	A
904-918	25' 0"	38' 4"	10	Peckham 14B3	GE 67	Laclede, 1901	111-125	B
962,968	28' 0"	40' 0"	10	Peckham 14B3	GE 80	St Louis, 1894	503, 509	C
974-984	28' 0"	40' 0"	10	Peckham 14B3	GE 80	Jackson & Sharp, 1900	66-77	D
1120-1199	32' 0"	46' 6"	11	Brill 27		Laclede, 1898	620-699	E
1400-1459	31' 3"	39' 1"	12-bench open	Brill 27G	Wh 68	J. G. Brill, 1904		
1460-1499	32' 4"	39' 4"	12-bench open	Brill 27G	Wh 68	J. Stephenson, 1904		
1557,1576	30' 8"	46' 4"	11	Brill 27G	Wh 68	J. G. Brill, 1904		
1900-1949	30' 8"	42' 10"	11	Brill 27G	Wh 68	J. G. Brill, 1903		
2317,2319	32' 0"	46' 4"	12			Newark Shops, 1910		
7000-7199	17' 9½"	27' 10"		OB 25-96		Osgood Bradley, 1920		

* Original trucks and motors shown

A. Former North Hudson County Railway.

B. Former Bergen Turnpike Company.

C. Former Jersey City Hoboken & Paterson St. Ry. Orig. JCH&R 108 and 120.

D. Former Elizabeth, Plainfield & Central Jersey St. Ry.

E. Former North Jersey St. Ry.

BERGEN PIKE CAR ASSIGNMENTS

Southern Segment (Hoboken-Little Ferry)	Years assigned
111-125 (BTCo)	1902-1903
904-918 (renumbered)	1903-1910
1437, 1442 plus other 1400s	Summer 1908
1147,1156,1180,1182,1192,1195-96,1198-99	1910-1918
1521	1910-1911
1905,1918-19,1927,1929,1931,1933,1937-39	1918-1926
1132,1147,1156	1926
1133,1139,1149,1919,1933,1937-39,2317,2319	Winter 1926–1927
1132,2317,2319	Summer 1927
1557,1576,2317	Winter 1927-1928

Northern Segment (Little Ferry-Hackensack)	
111-125 (BTCo)	1902-1903
904-918 (renumbered)	1903-1910
526,530	1906
974-980,984	1910-1913
962,968,974,977,978,980,984	1913-1921
7003,7013,7015,7085,7089,7093,7154,7184,7190,7198	1921-1926

BERGEN TURNPIKE TOLL GATES

Hoboken, Clinton St. between 14th & 15th streets,
Weehawken, Hackensack Plank Road north of 19th St.

No. 1   New Durham, Bergen Tpk., and Washington (54th) St.

No. 2   Fairview, Bergen Turnpike near Wolf's Creek

No. 3   Ridgefield Park, north end of Overpeck Creek bridge

No. 4   Little Ferry, west end of Hackensack River bridge

No. 5   Hackensack, Hudson St. south of Moonachie Road

The varied rolling stock used on the Bergen Turnpike line included the 1400-1459 series 12-bench open cars (1430 is pictured) built by Brill in 1904, and the 1120-1199 series closed cars (1165 is pictured) built by Laclede in 1898. Both cars were posed at the Newark Plank Road Shops of Public Service Railway.

7

THE PALISADE LINE
The Palisades Railroad Company
North Hudson County Railway Co.

The origin of the Palisade line is found in two separate corporations. In Hudson County it was the North Hudson County Ry. Co., formed in 1865 by merger of several small horse railroads. In Bergen County it was the Englewood Horse Ry. Co. formed in 1866. The Palisade line was the only street railway in Bergen County to use steam "dummies" to pull trains of cars and it was the last street car line to operate in Bergen County.

North Hudson County Ry. Co.

The first horse railway in the Hoboken area was the Hoboken & Hudson City Horse RR Co. chartered on 18 March 1859. The company built a line from the Hoboken ferry via Ferry St. and Hoboken Ave. to the "Five Corners" intersection between Summit Ave., Newark Ave. and Hoboken Ave. in Hudson City. Operations commenced in February 1860.

A second area line, the Jersey City and Hoboken Horse RR Co., was chartered on 23 March 1859 and authorized to build a horse railroad from the Jersey City ferry at the foot of Montgomery St. to the Hoboken ferry. The original line was built via Ferry St. in Hoboken and Grove St. in Jersey City terminating at Newark Ave. In 1870 cars were extended to the Jersey City ferry over the Jersey City & Bergen RR on Newark Ave.

The North Hudson County Railway had its origins in a stage coach line between the Hoboken ferry and Union Hill (Union City) which was opened by Nicholas Goelz and Peter Meicher on 20 June 1858. The line prospered from the start, but the poor roads contributed to passenger discomfort and a railway was considered. On 14 February 1860 the Hoboken

and Weehawken Horse Car Ry. Co. was chartered with John H. Bonn, a prominent real estate broker, as president; Jacob Schweitzer, a wealthy brewer, treasurer; and Nicholas Goelz, superintendent. Construction started in August, 1860 and horse cars began running in December.

The last horse railway organized in the Hoboken area was the Hoboken and West Hoboken Horse Car RR Co. organized in 1861. It built a line from a connection with the Hoboken and Hudson City Horse RR at Hoboken Ave. via a steep road (now Ravine Road) up the palisade bluff to Palisade Ave., thence north to West Hoboken.

On March 29, 1865 the State Legislature authorized the sale of the Hoboken & West Hoboken and the Hoboken & Hudson City to the Hoboken & Weehawken Horse Car RR which was renamed North Hudson County Railway Co. In 1870 the Jersey City & Hoboken RR was acquired. North Hudson County's office was established at 21 Hudson Place, Hoboken. The railway obtained a $1 million, 6-percent first mortgage from the First National Bank, Hoboken and assigned William G. Shepard and William W. Shippen as Trustees.

The North Hudson County Ry. built a narrow-gauge horse car line from the intersection of Union St. and Bergenline Ave. in Union Hill, north via Bergenline Ave. to Guttenberg, then east on Herman Ave. (70th St.) to Bulls Ferry Road, terminating at Anto Merket's Hotel and the old Guttenberg Post Office. A turntable was located at the Guttenberg terminal for turning the cars. Service was provided on a half-hour headway and sleds were often substituted for cars during heavy winter weather.

The Guttenberg Race Track (officially named the New Jersey Jockey Club) opened in 1885 and to accomodate track patrons, the North Hudson County Railway extended the Bergenline Ave. line from Herman Ave. northward to the county boundary at Nungessers. The extension ran in front of the race track entrance where "Pat" Sullivan's saloon was located. North Hudson County Railway replaced the old single-end horse cars with double-enders. In 1894 the line was reconstructed to standard gauge and electrified using single-truck cars.

Englewood Horse Railway Co.

The Englewood Horse Ry. Co. was granted a charter by the State Legislature on 6 April 1866. The company's authorized capitalization was $100,000, divided into $25 shares, with the power to increase to $250,000. The charter granted approval for a railway beginning at some point at or near Coytesville village in Hackensack Township, running northerly to a point at or near the intersection of Palisade Ave. and Summit St. in Englewood Heights, north to a point at or near the intersection of Clinton Ave. and Summit St. in Tenafly, then north along the top of the Palisades plateau to the state boundary. The charter prohibited the use of steam power on the railway. A covenant in the charter stipulated that if the railway was not completed by 4 July 1873 the charter will be voided. The railway was also authorized to make contracts or agreements with other incorporated railways in Hudson and Bergen counties.

The Palisades Railroad Co.

The Englewood Horse Railway's charter was amended on 29 February 1872 authorizing a name change to The Palisades RR Co. and construction and operation of a railroad from the New York state boundary, running south on or near the elevated ridge of the Palisades, crossing Palisade Ave. near Summit St. in Englewood, and continuing into Hudson County to a terminus on the Hudson River. The railroad was authorized to connect or consolidate with any railway in Bergen and Hudson counties.

The time allowed for completion was further extended in 1877, 1881, 1883, 1884, 1886 and 1888. The continuing delays were partially explained in the *Englewood Standard* on 14 October 1882, quoting President William B. Dana's report to the stockholders. "In order to begin with safety, it is necessary that $150,000 of the capital shall have been subscribed. The directors have subscribed $50,000; on this an assessment of 5 percent has been paid in. This money has been drawn upon for surveys and other expenses and $1,000 remains on hand. The company owes no debts."

"The directors employed surveyors to lay out a route with grades not to exceed 55 feet to the mile. The surveyors laid out a route called the gorge road route, the grade of which is 3 1/2 miles down the cliff. This route was found to be too expensive and not a very good one. There would be little traffic on it and it would not be acceptable to the Ontario Company. A new survey was made; the road thus laid down was down the cliff one mile, grade 138 feet. It is a good route and feasible, much cheaper than the first, and the traffic would be better, as the country through which it runs is better built up. The route is on the direct way to Hoboken."

At long last, the 4 April 1888 issue of *Railroad Gazette* reported The Palisades RR had contracted George F. Seward of New York City to build terminal facilities at the New York, West Shore & Buffalo Ry. ferry terminal at Weehawken and a standard gauge railway using 56 pounds per yard rails with a maximum grade of 126 feet per mile (2.4 per cent). The cost was estimated to be $275,000

and it was expected the Palisades road would have access to the Pennsylvania RR ferry terminal at Jersey City via the West Shore RR tracks. It was reported that $100,000 had been subscribed. The railroad filed with the NJ Secretary of State on 16 June 1888 for a route from Union Township to the county boundary (in Hudson County) and on 18 July 1889 from Oak Cliff (Cliffside Park) to Alpine in Bergen County. Its construction seems to have been stimulated by the Guttenberg Race Track which opened in 1885 and which scheduled "Flat" horse racing annually from October through May. The railroad's northern terminus was at the race track. Newspapers referred to the new line as the Palisade road and later as the Guttenberg steam road.

The Palisade Road Opens

Construction of The Palisades RR was taken over by the North Hudson County Ry. in 1889. The two companies shared the same principal stockholders but had different officers. On 14 August 1889 North Hudson County Ry. petitioned the Union Hill (Union Town) town council for a right-of-way across Bull's Ferry Road (Park Ave.) for a wooden trestle for the railroad. Plans and specifications were prepared for a double-track tunnel on a slight incline from a point nearly opposite Main St. (43rd St.) in Union Hill to Weehawken. The North Hudson County negotiated with the West Shore Terminal Co. for a terminus at the West Shore ferry. The line opened on 18 October 1889 from Union Hill to the Guttenberg Race Track, the opening day for the race track's 1889-1890 season. It was a muddy day for racing as it had rained all day and

Palisade road passengers were soaked while waiting for the trains.

Steam Passenger Trains

The Palisade road ran trains consisting of a steam motor and four passenger coaches. Electric traction was still in its infancy and cable traction was too expensive, as well as being impractical on a predomnantly rural line. Steam motors were already being used successfully at night by the North Hudson County on its Hoboken elevated line.

The first railway power house in Hudson County, the Palisade Ave. Station, provided power for the North Hudson County's cable railway on the Hoboken Elevated beginning in 1884. The Station was rebuilt in 1894 to generate 500-volt D.C. power. The original steam engines were modified to accomodate belt-driven electric generators. Other railway power houses followed: Hoboken in 1892; Grand St. in 1893; and Secaucus in 1895.

The North Hudson County owned nine steam dummy engines, two built by Baldwin for the Hoboken elevated and seven by H. K. Porter of Pittsburgh for the Palisades road. Steam motor 7, an 18-ton Rhode Island Locomotive Works tank engine, was acquired from a New York elevated railway. The Baldwins were transferred to the Palisade road by horse drawn wagon in September, 1892.

Porter called their steam motors "noiseless and smokeless motors"; Baldwin called theirs "noiseless steam motors." The motors were nearly noiseless as the steam exhausting from the cylinders escaped into the water tank and they showed no smoke when burning anthracite coal or coke as fuel.

NORTH HUDSON COUNTY STEAM DUMMYS					
No.	Builder	S/N	Shipped	Type	Cylinders
1	Baldwin	9434	Aug 1888	0-4-0	12 x 16
2	Baldwin	9431	Aug 1888	0-4-0	12 x 16
3	Porter	1075	Aug 1889	0-4-2T	10 x 14
4	Porter	1076	Sep 1889	0-4-2T	10 x 14
5	Porter	1077	Sep 1889	0-4-2T	10 x 14
6	Porter	1078	Sep 1889	0-4-2T	10 x 14
7	Rhode Island	?	Jan 1891		10 x 16
8	Porter	1298	Sep 1891	0-4-2T	12 x 18
9	Porter	1299	Sep 1891	0-4-2T	12 x 18
10	Porter	1300	Oct 1891	0-4-2T	12 x 18

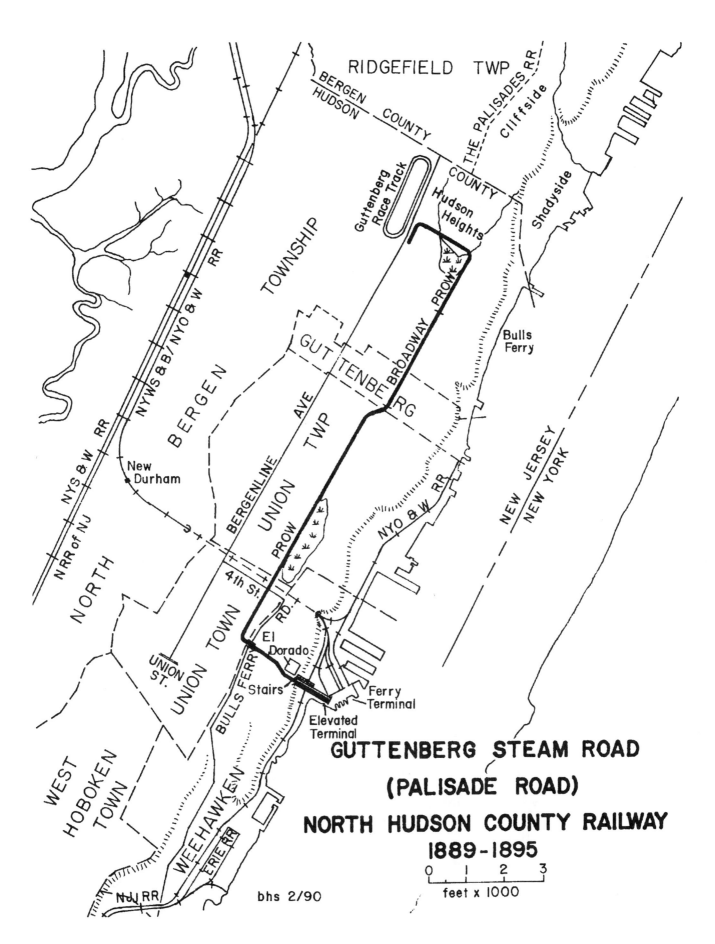

RIDGEFIELD TWP

THE PALISADES RR

Cliffside

Shadyside

Guttenberg Race Track

Hudson Heights

Bulls Ferry

BERGEN HUDSON COUNTY

COUNTY

TOWNSHIP

BERGEN

NYWS&B/NYO&W RR

NYS&W RR

NRR of NJ

New Durham

NORTH

GUTTENBERG TWP

BERGENLINE AVE

BROADWAY PROW

UNION TWP

PROW

NEW JERSEY
NEW YORK

NYO&W RR

4th St.

RD.

UNION TOWN

UNION ST.

El Dorado

BULLS FERRY

Stairs

Ferry Terminal

Elevated Terminal

WEST HOBOKEN TOWN

WEEHAWKEN

ERIE RR

NJ RR

bhs 2/90

GUTTENBERG STEAM ROAD
(PALISADE ROAD)
NORTH HUDSON COUNTY RAILWAY
1889-1895

0 1 2 3

feet x 1000

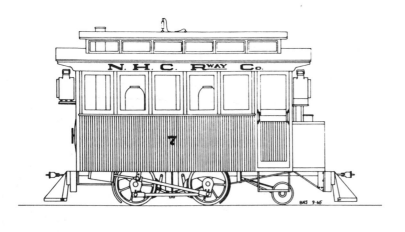

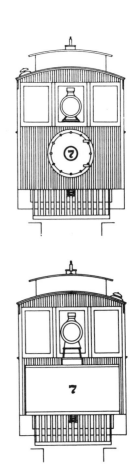

NHC Railway No. 7

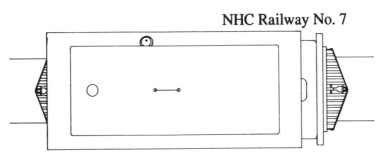

Twelve passenger cars, Nos. 21-32, with 24-foot 8-inch bodies and steam coach roofs were purchased from the Gilbert Car Co. of Troy, NY in October, 1889. They were similar to the Gilbert cars on the Manhattan Elevated Ry., but were provided with steps. Four identical cars (33-36) were acquired in March, 1890, and four more (37-40) in September, 1891. Nineteen were rebuilt as deck-roof electric cars in 1895 by the North Hudson County at the West Hoboken car house and renumbered 182 to 200. The fate of the remaining car is unknown. All of the cars were retired from service and scrapped by the end of 1915.

The North Hudson County Ry. owned ten double-truck cable cars (1-10) used on the Hoboken elevated which were received from the Pullman's Palace Car Co. in June 1885. These were replaced by new Brill electric cars in 1892 and may have been sent to the Palisade line to provide additional service after its extension in 1894. These cars, according to company records, were sold about 1898 to an unknown buyer.

The Weehawken Elevated Terminal

When the road opened in 1889, the southern terminus was at the Palisade bluff overlooking the West Shore RR's Weehawken ferry terminal. The North Hudson County Ry. provided a wooden stairway from the top of the bluff to the terminal. Construction by the Passaic Rolling Mills of an elevated terminus at the ferry commenced in 1891. The railway was built out from the Palisade bluff for a distance of 873 feet and was double-tracked for its entire length. The tower bents were 60 feet wide at the base, 24 feet wide at the top and the height of the station roof above the ground was 194 feet.

Three hydraulic elevators, designed by Thomas E. Brown, Jr. of Otis Brothers and Co., transported passengers between the elevated station and the ferry terminal. The hydraulic cylinders had an internal diameter of 38 inches and were 35 feet long. The power plant was located at the base of the elevator tower. The elevator

cars were built by Gilbert Car Co. They were constructed with a solid framework of hardwood, finished in mahogany, and measured 10 feet by 21 feet and 10 feet in overall height. Each car accomodated 120 passengers with a large number seated on willow chairs. The elevators were designed for a speed of 400 feet per minute (4.5 mph), but operating speed was held to half that. Approximately 45 seconds was required for the 148-foot ascent to the trains. The elevated terminal opened on 20 April 1892.

An amusement park named "El Dorado" was completed in 1891 at the edge of the Palisades bluff where the elevated viaduct joined the bluff. The chief attraction was an open air theater where the public saw spectacles such as "Egypt Through The Centuries." Thousands of New Yorkers crossed the Hudson River to visit El Dorado. Ferries from Manhattan, Brooklyn and Jersey City landed passengers at the West Shore terminal where they either climbed 180 feet up the wooden stairway or rode the elevators and took the 900-foot train ride to the

El Dorado station. El Dorado was destroyed by fire early on the morning of 4 November 1898.

The Guttenberg Track closed in 1893. The final race was held in September and a record breaking throng came to see an exciting contest between *Tammany* and *Lamplighter*. The race track began to deteriorate after "two wheelers" (trotters) took over from "flat" racing. The track left nothing but odors and was commonly referred to as "The Gut." The New Jersey Legislature investigated betting at the track and found such outrageous scandals that it enacted an anti-gambling bill in 1894.

The Railroad to Alpine

The Palisades RR surveyed during the winter of 1892-1893 for a railroad from the Hudson County boundary line, running north through Bergen County to Fort Lee in Ridgefield Township and then to Alpine in Harrington Township.

On 4 January 1893, an agreement was made providing for the operation of the new railroad by the North Hudson County. The Palisades Co. agreed to build a double-track railroad at its own expense from the county line north to Fort Lee, and a single-track line from Fort Lee to Alpine. The North Hudson County Ry. was to build an extension of the Guttenberg line from the race track to the county line and was to operate and maintain both railroads as a through line to Weehawken ferry as soon as the new road was completed to Fort Lee. Not less than 20 trains each way were to run each weekday between Fort Lee or Englewood and Weehawken, at least ten running to Alpine as soon as the road was completed to that point. No Sunday trains were to run north of Ridgefield Township unless both parties agreed. The North Hudson County also agreed to build steam railroad connections to allow freight and express business.

The El Dorado Viaduct and the elevated terminal at Weehawken. The electric car at the foot of the second elevated tower from the left is on the surface line which replaced the elevated operation in 1895. The car was one of a group delivered by Stephenson in August 1896.

The North Hudson County agreed to increase service when business warranted and to provide cars equal to the Gilbert cars already in use on the Guttenberg line. The North Hudson County was to receive five cents from the gross passenger receipts for each passenger carried from the Weehawken ferry to points on the Palisades road and a smaller pro-rated amount for passengers riding from other points on the Guttenburg line. The balance was divided two-thirds for the NHC and one-third for the Palisades RR. It was

PALISADES RAILROAD.

TRAIN SERVICE BETWEEN WEEHAWKEN AND FORT LEE.

WEEK DAY TIME TABLE.

Effective May 13, 1894.   NORTHBOUND TRAINS.

STATIONS.	3	7	13	17	25	109	53	65	69	73	77	81	85	95	99	107
	A.M.	A.M.	A.M.	A.M.	A.M.	P.M.	P.M.	P.M.	P.M.	P.M.	P.M.	P.M.	P.M.	P.M.	P.M.	P.M.
Weehawken Leave	5.40	6.20	7.20	8.00	9.20	.....	2.00	4.00	4.40	5.20	6.00	6.40	7.20	8.55	10.00	11.55
Hudson Heights	5.53	6.33	7.33	8.13	9.33	.....	2.13	4.13	4.53	5.33	6.13	6.53	7.33	9.08	10.13	12.08
Cliff Side						1.51										
Edgewater	5.57	6.37	7.37	8.17	9.37	1.54	2.17	4.17	4.57	5.37	6.17	6.57	7.37	9.12	10.17	12.12
Shady Side																
Fort Lee Arrive	6.03	6.43	7.43	8.23	9.43	2.00	2.23	4.23	5.03	5.43	6.23	7.03	7.43	9.18	10.23	12.18
	A.M.	A.M.	A.M.	A.M.	A.M.	P.M.	P.M.	P.M.	P.M.	P.M.	P.M.	P.M.	P.M.	P.M.	P.M.	A.M.

SOUTHBOUND TRAINS.

STATIONS.	6	10	14	20	28	36	56	104	68	72	76	80	84	88	92	98	102
	A.M.	A.M.	A.M.	A.M.	A.M.	A.M.	P.M.	P.M.	P.M.	P.M.	P.M.	P.M.	P.M.	P.M.	P.M.	P.M.	P.M.
Fort Lee Leave	5.50	6.23	7.10	8.08	9.30	10.50	2.05	2.25	4.10	4.50	5.30	6.10	6.50	7.30	8.05	9.30	10.30
Shady Side																	
Edgewater	5.56	6.29	7.16	8.14	9.36	10.56	2.11	2.31	4.16	4.56	5.36	6.16	6.56	7.36	8.10	9.36	10.36
Cliff Side								2.34									
Hudson Heights	6.00	6.33	7.20	8.18	9.40	11.00	2.15		4.20	5.00	5.40	6.20	7.00	7.40	8.13	9.40	10.40
Weehawken	6.12	6.45	7.32	8.30	9.52	11.12	2.27		4.32	5.12	5.52	6.32	7.12	7.52	8.25	9.52	10.52
Arrive	A.M.	A.M.	A.M.	A.M.	A.M.	A.M.	P.M.	P.M.	P.M.	P.M.	P.M.	P.M.	P.M.	P.M.	P.M.	P.M.	P.M.

Palisades Railroad Schedule No. 1

SUNDAYS AND HOLIDAYS.

NORTHBOUND TRAINS.

STATIONS.	3	13	33	37	41	45	49	53	57	61	65	69	73	77	81	85	95	99	107
	A.M.	A.M.	A.M.	A.M.	P.M.	P.M.	P.M.	P.M.	P.M.	P.M.	P.M.	P.M.	P.M.	P.M.	P.M.	P.M.	P.M.	P.M.	P.M.
Weehawken Leave	5.40	7.20	10.40	12.00	12.40	1.20	2.00	2.40	3.20	4.00	4.40	5.20	6.00	6.40	7.20	8.55	10.00	11.55
Hudson Heights	5.53	7.33	10.53	11.33	12.13	12.53	1.33	2.13	2.53	3.33	4.13	4.53	5.33	6.13	6.53	7.33	9.08	10.13	12.08
Cliff Side																			
Edgewater	5.57	7.37	10.57	11.37	12.17	12.57	1.37	2.17	2.57	3.37	4.17	4.57	5.37	6.17	6.57	7.37	9.12	10.17	12.12
Shady Side																			
Fort Lee Arrive	6.03	7.43	11.03	11.43	12.23	1.03	1.43	2.23	3.03	3.43	4.23	5.03	5.43	6.23	7.03	7.43	9.18	10.23	12.18
	A.M.	A.M.	A.M.	A.M.	P.M.	P.M.	P.M.	P.M.	P.M.	P.M.	P.M.	P.M.	P.M.	P.M.	P.M.	P.M.	P.M.	P.M.	A.M.

SOUTHBOUND TRAINS.

STATIONS.	10	20	36	40	44	48	52	56	60	64	68	72	76	80	84	88	92	98	102
	A.M.	A.M.	A.M.	A.M.	P.M.	P.M.	P.M.	P.M.	P.M.	P.M.	P.M.	P.M.	P.M.	P.M.	P.M.	P.M.	P.M.	P.M.	P.M.
Fort Lee Leave	6.23	8.08	10.50	11.30	12.10	12.50	1.30	2.05	2.50	3.30	4.10	4.50	5.30	6.10	6.50	7.80	8.05	9.30	10.30
Shady Side																			
Edgewater	6.29	8.14	10.56	11.36	12.16	12.56	1.36	2.11	2.56	3.36	4.16	4.56	5.36	6.16	6.56	7.36	8.10	9.36	10.36
Cliff Side																			
Hudson Heights	6.33	8.18	11.00	11.40	12.20	1.00	1.40	2.15	3.00	3.40	4.20	5.00	5.40	6.20	7.00	7.40	8.13	9.40	10.40
Weehawken	6.45	8.30	11.12	11.52	12.32	1.12	1.52	2.27	3.12	3.52	4.32	5.12	5.52	6.32	7.12	7.52	8.25	9.52	10.52
Arrive	A.M.	A.M.	A.M.	A.M.	P.M.	P.M.	P.M.	P.M.	P.M.	P.M.	P.M.	P.M.	P.M.	P.M.	P.M.	P.M.	P.M.	P.M.	P.M.

All regular trains stop at Cliff Side on signal to receive and discharge passengers.

FRANK L. HALL,
Secretary Palisades R. R. Co.

also to receive one-third of a mileage pro rata of non-passenger receipts.

Palisades RR Construction

Construction of The Palisades RR commenced on 14 May 1893. According to terms of the contract with the Hudson County Contracting Co., signed on 1 May 1893, the route to Fort Lee was to be completed by 1 November, but delays were encountered and the completion date was extended to February, 1894. The contract called for four miles of double-track railroad from the county line to Fort Lee.

At the intersection of Anderson and Palisade avenues and Gorge Road at Cliffside Park, a trestle was built, nineteen feet high and 156 feet long. The steel girders rested upon huge granite abutments and intermediate steel columns. A large fill about 1800 feet long with a maximum height of 14 feet was made across the Watkins property to bring the line up to grade. The fill material was taken from the tunnel being excavated for the NYS&W RR through the Palisades between Fairview and Edgewater. The bridge and fill were completed by the end of January, 1894. The trestle foundations were found still to be in good condition during an inspection in August, 1960.

At Fort Lee, south of Main St., a deep rock cut was excavated for a distance of 1800 feet at a maximum depth of 14 feet. The railroad was extended north of Main St. to a point opposite Abbott's factory where a switch was placed. This was the northern terminus until 1895. The entire railroad line within Bergen County was built on a private right-of-way similar to a rapid transit railway. The track consisted of 56 pounds per yard rails, Georgia yellow pine ties and stone ballast.

The Extension to Fort Lee

The first construction train to use the new railroad was on 18 January 1894 when the North Hudson County Railway completed its connection to the county line. The line was completed to Fort Lee early in May, 1894. The opening of service between Weehawken and Fort Lee was celebrated with a special train on Thursday, 10 May. The train, carrying company officers and invited guests, left Weehawken at 3:05 p.m. and consisted of four passenger cars, elaborately decorated with flags, and one steam dummy. At the Edgewater Road station the train stopped for half an hour and the passengers alighted and walked to the edge of the Palisades. The train arrived at Fort Lee at 3:50 p.m. to be greeted by 500 residents described as a "living mass of humanity." The embankment on either side of the 1800-foot rock cut was black with men, women and children who cheered and waved handkerchiefs. Fort Lee village was handsomely and profusely decorated with flags, bunting and flowers in honor of the occasion. When the train came to a standstill on the Main St. grade crossing the passengers alighted and proceeded to Schlosser's Hotel where luncheon was served. At 4:45 p.m. the officers and guests again boarded the cars, the locomotive blew a shrill blast and the train proceeded slowly on its homeward journey. A large number of Fort Lee citizens congregating on the grade crossing at Main St. cheered as the train departed and until it had passed out of sight.

The Fort Lee substation was built at the time of electrification to provide power to the upper end of the Palisades line. View taken on 28 January 1916.

At this time the officers of The Palisades RR were: George S. Coe, President; William E. Bond, Vice President; William S. Opdyke, Treasurer; and Frank L. Hall, Secretary. The Chairman of the Operating Committee was Robert W. de Forrest. The Chief Engineer for the railroad was Charles B. Brush.

Regular Service Begins

Regular service began on Sunday, 12 May 1894 although its timetables were effective 13 May. On weekdays the first train left Fort Lee at 5:40 a.m. for Weehawken. The last train for Fort Lee left Weehawken at 11:55 p.m. The trip between Fort Lee and the Weehawken ferry required 22 minutes. The West Shore RR maintained ferry service to 42nd St. and Franklin St. in Manhattan. Passengers taking ferries from Franklin St. were advised to leave on the boat 25 minutes before train time and from 42nd street 15 minutes before train time. There were 15 trains each way on weekdays and 19 trains on Sundays and Holidays. The fare between Fort Lee and Weehawken was 35 cents for a round trip.

Trains consisted of two passenger cars and a steam dummy. The cars seated 80. Trains were sometimes delayed in Ridge-field Township by cows. "The bovines get on the tracks and seem to enjoy the clanging of the steam motor's bell and blast of the whistle and invariably refuse to move along until the fireman gets out of the cab and drives them off." Trains were limited to 20 mph and could cover the six-mile trip in 18 minutes non-stop.

The Coytesville Extension

The railroad broke ground for the Coytesville extension to the Ridgefield Township line on 14 January 1895. A force of 50 men and a number of teams began clearing the route. The single-track extension was completed during the last week of April and service between Coytesville and the Weehawken terminal commenced on 6 May. The round-trip fare between the two terminals was 40 cents.

Many Coytesville residents turned out to welcome the trains. All day long people congregated on the Coytesville station platform and gazed with apparent delight and satisfaction as the trains came and went. One old gent, who for 45 years had been patiently waiting for the road to be constructed, stood on the platform from the arrival of the first train in the morning until late into the afternoon tell-ing those who gathered at the platform how lines had been surveyed by various engineering survey parties and then abandoned, and finally he had lived to see the long proposed road constructed and in operation.

Electrifying the Palisades RR

In 1892 the Hoboken Generating Station was completed by the Hudson Electric Light Co. and contained three 850-kw, 500-volt D.C. generators which supplied traction power to the North Hudson County system. In 1894 the old North Hudson County's Palisade Ave. cable power house was converted into an electric generating station. The cable equipment was removed and the cable steam engines were modified to drive belt-driven generators to provide 500-volt D.C. power for the railway. The original 1884 steam boilers remained unchanged. The Palisade Ave. Generating Station was shut down in March, 1905 and held in cold shutdown until 1909. In 1910 a 3000-kw, 600-volt D.C railway rotary convertor was installed. The two stations provided sufficient power to enable North Hudson County Railway to complete electrification of its system. The Palisade road was the last to be electrified.

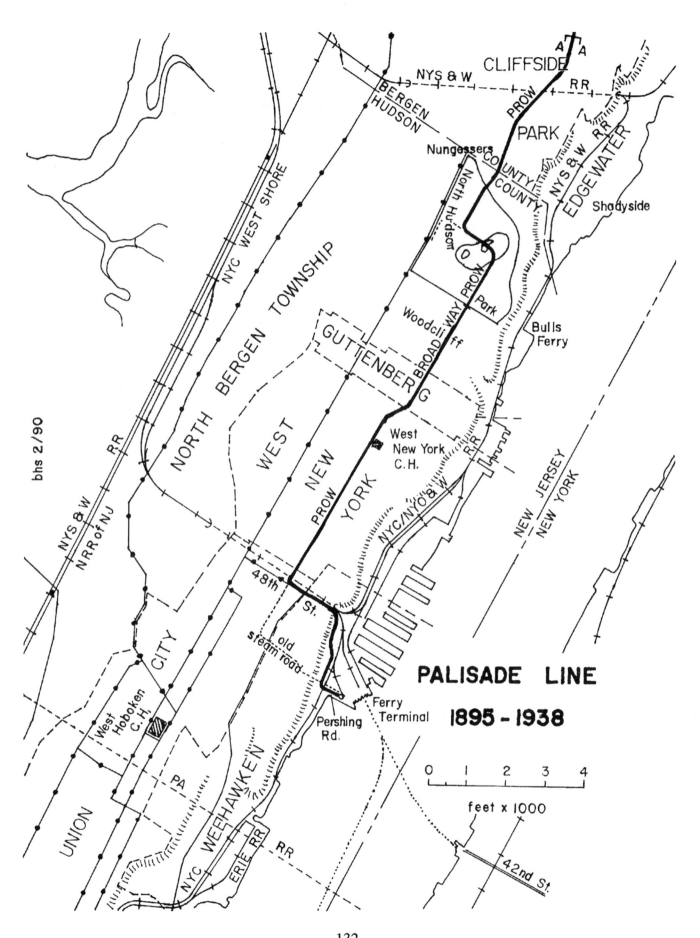

bhs 2/90

CLIFFSIDE

A A

NYS & W   RR

PROW

PARK

BERGEN
HUDSON

COUNTY

NYS & W
RR

EDGEWATER

Nungessers

COUNTY

Shadyside

North Hudson

NYC WEST SHORE

NORTH BERGEN TOWNSHIP

PROW

Park

Woodcliff

Bulls
Ferry

GUTTENBERG

BROADWAY

WEST

PROW

West
New York
C.H.

RR

NEW

YORK

NYC/NYO & W

NEW JERSEY
NEW YORK

NYS & W
RR of NJ

RR

UNION

CITY

48th
St.

old
steam road

West
Hoboken
C.H.

PA

Pershing
Rd.

Ferry
Terminal

PALISADE LINE

1895 - 1938

WEEHAWKEN

NYC

ERIE RR   RR

0   1   2   3   4

feet x 1000

42nd St.

132

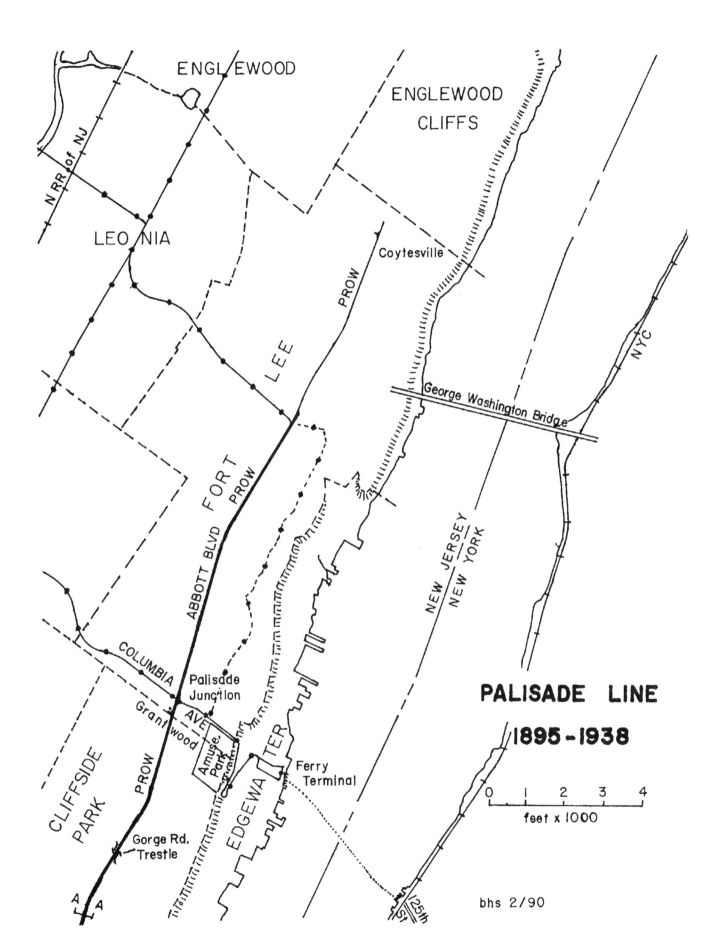

ENGLEWOOD

ENGLEWOOD
CLIFFS

N RR of NJ

LEO NIA

Coytesville

LEE PROW

NYC

FORT PROW

ABBOTT BLVD

George Washington Bridge

NEW JERSEY
NEW YORK

COLUMBIA

Palisade
Junction

Grantwood

AVE

EDGEWATER

Amuse.
Park

Ferry
Terminal

CLIFFSIDE
PARK

PROW

Gorge Rd.
Trestle

A   A

125th
St

PALISADE LINE

1895-1938

0   1   2   3   4

feet x 1000

bhs 2/90

133

The original Palisades electric car fleet included North Hudson County car 180, later Public Service 518 (above), one of ten cars built by Stephenson in 1896, and Public Service 525, originally NHC 200, one of 20 built by Gilbert between 1889 and 1891 for service on the Hoboken elevated and electrified in 1895.

Electric cars commenced service from Weehawken to the county line on 30 June 1895. Steam trains continued to provide service between the county line and Coytesville. This was inconvenient for passengers who had to change cars at Hudson Heights where there were neither benches nor a shelter. Furthermore, the electric cars invariably failed to connect with either the ferries or the steam trains.

During May, 1895 work was underway for a new trolley road down the steep grade alongside Pershing Road in Weehawken between 4th (48th) St. and the West Shore ferry terminal. The new road was opened in July, 1895 and Palisade electric cars used the new route to the West Shore ferry terinal. The old elevated viaduct and terminal with its elevators were abandoned. Dismantling was completed in 1897.

Electrification of the road north of the county line to Coytesville continued into July and August, 1895. The first electric car to run through to Coytesville was North Hudson County Railway car 195, which left Hoboken at 4:30 p.m. on 20 August carrying company officers and guests. Motorman Albert Darlitz and Conductor G.E. Middleton were in charge of the car. The special reached Coytesville at 5:30 p.m. Its passengers alighted and walked to the edge of the Palisades where a sumptuous repast was offered. The car had been decorated with 200 incandescent lamps by Chief Electrician A.K. Bonta and Motorman Darlitz turned on the current which illuminated the whole village and presented a spectacle never before witnessed in the county. At 8:20 p.m. General Manager W.H. Starr gave the signal to start back to Weehawken.

The trip from Coytesville to Fort Lee was made in about three minutes. At Fort Lee the trolley was greeted by no less than 500 enthusiastic citizens. South of Main St. where the railway ran through the rock cut, the car was greeted by women and children who waved their handkerchiefs and cheered. A stop of about ten minutes was made to allow them to examine the car. When the special arrived at 4th (48th) St. in Union Hill it was switched onto the Bergenline Ave. route's track and made its way to Nungessers Hotel at the county line. After a ten-minute stop the car returned to Hoboken.

A North Hudson County spokesman said, "The electrification of the Palisade road north of the county line was practically completed save for stringing the main feed wires which was scheduled for the early part of the week of August 26, 1895." Due to the incomplete condition of the trolley wire, the special car carried Chief Electrician A.K. Bonta and two electricians, John Long and James Harper, in case problems arose.

The Fort Lee Trolley Collision

Two Palisade road trolleys, Nos. 185 and 192, loaded to the steps with excursionists were involved in a serious collision at Main St., Fort Lee on 6 September 1897. The cars were chartered by the Lyric Amateur Orchestra of Union Hill for an annual outing. Car 185 was in the lead and stopped around 10:30 a.m. at Main St. to discharge its passengers. Car 192, about 150 yards behind, loomed into view and had plenty of time to stop. The motorman pulled on the hand brake and it failed to work. The cars collided with a terrific crash and the passengers were hurled about amid fragments of splintered wood and broken glass.

James Dauvereous, motorman on car 192, was pinned in the wreckage and was unconscious. The entire front platform, motor controller and platform roof were smashed to splinters. The standing car, No. 185, strangely enough, was not badly wrecked. The injured were attended to by Dr. Max Well at the house of Mrs. Charles Bender who kindly received them.

All of the members of the Lyric Amateur Orchestra carried their instruments, many of which were broken in the crash.

North Hudson County Ry. Reorganization

On 25 January 1899, at the annual stockholders' meeting of the North Hudson County Railway, the following new directors were elected: David Young, William G. Shailer, J.F. Shanley, J.I. Waterbury, John Kean, John Omberson, John D. Crimmins, Allan L. McDermott and Edward F.L. Young. Concurrently, all of the above men were also elected directors of The Palisades RR Co.

David Young was named NHC president; John S. Shanley, vice president; William C. Doubleday, secretary; and George W. Coe, treasurer. Warren S. Hall was appointed general superintendent, a new office; David Young replaced William H. Starr as general manager; James Craig was appointed chief engineer and superintendent of motive power; T.S. Evans, superintendent of tracks and property; William Jackson, superintendent of line construction; and Hugh Brooks and Chris Holden, division superintendents.

Street Railway Co. Mergers

Many of the men named above participated in the 1899 merger of street railway properties extending from Hudson County through Bergen County and into Passaic County. In 1898, B.M. Shanley formed the North Jersey St. Railway by merging traction companies in Hudson and Essex counties. In 1899 he gathered together a number of small street railway companies in northern Hudson County and Passaic County and consolidated them into the Jersey City, Hoboken and Paterson St. Railway Co. The JCH&P is discussed in Chapter 9.

The Palisades RR Co. was included in the merger. David Young and William C. Doubleday signed the Agreement of Consolidation and delivered the Palisades company deed on 28 October 1899 to Spencer Weart, Master in Chancery Court at Jersey City. The capital stock of The Palisades RR Co., consisting of 2517 shares at a par value of $100 each, was converted into 15,102 shares of the capital stock of the new company. Each

Palisades stockholder received six shares of capital stock of the new company for each Palisades share.

The North Hudson County Ry. and the Paterson Ry. companies did not participate in the consolidation. Edward F.C. Young was a large stockholder in the North Hudson and Paterson companies who offered in writing to sell his stock for $4.5 million. The offer was accepted by the JCH&P directors at their first meeting. However, it was not until July 1901 that the shares held by other local investors were finally purchased. On 2 August 1901 the property and franchises of the North Hudson County Ry. and the Paterson Ry. were merged into the JCH&P, which now owned 139.27 route miles with 415 passenger and 31 work and miscellaneous cars.

Palisades Railroad Boycott

A Commuters' Association organized on 31 May 1900 at Schlosser's Hall at Fort Lee, and appointed Allen S. Williams of Coytesville as chairman. The main complaint were the fares on The Palisades RR between Coytesville and Weehawken: 30 cents round trip for excursion fares and 40 cents otherwise. The Coytesville commuters agreed to boycott the Palisade trolleys and to walk one mile to the Hudson River trolleys on Main St. The Association resolved that the company should issue 20-cent excursion tickets, provide more frequent trips during business hours, and sell tickets of a more convenient size. The existing tickets were twelve inches long!

A committee from the Association met with JCH&P President Young on 20 June 1900 to discuss the boycott. Young agreed to lay the matter before the Board of Directors which agreed to a 20-cent round-trip excursion fare between Coytesville and Weehawken.

Public Service Corp. of New Jersey

The Public Service Corporation of New Jersey was incorporated on 6 May 1903. On 16 May, David Young sold his controlling interest in the JCH&P to the new corporation and the Palisade road became Public Service's Palisade line, a name that lasted until 1938. The street railways acquired by Public Service con-

The 1800 series was built by Stephenson in1907 and replaced the older 500-series and 160-series cars on the Palisade line.

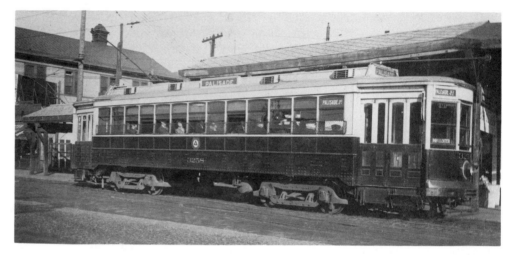

Car 3268 at Weehawken on 21 May 1938. These were built by Cincinnati Car Co. in 1918 and were originally used in Camden.

tinued operating as separate systems although all of the rolling stock was repainted chrome yellow and light cream and renumbered into a unified series.

The JCH&P and the Hudson River line opened a joint line between Englewood and the Weehawken ferry terminal on 4 August 1905 described in Chapter 2. The line was unsuccessful and was discontinued on 14 October. Public Service assigned low numbered 1900-series cars to the line and after its demise these cars remained on the Palisade line. A few car numbers identified in newspapers were 1926, 1930 and 1933. On 11 December 1905 Public Service instituted all night "Owl Service" on the Palisade line between Weehawken and Coytesville.

The Hudson River line opened a new route via Morsemere that crossed the Palisade line in Grantwood on 25 May 1905. The new crossing was named Palisade Junction.

Public Service Railway

The Public Service Corporation formed the Public Service Railway Co. on 30 July 1907 which reorganized railway operations into five divisions. The Palisade line became a Hudson Division line operating from the West Hoboken car house. Until 1907, the name "Public Service" did not appear on the sides of its street cars. Henceforth, "Public Service" in black letters was applied to each side of the chrome yellow passenger cars on the side panel below the windows.

Strikes — 1918-1923

The work stoppages already discussed in chapter 4, affected the Palisades line. No service ran for two days during the 1918 strike. In 1919, service was provided through Bergen County between Coytesville and Union Hill on an infrequent schedule. In 1923, the only car to operate anywhere on the Public Service Railway system during the strike was the U.S. Mail trolley car on the Palisade line

between Hoboken and Coytesville. Normal service was restored on the Palisade line on 21 September 1923.

The strike settlement enabled Public Service Ry. to use one-man cars. They were placed on the Palisade line beginning 6 April 1925, using some of the two-man cars converted during 1924. Conversion required installation of pneumatic door opening devices, removal of bulkheads and bulkhead doors and the lengthening and reversing of car platforms.

Line Changes — 1925-1928

The northern terminus was cut back from Coytesville to Palisade Junction on 1 July 1925. All night service continued to Coytesville until 10 July 1927. Regular service north of Palisade Junction was provided by the Coytesville line which ran between the Edgewater ferry terminal and Palisade Junction on the Hudson River line, then used the Palisade line tracks to Coytesville. The Coytesville line was reduced to rush hours only beginning on 10 July 1927.

Palisade car 3261 in front of the Palisade post office at Palisade Junction in August 1938. The car in the rear is on the Hudson River line.

8600-series Yellow Coach buses replaced streetcars on the Palisade line. (below)

The Palisade line was extended from Palisade Junction to the Edgewater ferry on 6 February 1927 but was cut back to rush hours only on 6 May. The line was cut back to Palisade Junction on 15 June 1928. During 1927, Public Service began assigning route numbers to its trolley lines and the Palisade line became route 23—Palisade.

During the twenties new bus lines began competing with the old established trolley car lines. One bus line parallelling the Palisade car line, started by independent operators, was purchased by Public Service in 1924 and became the 22—Hillside bus line. Public Service extended the 22—Hillside bus over Palisade Ave. through Cliffside Park to the Palisades Amusement Park on 16 September 1928. On 1 July 1929 Public Service extended the line to Coytesville but it was cut back to the amusement park in 1938.

Decline and Abandonment — 1929-1938

Public Service Ry. and Public Service Transportation merged on 10 January 1928 to form Public Service Coordinated Transport Co. The merger was followed by the 1929 depression. The loss of business and the increasing use of buses doomed Bergen County's trolley lines. On 31 October 1931, the George Washington bridge was opened. Public Service Coordinated Transport (Interstate Transportation) and independent bus companies

quickly established new bus routes over the bridge into Manhattan. This accelerated the diversion of passengers from the trolleys.

Buses were substituted for Palisade line trolleys beginning 4 September 1938. Car 3257 made the last run to Coytesville, bearing a sign saying "GOOD-BYE PALISADE TROLLEY, ULTRA-MODERN BUSES SEPT 4." The Palisade line was the last trolley to operate in Bergen County.

Public Service assigned buses 8628-8657, Yellow Coach model 726 coaches built in 1938 with GMC 6-71 diesel engines, to the 23—Palisade bus line. The buses were painted chrome yellow with light cream trim and black lettering and maroon striping. Public Service pro-

claimed these buses, seating 36, to be the first of this size placed in street transportation service anywhere in the world!

Public Service paid taxes on the Palisade right of way until the 1950s. When it stopped, Cliffside Park placed a tax lien on the right of way from Walker St. to the county line. The borough took title in 1955 and built playgrounds on the property at Main and Walker streets and behind School No. 3 from Jersey Ave. to Park St. Public Service sold the north portion to the borough and this became Parking Authority parking lots. During 1960 Cliffside Park Tax Collector Vincent T. McKenna reported the foundations for the Gorge Road trestle were in good condition and poles used for the trolley wires were still standing.

The 2050-2071 series cars held down the Palisade car line assignment from 1908 until replaced by the 3200s in 1937. Car 2059 is shown here at the Weehawken terminal.

Palisade Electric Cars

The original electric cars on the Palisade line were the former steam dummy trailers which were electrified in 1895 and numbered 182 to 200. They were renumbered 520 to 538 by Public Service in 1903. Five of the cars were transferred to the Camden Division in 1907 and eight became service cars. The last survivor was scrapped in 1922.

An additional ten double-truck cars with 24 foot 10 inch bodies built by John Stephenson & Co. of New York City and numbered 172 to 181 were delivered to North Hudson County in August 1896. These became Public Service 510-519. Three went to Camden and six were converted to service cars. The last was scrapped in December, 1921.

Twelve more cars with 32-foot bodies were acquired from the Laclede Car Co. of St. Louis in December 1899 by North Hudson County and numbered 160 to 171. These became Public Service 1506 to 1517 and remained in service on other lines until the early 1930s.

During 1907, cars from the Public Service 1800-1846 series were used on the Palisade line. The single-end cars were built by John Stephenson in 1907 and had bodies 30 feet 8 inches long. The cars were converted to Pay-as-you-enter with longer rear platforms at the Stephenson plant in 1908.

As single-end cars, the 1800-1846 series required construction of wyes at Coytesville, Palisade Junction in Grantwood, and Hudson Heights. A loop already existed at the Weehawken ferry. The Grantwood wye was located on the south side of the Fort Lee substation. Palisade cars turning back at Palisades Junction backed from the northbound track through a crossover onto the southbound track and then into the wye at the substation, then headed back to Weehawken.

Nos. 1823 and 1828 were involved in a rear-end collision on 20 July 1907 in Cliffside Park. Car 1828 was reported to have been badly wrecked.

In 1908, Public Service Ry. received 150 new single-end Pay-as-you-Enter cars from the Cincinnati Car Co. numbered 2050-2199. Twenty-two (2050-2071), were assigned to the Palisade line. The Pay-as-you-Enter design required longer rear platforms to provide for separate exit and entrance door openings in the platform and rear bulkhead. The cars were built with storage air brakes and, therefore, had no air compressors. Instead the reservoir tanks were charged with air from compressor stations at carhouses and terminals, the charge being more than sufficient for the car's trip. The group was scrapped in 1938 and 1939.

On 10 May 1937 Public Service assigned cars from the 3250-3282 series to the Palisade line. Built by Cincinnati Car Co. in 1918, they were bought by the Emergency Fleet Corporation, a government agency, for wartime service in Camden. They were transferred to North Jersey about 1931. As double-ended cars, they allowed the abandonment of the West Shore Ferry terminal loop and the use of the stub end spur track at that point. They were the last cars used in Bergen County. Because of their relative youth and large size, they remained in service elsewhere through World War II and were scrapped between 1945 and 1954.

Palisade Car Assignments
Winter 1937-1938
24 assigned, 19 operated
    2050-2056, 2058-2064, 2066-2073, 2132, 2190.
Summer 1938
18 assigned, 14 operated
    3257-3258-3260-3262, 3265, 3267-3271, 3273-3275, 3277, 3279, 3281, 3289.

8

SADDLE RIVER TRACTION COMPANY

The area of Bergen County directly across the Passaic River from Passaic City above the confluence with the Saddle River was designated as Saddle River Township in 1716. Two municipalities were separated out of the township, Lodi Borough on 22 December 1894 and Garfield Borough on 15 March 1898. The Saddle River Traction Co. was constructed through these communities. The Lodi trolley route was the goal of several earlier companies namely, Passaic, Garfield and Clifton Railway Company and Paterson Railway Company. The latter lines never managed to build their trolley routes into Bergen County.

PASSAIC, GARFIELD AND CLIFTON RY. CO.

The Passaic, Garfield and Clifton Railway Company was incorporated on 14 August 1889 and capitalized at $60,000. The charter authorized it to construct and operate an electric railway in Saddle River Township, Passaic City and Acquackanonk Township. The incorporators were George V. DeMott of Clifton, Mayor Gilbert D. Bogart of Garfield, and Richard Morrell and Mayor Walston R. Brown of Passaic City. Brown and Bogart were cited as the principal motivators and were president and secretary respectively. A. G. Earle was the superintendent. The company office was established in the rear of Charles A. Stelling's jewelry store on East Main Avenue in Passaic.

Franchises were granted by Passaic City on 25 November 1889 and Acquackanonk Township in December permitting construction from the Garfield bridge on Wall Street in Passaic via Passaic Street to Main Avenue, thence to Piaget Avenue. Construction began in January, 1890 at the Garfield bridge but was delayed until April because of the cold winter. The railway was completed from the bridge to Highland Ave. on 1 June 1890.

The cars were late in delivery, which delayed opening the line until July, 1890. On July 26th, two of the new cars left the Harrison Street car house on Main Avenue at 4:30 p.m. with company officers and guests on board for a 16-minute trip to the Garfield bridge. The entire route was thronged with men, women and children and by the return trip the crowds had doubled. The excitement continued into the evening and over one thousand persons rode between 5:30 pm and 10:00 p.m. for a fare of five cents. Regular service commenced with two cars on 28 July. After raising the track which had sunk into soft backfill in a recently-filled sewer excavation on Main Avenue, the schedule was resumed on July 29th.

The railway continued construction through Acquackanonk Township towards Paterson during 1890. The New York, Lake Erie and Western Railroad refused a grade crossing of its race track spur at Main Avenue. It was necessary to run a shuttle car between Crooks Avenue and the NYLE&W. The railroad consented to a crossing in December, 1890.

The PG&C owned five single-truck passenger cars with 26-foot bodies, six windows on each side and open platforms, and one construction car. The passenger cars were painted chrome yellow with light cream trim and the lower side panels were lettered "Passaic, Garfield and Clifton Railway."

Passaic Garfield and Clifton car 3 was built by Brill in 1890 and was one of the original electric cars used on the line.

PATERSON RAILWAY CO.

The Passaic, Garfield and Clifton was merged into the Paterson Railway Co. on 19 May 1891. The Paterson Railway Company had been incorporated as a consolidation of three Paterson companies on 2 May 1888.

The PG&C cars were repainted carmine red and light cream. The first car to emerge in the new colors was No. 6 on 16 September 1891. Paterson Railway upgraded the PG&C route with six additional turnouts and, during April, 1894, double-tracked Main Avenue between Paterson and Passaic.

On 17 July 1893, the Paterson Railway petitioned the Bergen County Freeholders for a franchise for a single-track railway on Passaic Avenue and Main Street, crossing the Garfield (Passaic River) and Saddle River bridges in the Lodi area of Saddle River Township. The bridges were too weak to carry street cars and the petition was denied.

SADDLE RIVER TRACTION COMPANY

The Saddle River Traction Co. was incorporated on 22 June 1897 and was authorized to issue capital stock up to $1.0 million with an initial subscription of $25,000. The incorporators were Bird W. Spencer, Michael F. Burns and Gilbert D. Bogart. Spencer was also affiliated with the Passaic & Newark Traction Co. and the New York, Lake Erie and Western RR. The company filed a proposal on 24 June 1897 to build from the Garfield bridge via Passaic Ave. to Main Street, Lodi.

The company petitioned the Saddle River Township Committee for a franchise on 28 July 1897. Also at the meeting was a competing company called the Passaic and Hackensack Railroad Co. Surveyors were hired to determine which company possessed the longest linear feet of abutting property owner consents along the proposed route. Believing the Garfield bridge would eventually be rebuilt to support the weight of trolleys, the Saddle River Township Committee granted Saddle River Traction a franchise on 24 September 1897. The ordinance granting the franchise was introduced on October 13th and adopted on November 3rd. The franchise authorized the traction company to construct and operate over Passaic Street to the Erie Railroad, thence over Midland Avenue, Clark Street, and Farnham Avenue to Arnot Place.

Lodi Borough granted a franchise to Saddle River Traction on 21 December 1897 for a line over Charles Street, Westervelt Place, Arnot Street and Nicholson Street to Main Street. The company was required to build a public bridge across the Saddle River at Arnot Street.

Marsellus versus Bogart

Construction of the Saddle River line was delayed for over a year. According to *Passaic and Its Environs*, "A few men led by Henry Marsellus did everything they could to block the efforts of the Saddle River Traction Company to construct a trolley line from the Garfield bridge to Lodi. It is doubtful if this opposition would have arisen had it not been that Marsellus was an implacable foe of Gilbert Bogart. Marsellus whose wife, Catherine, owned an old farm inherited from her father, and without whose consent, the trolley could not be built directly to Lodi on Passaic Street, as she owned the necessary frontage to prevent it, soon killed that route.

"Bogart set out to work out a new route, which was from the bridge via Passaic Street to and through Midland Avenue, northerly to Charles Street, and thence through Charles Street to Passaic Street. But 'Boss Eel,' as Marsellus was known, killed this route between Marsellus Place and Charles Street, because his wife and other owners of land refused to give their consents." Henry Marsellus also was known as the "bass" of Garfield.

"It now looked as if there could be no direct trolley line between Passaic and Lodi. At this point, Bogart engaged Lawyer Thomas A. Moore to devise another route to Lodi. Moore suggested a route, which was adopted, along Harrison Avenue to Charles Street. Even this the 'Boss Eel' strenuously opposed and would have won for the third time had it not been for Thomas A. Moore who discovered that one of the objectors was a life tenant and not the owner, who lived hundreds of miles away. To this tenant, Moore dispatched an assistant with maps and documents. The tenant, being in favor of the trolley, signed the petition."

Construction of the Railway

C.R. Wise of Passaic was appointed Chief Engineer of Saddle River Traction in 1897. Construction began at the Garfield bridge and proceeded towards the Erie's Bergen County Railroad grade crossing.

The Erie opposed a crossing because of a sharp curve which did not allow train crews sufficient distance to see ahead and make an emergency stop if a trolley stalled on the crossing. The traction company and the railroad agreed to depress Passaic and Midland avenues to a point 15 or 16 feet below the existing surface of Passaic Avenue at the railroad. The approach was to be about 270 feet long from the east, and about 160 feet from the west, both on an eight percent grade. Midland Avenue and intersecting streets were to be graded to conform. The cost, including damages to adjacent property owners, was estimated at about $24,000. The Erie was to pay three-fourths and Saddle River Traction one-fourth of the bill. In June, 1898 the two railway companies applied to Chancellor Alexander T. McGill, Court of Chancery of New Jersey to define the mode of crossing. However, Garfield Borough authorities applied to reduce the grade to six percent or require a grade crossing. McGill amended his decree to require the six percent grade, increasing the length of the approaching grades to 550 feet in the east and 200 feet in the west. It was estimated the change would increase the cost to $30,500 and on 6 July 1898, Bogart threatened to give up the franchise because of the increased cost of construction and damages to additional property owners. On 22 August, McGill decreed a grade crossing with necessary safety devices. A complete description of the decree can be found in *Atlantic Reporter* 41-A107.

The Erie Railroad was determined to have an underpass and on 11 November 1898, notified Saddle River Traction it that the railroad would construct the underpass at the six percent grade decreed by McGill in June. The traction company would be responsible for the cost of storm sewer construction. Contractor John Garretson began work on the underpass

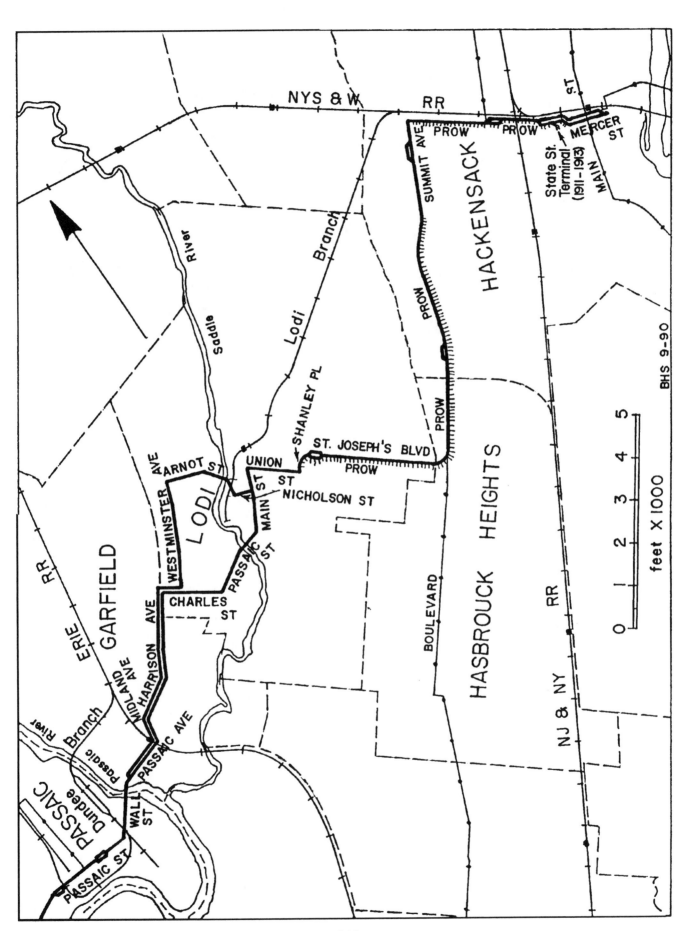

NYS & W   RR

HACKENSACK

State St.
Terminal
(1911-1913)

MERCER
ST

ST

MAIN

PROW   PROW

SUMMIT AVE

PROW

PROW

SHANLEY PL

St. JOSEPH'S BLVD

PROW

UNION
ST

NICHOLSON ST

ARNOT ST

HASBROUCK HEIGHTS

River

Lodi

Branch

Saddle

WESTMINSTER AVE

LODI

MAIN ST

PASSAIC ST

BOULEVARD

GARFIELD

ERIE   RR

CHARLES
ST

HARRISON AVE

MIDLAND AVE

NJ & NY   RR

BHS 9-90

feet X 1000

5
4
3
2
1
0

PASSAIC AVE

Branch

River

WALL
ST

Passaic

Dundee

PASSAIC

PASSAIC ST

141

Paterson Railway car 72, built by Jackson & Sharp in 1895 and delivered in 1896, was used on the Riverside line from Paterson, through Passaic, to the Garfield Bridge. This class of cars was probably used into Saddle River after the line was extended in the summer of 1899.

on 8 December and was ordered to cease the next day because three property owners had not yet settled with the traction company. Construction resumed on December 13th.

Garfield authorities applied for a permanent injunction against the underpass which was denied by McGill on 20 December 1898. The authorities took alternative action on 27 December and obtained an indictment from the Bergen County Grand Jury against contractors Garretson and Troast, engineer Lesher and four others. They were arrested at 3:00 p.m. and arraigned at the County Court House. Bail was posted for all seven. In March 1899, Chancellor McGill once again decreed an underpass. Excavation resumed on 1 May, the railway and traction companies having settled with the affected property owners.

The Garfield Bridge

The Garfield bridge had been built in 1884 and had an 18-foot roadway. The Bergen and Passaic County Freeholders inspected the bridge on 16 September 1897 to determine its condition. They found a constant stream of teams and pedestrians using a rickety old span which shook and trembled under the weight and motion. The Freeholders voted to replace the old span and appointed a joint committee to oversee preparation of specifications and construction of a new bridge.

The committee approved plans for the bridge on 8 July 1898. A contract was awarded to F. R. Long & Company on 5 September to build the bridge at a cost of $28,950. Construction was to start on 1 October 1898 and to be completed in 71 days. The old bridge was closed on October 5th and on October 10th, the Freeholders agreed to have F. R. Long & Company construct a temporary foot bridge at a cost of $375. The new Garfield bridge with its 30-ft wide roadway was opened for public travel on 3 May 1899.

Meanwhile the joint committee and traction company negotiated the terms for a single-track railway across the new bridge. In December 1898, the committee wanted the traction company to pay

$450 to lay a track, $350 annual rent for six years, then $600 per year for four years. The lease would expire in ten years. On 6 March 1899 Saddle River Traction proposed an annual payment of $300, evenly divided between Bergen and Passaic counties. On 17 March, the Bergen and Passaic County Freeholders signed a 15-year lease with Saddle River Traction granting permission to use the bridge for $300 a year. Rails for the bridge arrived on 8 April and workmen laid them that day.

Poles for the overhead system were placed during May, 1899 and had reached Charles Street by May 22nd. The Paterson Railway and Saddle River Traction agreed on 12 January 1899 on the division of fares. Saddle River Traction received one-half of every fare on the Garfield end of the railway; 2.5 cents went to Paterson Railway to transfer passengers.

The Lodi Line Opens

The Saddle River Traction line opened to Lodi in a blinding rain storm on Sunday, 24 December 1899. A special car from Newark, possibly the *Ampere*, was chartered for the first trip. Among those who made the trial trip were Mayor Bogart, Bird Spencer, Mr. Schatzkin,

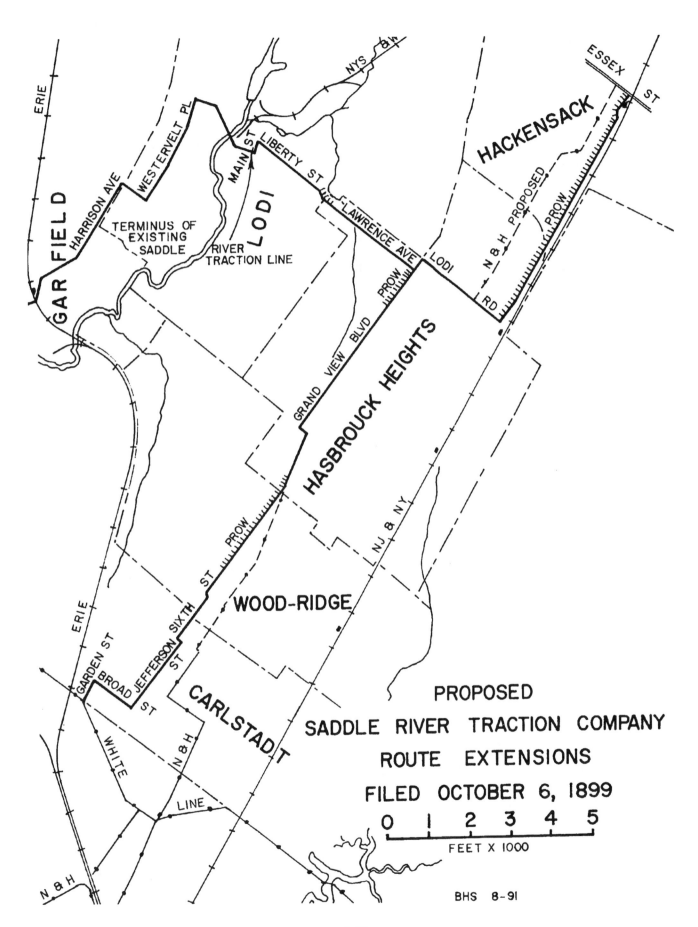

GAR FIELD

HARRISON AVE

WESTERVELT PL

ERIE

TERMINUS OF
EXISTING SADDLE
RIVER
TRACTION LINE

MAIN ST

LIBERTY ST

LODI

NYS

LAWRENCE AVE

LODI RD

PROW

HACKENSACK

ESSEX ST

N & H PROPOSED PROW

GRAND VIEW BLVD

HASBROUCK HEIGHTS

PROW ST

SIXTH ST

JEFFERSON ST

BROAD ST

GARDEN ST

ERIE

WOOD-RIDGE

NJ & NY

CARLSTADT

WHITE

N & H

LINE

N & H

PROPOSED

SADDLE RIVER TRACTION COMPANY

ROUTE EXTENSIONS

FILED OCTOBER 6, 1899

0 1 2 3 4 5

FEET X 1000

BHS 8-91

143

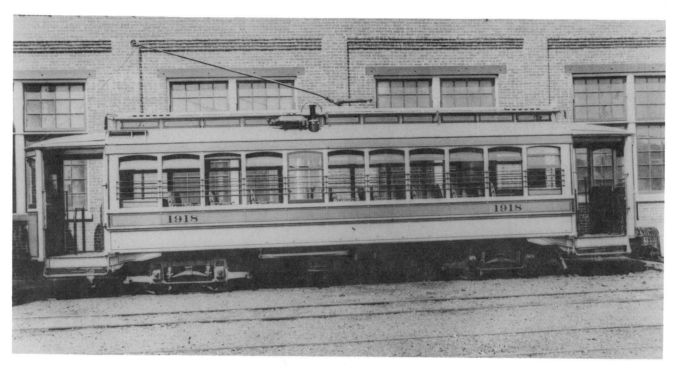

Public Service 1900-49 series cars were assigned to the Saddle River line in 1904 to open through service between Hackensack and Paterson and are typical of the large cars used on the light-traffic line.

Mayor Mercer of Lodi and Borough Clerk Holmes. The car started at the Garfield bridge at 11:00 a. m. Going through the Erie RR underpass, the car derailed with a shower of sparks. It ran as far as Mayor Mercer's home in Lodi and returned. Just as the car reached the home stretch, the sun broke out from behind the clouds. This was accepted by Mayor Bogart as an omen of the future prosperity of the road. "It has taken ten years to get across the Garfield bridge," said Mayor Bogart. "We started when ex-Mayor Brown first commenced to run the Passaic, Garfield and Clifton road in 1889, the first electric railroad in New Jersey, by the way. We failed miserably and have been failing from time to time ever since. It has been storm and battle for ten years, and now the sun is shining through the clouds."

One car operated on a half-hour headway between Garfield bridge and Lodi on 25 December 1899, and although there had been no previous notice, it was filled on every trip all day long. It carried over 1,200 passengers and in one hour, from 4 to 5, 120 fares were rung up. At one time

there were 40 people on board. On 26 December, every third car from Paterson was extended over the Garfield bridge to Lodi. Paterson Railway named its route the Riverside Line.

Beyond Lodi to Hackensack

As discussed in Chapter 3, Saddle River Traction and Newark and Hackensack Traction disputed entry into Hackensack. The area between Hasbrouck Heights and Hackensack was part of Lodi Township until 1905 and it was necessary to pass through the township to reach Hackensack. The companies' representatives appeared before the Lodi Township Committee on 13 October 1899. Each offered reasons why it should receive the franchise. No action was taken by the committee.

On 25 October, the companies appeared before the Hasbrouck Heights Borough Council. David Young, representing the Saddle River line, proposed a railway from Lodi Borough via Lodi Road and Union Street to the NJ&NY Railroad, then north into Hackensack, with a spur through Hasbrouck Heights south from Lodi Road over Grandview Boulevard to the Wood-Ridge line. Young said the railway would be operational by 1 August 1900. In the end, Newark and Hackensack Traction received franchises in both Hasbrouck Heights and Lodi Township.

Jersey City, Hoboken and Paterson Street Railway

Saddle River Traction was one of seven traction companies merged to form the Jersey City, Hoboken and Paterson Street Railway Company, which was incorporated on 1 November 1899. The Articles of Agreement for Consolidation was signed and sealed by Gilbert D. Bogart, President and Bird W. Spencer, Secretary for Saddle River Traction on 23 October 1899. The deed of Saddle River Traction was delivered to Spencer Weart, Master in Chancery of New Jersey, at Passaic on 24 October. The Saddle River stockholders adopted the consolidation agreement on 30 October 1899. Bird W. Spencer became one of the first directors of the new street railway.

The $100,000 capital stock of Saddle River Traction which consisted of 1,000 shares with a par value of one hundred dollars each, was converted into 1,200 shares of the capital stock in the JCH&P. Saddle River stockholders received 1.2 shares of JCH&P capital stock in exchange for each Saddle River share.

The Paterson Railway did not immediately enter the consolidation, but there was coordination with the JCH&P to permit through operation. The Saddle River line was now a JCH&P route that connected with the Paterson Railway's Riverside cars at the Garfield bridge. Through cars between Paterson and Lodi were not operated after 31 March 1900. Paterson cars terminated at the Garfield bridge, requiring passengers to transfer to the Lodi car. The JCH&P operated a former Paterson, Passaic and Rutherford single-truck car between the Garfield bridge and Lodi. JCH&P purchased all outstanding shares of Paterson Railway stock on 23 July 1901. A merger agreement became effective on 2 August 1901.

Franchise Problems and Extensions in Garfield and Lodi

The Lodi Borough Council passed an ordinance on 2 August 1900 giving the JCH&P authority to construct an extension on Union Street towards Hackensack. However, the council was dissatisfied with existing service, particularly with JCH&P's failure to run on schedule. Service delays were primarily caused by frequent derailments on the line's curves. At its 20 August 1900 meeting the council provided for repeal of the trolley franchise ordinance. JCH&P President David Young responded at the council's 1 October meeting when he proposed to eliminate the numerous curves by building a new line straight through Passaic Avenue between Garfield and Lodi. In the event of failure to obtain a franchise in Garfield, the JCH&P proposed to run down Charles Street to the cemetery and make a straight route to Main Street. Young noted that the JCH&P had been surveying the proposed routes. With the prospect of better service, the council tabled the rescinding ordinance.

The truce lasted until 2 October 1901 when a Garfield resolution gave notice to the JCH&P that the franchise would be rescinded unless the Paterson Railway cars terminated at the Erie's Garfield depot instead of at the Garfield bridge on Wall Street, Passaic, to eliminate a change of cars at the bridge. The council described the Lodi cars as being unfit for cattle. The JCH&P responded to the attacks by securing an injunction from the New Jersey Supreme Court restraining the borough from rescinding the trolley franchise. Garfield Mayor Hepworth was served with the injunction on 11 October 1901.

In order to improve relations, the JCH&P put a large gang of men to work in Lodi. Sharp curves were reduced and the roadbed levelled and tamped. One of the tracks on the Heights was taken up and relaid through Charles Street and Passaic Avenue to Main Street, forming a belt line. The new line was completed in early December, 1901. Lodi-bound cars were to descend the Charles Street hill and run on Passaic Street to Main Street, returning over the old route on the Heights. However, Lodi officials would not permit a switch at Nicholson Street for the belt line. The Bergen County Freeholders prevented the laying of tracks on the Passaic Street bridge over the Saddle River. Thus the Passaic Street route had a break at that point and Lodi cars had to use the Heights route in both directions.

In late 1903, a new Saddle River bridge was built by the American Bridge Company of New York but trolleys were not permitted to use it because of a disagreement between the traction company and the county over financial arrangements. By an agreement dated 6 April 1905 Public Service was finally granted permission to use the Passaic St. bridge. Public Service paid the county $2,500 and agreed to pay one-fourth of maintenance and repair costs. Through cars via the bridge and Passaic Street commenced on 22 June 1905. Hackensack-bound cars used this route while the Passaic and Paterson-bound cars used the Heights route.

The Hackensack Extension

Meanwhile slow progress was made on a Hackensack extension. President David Young and other JCH&P officials toured the Lodi trolley route on 21 March 1902 and inspected a proposed route for the extension. This was to run east over Union Street and Lodi Road to the foot of Main Street in Hackensack where it would connect with the Bergen Pike car line. The officials returned on 24 May 1902 to survey other routings, including a proposal to connect with the Newark & Hackensack line in the wetlands below Polifly Road.

The line was extended via Main and Union streets as far as Prospect Street and cars began running on 15 November 1902. However, the line was still incomplete when Public Service Railway was orga-nized on 6 May 1903. No progress was made until January, 1904 when Hudson River Traction, successor to the N&H, and Public Service Corporation agreed on a connection. HRT General Manager Frank R. Ford announced on 10 January that "... the route will be over the new tracks on Hackensack Heights to a point 500 feet north of Lodi Road in Hasbrouck Heights, thence through the Sanford farm, making a connection with the White Line tracks on Lodi Avenue in Lodi.

"All that is needed to make the connection between the White Line and the Hudson River Traction Company is to build about 0.75 of a mile of track on the Sanford farm which has been purchased by the Hudson River Traction Company. The farm is 6000 feet long and 250 feet wide. In order to make fast operating time, the Hudson River Line chose to build on private property."

Construction commenced on 4 April 1904. The spur was completed on 10 May and was opened on 14 May. Hudson River Traction owned the spur and operated a shuttle car on a half-hour headway until Public Service had prepared its cars.

Through cars began operating on a half-hour headway at 6:00 a.m. on 16 May 1904. The Lodi cars terminated at the NYS&W Railroad depot on Mercer Street in Hackensack and at the Broadway/Van Houten Street loop in Paterson. Public Service assigned fourteen virtually new Brill semi-convertible cars from the 1900-1949 group to the new service. Fare was 10 cents to Lodi and Garfield.

Responding to complaints about the double fare, beginning on 18 June 1904, the fare was set at five cents between Hackensack and Lodi and the second fare was not collected until the cars turned the corner beyond the Lodi Post Office.

Public Service's Main St. Line

The Paterson Railway/JCH&P Riverside line was renamed as the Main Street line by Public Service Corp. in 1903. When Public Service Railway was formed on 20 August 1907, the line was assigned to the Passaic Division. Main St. cars operated from the Broadway Terminal at Paterson. There was no barn and cars were stored outdoors in a yard. Broadway Terminal remained as the base of operations until 1 August 1924, shortly

Right: The United Bus Line was one of the small independent operations which competed with Lodi street cars until they were purchased in 1924.

Below: Public Service bus 4703 was built by Yellow Coach in 1929 as bus 2683. It was rebuilt and renumbered in 1940 and is typical of buses used on the 44- Lodi line during World War II.

before abandonment, when the line was transferred to the Market Street car house.

On 8 June 1911, Public Service established transfer points at Main and Mercer streets and at First Street and the private right of way in Hackensack. Passengers on the Main Street, Hudson River, Hackensack and Bergen Pike lines were permitted free transfers between lines to points within Hackensack. Public Service established new fare zones effective 5 August 1912: a five-cent fare between Frederick Street, Lodi and Hackensack and a five-cent fare from any point in Lodi to to any point in Passaic City.

The Hackensack terminus was relocated in July, 1911 to the corner of State and Trinity (Gamewell) streets. A wye permitted turning the single-end cars operating on the line. The terminus was

changed again on 11 August 1913 to Mercer Street at the Susquehanna depot. This required the use of double-end cars.

The Main Street line was severed in Lodi on Main Street from 22 May 1917 until 23 June 1917 because of sewer construction. A portion of the line that was temporarily severed was served by a shuttle, old single-truck car 439.

When Public Service Railway was shut down by the 1923 strike, there were no cars operating in the Passaic Division. The strike ended on 21 September and the first Main Street car to resume service arrived in Hackensack at 4:00 p.m.. Independent jitney buses began running during the strike. Operating straight through on Passaic Street in Garfield and Lodi, they could provide faster service to Passaic. Their continued operation cut into

revenues on the Main Street line and one-man operation began on 16 December 1923. At the same time the line was redesignated as the Main and Lodi line.

Continued patronage losses were complicated by a 1924 sewer project in Passaic Street which promised to disrupt service. In response, Public Service applied to the PUC for permission to abandon the Main Street line. Permission was granted on 28 August 1924 and the line was abandoned on 31 August. Passaic (White Line) cars were rerouted to provide replacement service from Paterson via Main Street to Passaic and State streets in Passaic. The old White Line route through Passaic was served by the Lakeview line, a new route running from Paterson's City Hall loop as far as Passaic and State streets. Service from Passaic through Garfield and Lodi to Lodi Junction (Grandview Blvd. in Hasbrouck Heights) was provided by the 44 — Lodi bus, transfers being given to Hackensack line cars. Some 44 — Lodi buses were extended to Hackensack via Rochelle Park and Maywood on 22 October 1924.

The 44 — Lodi bus line replaced 26 independent buses operating between Passaic, Garfield and Lodi on a 3- to 4-minute headway. The independents' permits were purchased by Public Service Transportation between 14 December 1923 and 1 November 1926. The independent buses were renumbered 288 through 329 and 1810 through 1814. Included were six Whites, five Giants, three G. M. C.'s, three Macks, two Packards, and one each Apex, Brockway and Pierce-Arrow. They were replaced by new buses from the following series assigned to the Passaic garage: 506-510, Macks, August 1924; 537-547, Macks, March and April 1925; and 559-562, 570-573, Yellow Coach, June 1924.

EQUIPMENT NOTES
JCH&P Cars

By the time the Saddle River Traction line was opened in 1899, it had been merged into the Jersey City, Hoboken and Paterson. There was no indication that Saddle River Traction intended to purchase cars but rather intended to run the Paterson Railway's Riverside cars through to Garfield and Lodi. One car was used from 1899 to 1904 to operate a shuttle between the Garfield bridge and Lodi, about two miles one way.

The complex car renumberings by the JCH&P make it difficult to trace their identity. Reports indicated that cars 711 and 725 were in service in 1901. The only car 711 known on the JCH&P was new, a closed car with a 25-foot 6-inch body delivered by St. Louis Car Co. in December 1900. Car 725 was a 23-foot Jackson & Sharp-built closed car purchased by Paterson Railway in September 1896.

Thereafter, the quality of equipment seems to have deteriorated. A car numbered 144 or 411 was reported in service in 1902. No car 411 has been found in rolling stock records. Car 144 may have been a former North Hudson County Railway horse car.

Car 177, was blamed for a carbarn fire that destroyed fifty open cars of the JCH&P on 30 January 1902. It appears to have been an 18-foot Brill formerly owned by the Paterson, Passaic and Rutherford Electric Railway and built in 1893. The Harrison Avenue carbarn located on Main

Avenue in Passaic was used mainly for winter storage of summer cars by the Paterson Railway. The fire lasted only twenty minutes, but the entire building was laid waste. The fire originated from an overheated stove in car 177, which was known among the trolley men as the "hoodoo." The car had the reputation of derailing daily and causing numerous blockades on the Saddle River line. No. 177 stood at the extreme front of the barn and the other cars could not be run out of the barn as their trucks had been transferred to the winter closed cars.

Car 114, described as a discard from the White Line, was assigned as the replacement car on the Lodi line and also derailed frequently. It appears to have been a 28-foot closed car built for the opening of the White Line in 1894. May 1, 1902 was a typical day. The car left the Garfield bridge at 4:40 p.m. with a number of passengers including Mayor George Mercer. It made great progress until the top of the hill at Charles Street was reached. The motorman turned off the power going downhill so as to run slowly around a very sharp curve into Westminster Avenue. It was at this curve No. 114 derailed on almost all the previous trips during the day and every precaution was taken to prevent another. The car moved so slowly the passengers thought they were in a funeral procession. Precautions were in vain as No. 114 derailed again.

In Passaic City for three days in mid-June, 1902, the JCH&P reconstructed its track on Passaic Street with heavier rail. JCH&P car 117 was used as a shuttle car between Columbia Avenue and the Garfield bridge during the reconstruction. The JCH&P had assigned 12-bench open cars 1726 and 1727 to the Riverside line and they often spread the rails on Passaic Street prior to June, 1902. These cars were built for Paterson Railway by Jackson & Sharp in 1896.

Public Service Cars

Over the years, Public Service used a variety of cars on the Main and Lodi line. The vital statistics of these cars are shown in the table below :

When Public Service initiated through service over the Lodi route between Paterson and Hackensack in 1904, it provided Brill 1900-series semi-convertible cars with cross seats.

During 1905 the 1900s were reassigned to the Palisade and White lines and were replaced by double-end 1700-series cars. The 1700s were converted to pay-as you-enter type at the Plank Road shop and at the works of John Stephenson Company during 1908. Some were converted from double-end to single-end cars.

The 1900s were involved in various derailments and collisions. On 26 August 1904 two collided at Passaic and Columbia streets in Passaic because of both motormen trying steal the next switch on the single track. On 11 March 1905, car 1933 derailed in Hackensack between Union and Park streets while on the Hudson River Line's track; and an empty 1900 deadheading back to the Harrison Avenue carbarn ran into the rear of a Hudson River Line work car carrying stone ballast at 8:30 p.m. in Hackensack on the private right of way downgrade towards First Street on 13 October 1905.

The 1700s suffered similar mishaps. Main Street car 1704 was standing on Mercer Street in front of the Susquehanna Railroad depot at midnight on 16 October 1905, when Hudson River car 55, bound for Paterson, failed to stop and crashed into the rear of 1704. Car 55's headlight was smashed. Another 1700 bound for Paterson on 30 December 1905 and carrying 75 passengers lost its air brakes while descending Westminster Avenue hill. When the motorman attempted to apply the hand brake he found this, too,

Series	Body Length	Length Overall	Win- dows	Trucks	Motors	Controllers	Seats	Builder
1100-1119	32' 0"	42' 10"	11	2 — Brill 27G	4 — GE 80C	2 — K6	31	Brill, 1898
1700-1721	30' 8"	44' 7"	11	2 — Brill 27G	4 — Wh 68	1 — K6 SE	33	Cincinnati, 1904
1700-1721	30' 8"	46' 4"	11	2 — Brill 27G	4 — Wh 68	2 — K6 DE	31	Cincinnati, 1904
1900-1949	30' 8"	42' 10"	11	2 — Brill 27G	4 — Wh 68	2 — K6	42	Brill, 1903

was out of order. The car derailed on the sharp curve at Charles Street, struck a utility pole and turned over. Most of the passengers were cut with broken glass and splinters from the roof of the car. The car was heated by a stove and coals from it started a fire which added to the excitement. On 2 January 1905, car 1711 was bound for Paterson in Lodi with 95 passengers on board. When it descended Westminster Avenue hill it failed to negotiate the curve into Charles Street and tipped over on its side. The passengers suffered mainly cuts and bruises, but were so angry they nearly rioted, threatening to kill the motorman. Hackensack bound car 1712 was travelling north on Westminster Avenue on 8 January 1906. Upon nearing Arnot Street the motorman found the brakes didn't work. No. 1712 turned into the curve at an excessive speed and derailed skidding 90 feet to stop at the brink of a 20-foot embankment. On 13 March 1906 a 1700 came down the Charles Street hill and went out of control when the brakes failed. The car derailed at the curve, smashed into the curb and plowed 50 feet across a lawn into a house. Several men were playing cards in the room through which the trolley stuck its vestibule.

Reverend Father Aschert spoke at length about the trolley accidents at the 28 March 1906 Lodi Borough Council meeting. He urged the council to give Public Service permission to run cars over the Saddle River bridge on Passaic Street. Councilman Demarest said: "I don't see what difference it will make in avoiding accidents if we do grant the company's request. The cars are in such poor condition and no effort seems to be made to repair them. The hills will have to be used both going and coming from Passaic and unless the cars are repaired, the accidents will continue."

In Hackensack about 7:30 a.m. on 13 February 1908 a Main Street line car and a Hudson River Traction Newark car collided headon on the private right of way at the east end of the Hudson River Line's bridge above the NJ&NY Railroad. The Main Street line car telescoped through the vestibule and into the smoking compartment of the Hudson River car fatally injuring the Hudson River motorman.

The last cars to operate over the Main and Lodi line were 14 Public Service cars from the 1100-1119 series, built by J. G. Brill in 1898 and numbered 1100-1108, 1110, 1112, and 1114-1116.

During 1914 a single-truck 9-bench open car (No. 439) was reported in service on the Lodi portion of the line. It was built by Stephenson in 1894 for the Consolidated Traction Co. and had originally operated on the Bayonne line.

Color Schemes

Paterson Railway cars were painted carmine red with light cream trim. Striping and lettering appeared to be gold or light cream.

JCH&P cars were solid carmine red with gold or light cream trim.

Public Service passenger cars were chrome yellow on the top panel and vestibule ends. The bottom panel and window posts were light cream. Wide striping and trimming was tuscan red and fine striping and lettering was black.

Lodi's Trolley System

The following poem was printed in the Hackensack *Bergen Record* on 9 May 1906. It describes the frustrations the citizens of Lodi experienced with the delays in opening the Main St. line.

Riding home on a Lodi car
    is nothing but a joke,

The tracks are either smeared with tar,
    Or the running gear is broke.

When going round a bend, the car
    will assuredly jump the tracks,
The passengers get such a jar,
    it almost breaks their backs.

And coming down the Lodi hills,
    the brakes will fail to work.
The Public Service stands the bills,
    the public stands the jerks.

There are a thousand other things
    that to the trolleys happen,
But what most sorrow to you brings
    they always catch you napping.

You're holding tightly on a strap
    or to your seat are clinging.
When suddenly you hear a crack
    and screams in your ears are ringing.

And when you try to find your hat,
    you see it on the floor.
The people used it as a mat
    when they ran out the door.

But surely there will be an end
    to all this trouble soon.
The company will make amend
    before another moon.

For every trouble has an end
    so Tom McCarter claims.
They Public Service will send
    that will not give us pains.

Passaic Street, it will be used,
    the bridge will now be crossed.
We will no longer be abused,
    or from the cars be tossed.

Oh let us hope it all is true,
    and let us all be jolly.
What we ne'er could safely do
    we'll use a Lodi trolley.

Rejoice then, Lodi, at the news,
    the time is not so far,
When you can with safety use
    a Lodi trolley car.
                        A. VIKTUM

9

JERSEY CITY, HOBOKEN & PATERSON STREET RAILWAY COMPANY

The Jersey City, Hoboken and Paterson Street Railway Co. was one of the largest traction companies in northern New Jersey prior to formation of Public Service Railway in 1907. The JCH&P was created by merger of seven relatively small traction companies on 1 November 1899. Subsequently, five additional traction companies and one elevating company were added by merger.

To present the history of the Jersey City, Hoboken and Paterson in detail would require an entire book devoted solely to the review of no less than 23 predecessor traction companies that were the roots of the JCH&P family tree.

When the JCH&P was taken over by Public Service Corporation of New Jersey in 1903, the company owned 139.27 route miles and 374 passenger cars. The capital liability per mile of track was $264,551.00. For the year ending December, 1902, the net earnings were $854,893.36. After deducting interest and taxes, the profit was $5,595.94!

The scope of this chapter is limited to the operations of the JCH&P "White Line" route through Bergen County. Noteworthy anecdotes elsewhere on the system are included in this review.

THE MORRISSE SYSTEM

In Bergen County the roots of the JCH&P are found in two companies: The Passaic, Rutherford and Carlstadt Electric Railway Co. and The Jersey City, Hoboken and Rutherford Electric Railway Co. Note that "The" is part of the corporate name of the two companies. The PR&C entered Bergen County from Passaic City on the west and the JCH&R entered Bergen County from the Secaucus area of North Bergen Township on the east. Both companies planned to build over the Paterson and New York Plank

Road and both planned to terminate in the vicinity of Park Avenue in East Rutherford. This connected both traction companies in an end-to-end arrangement and offered through travel between Hudson, Bergen and Passaic counties. The two companies were part of a link in a chain of lines between Paterson and Hoboken of which James A. Morrisse was the principal promoter.

The Passaic, Rutherford and Carlstadt Electric Railway Co.

The PR&C was incorporated on 29 September 1892 and was authorized to construct a street railway over a circuitous route beginning in Paterson City, through Acquackanonk Township, Passaic City, Lodi Township, and along the Paterson and New York Plank Road to Boiling Springs to a terminus at the Erie Railroad on Park Avenue.

In Paterson, the PR&C was authorized to terminate at the intersection of Knickerbocker and Railway avenues where it made an end-to-end connection with The Paterson and Passaic Electric Railway Company (another Morrisse enterprise). In Passaic, property owners fought, hampered and delayed construction and the PR&C was compelled to alter its route through the city twice.

In the Wallington area of Lodi Township, property owners abutting the proposed route gave their full support to the company. Wallington Borough was separated from Lodi Township by referendum of 31 December 1894, effective on 2 January 1895. Carlstadt granted a franchise to the PR&C on 21 February 1893. Because The Passaic, Rutherford and Carlstadt wanted to operate over the Paterson and New York Plank Road, a county road, between the Passaic River and Boiling Springs, it was necessary for

the company to petition the county freeholders. The Bergen County Board of Chosen Freeholders granted permission on 6 March 1893 to build on the plank road. By August nearly two miles of track had been completed from the Passaic River bridge to Boiling Springs Township. The township became East Rutherford Borough on 28 March 1894.

The Paterson, Passaic and Rutherford Electric Ry. Co.

Because The Passaic, Rutherford and Carlstadt Electric Railway was having both legal and financial difficulty in securing a route through Passaic and Morrisse saw a need to consolidate the several small traction companies into a financially stronger corporation, he established a new company. The Paterson, Passaic and Rutherford Electric Railway was incorporated on 21 November 1893 as a consolidation of The Paterson and Little Falls Consolidated Railway, The Paterson and Passaic Electric Railway and The Passaic, Rutherford and Carlstadt Electric Railway. The consolidation provided a continuous route from Boiling Springs to Singac via Passaic and Paterson, a distance of 20 miles. The officers were Charles A. Johnson, President; Louis Fitzgerald, Treasurer; and A.H. Hayward, General Manager.

The route through Passaic had been settled in June 1893 by the PR&C, but the franchise was not granted until 6 January 1894. Construction proceeded slowly through Passaic because of the continued opposition by several property owners along the route. Protracted litigation was settled only by large payments to the property owners. In time this contributed to the bankruptcy of The Paterson, Passaic and Rutherford.

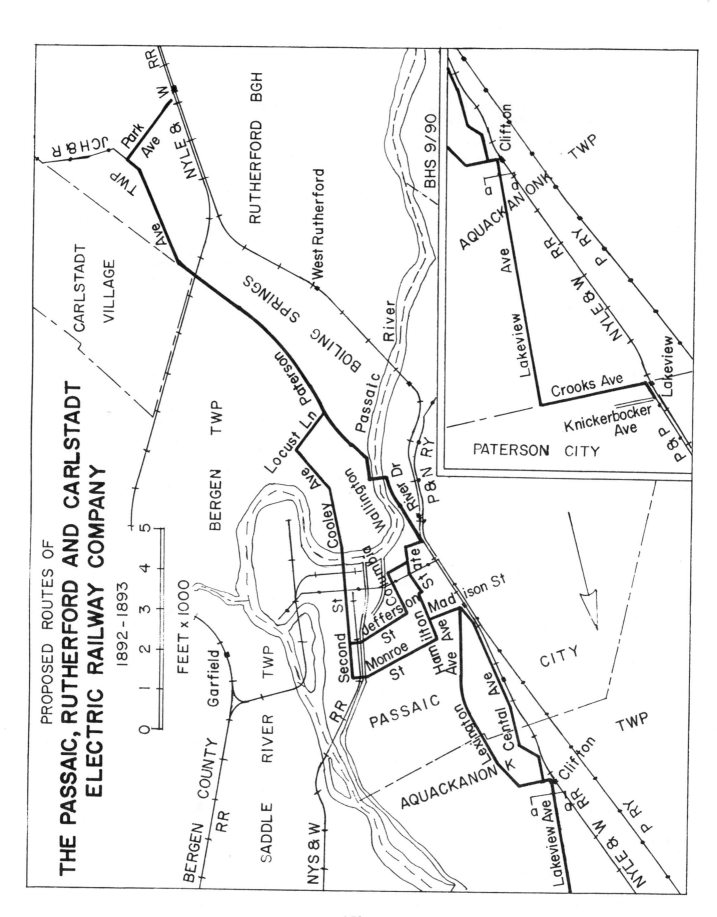

PROPOSED ROUTES OF

THE PASSAIC, RUTHERFORD AND CARLSTADT ELECTRIC RAILWAY COMPANY

1892 - 1893

FEET x 1000

0 1 2 3 4 5

150

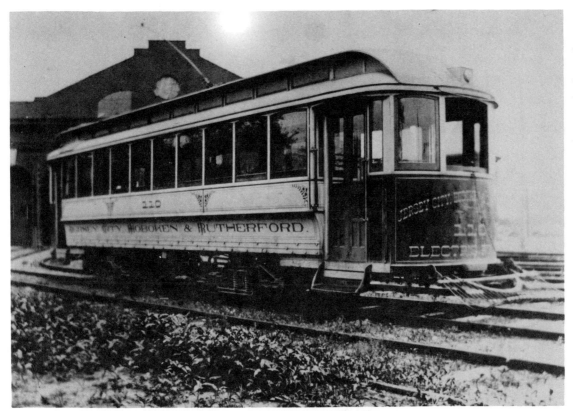

JCH&R car 110, later JCH&P 505 and Public Service 964, was received from St. Louis Car Co. in 1895 for service from Hoboken to Paterson over the so-called "White Line." The St. Louis trucks were unsatisfactory and were quickly replaced.

In constructing the line between Lodi and Boiling Springs, it was necessary to build a 1200-ft. long retaining wall for the Paterson and New York Plank Road where it crossed a depression on the south side of the road. The retaining wall was needed to bolster the side of the road as the railway tracks were laid at the side.

The first five cars purchased by The Paterson, Passaic and Rutherford arrived during the third week of February, 1894. By 4 May, track construction was completed on the Paterson and New York Plank Road between Wallington and East Rutherford. The PP&R was completed on 1 June 1894 and on Tuesday, 3 July the first car ran through to the East Rutherford terminus at Park Avenue.

The Paterson, Passaic and Rutherford was designed, engineered and built by Lemuel William Serrell. A brick car house with a steel truss roof covered with corrugated steel, and with a capacity of approximately 15 single-truck cars was built in Carlstadt on property adjacent to the Erie Railroad's Bergen County line and faced Paterson Avenue. It was built on low ground and a peat bog was removed to a depth of two feet to provide a stable foundation. The car house, 68' 6" wide by 134' long, contained five storage tracks. A 25' by 50' extension, contiguous to the west side, contained a machine shop,

storeroom, superintendent's office, conductors' room, passenger waiting room and a starters' office. A Howard clock was installed near the peak of the car house roof facing Paterson Avenue, enabling conductors to set their watches without leaving the car.

The power supply for the PP&R was furnished by the Edison Electric Illuminating Company's station on Paterson Street near Market Street. The Edison Company built a new power station in 1895-96 at Prospect and Van Houten streets on a raceway from the Passaic River which furnished ample cooling water. The station was put in service on 1 February 1896 furnishing lighting power to the city, and 500 volt d.c. power to the Paterson street railways. PP&R feeders extended nine miles to East Rutherford. The six feeders had a total of 36 miles of No. 0000 copper wire. The traction company laid a 500,000 circular mil armored submarine cable under the Passaic River.

In 1894 PP&R cars were painted white to distinguish them from the cars of the Paterson Railway which were painted carmine red. As a result the PP&R line came to be known as the "White Line."

The PP&R was leased to New Jersey Electric Railway on 15 May 1895. Passaic City granted a franchise to the NJE to operate over PP&R tracks on 11 July.

The Jersey City, Hoboken and Rutherford Electric Ry. Co.

The Jersey City, Hoboken and Rutherford Electric Railway Co. was incorporated on 5 December 1892. It was authorized to construct a street railway beginning in Boiling Springs Township and proceeding east over the plank road forming the boundary between Lodi and Boiling Springs townships, crossing the Hackensack River into North Bergen Township (Secaucus area), thence to Jersey City, thence along the dividing line between Jersey City and the Town of West Hoboken, its terminating point. The JCH&R was capitalized at $500,000.

At the first Board of Directors' meeting on 10 December 1892, Charles A. Johnson was elected President; James A. Morrisse, Vice President; Louis Fitzgerald, Treasurer; and Charles H. Russell, Secretary. The board announced the line would run from the Barclay Street ferry landing (DL&W RR) in Hoboken to Boiling Springs in Bergen County where it would connect with the PR&C.

Since most of the available through streets in Hoboken and Jersey City were already occupied by street railways, the JCH&R was forced to seek franchises over back streets in Hoboken and Congress Street in Jersey City.

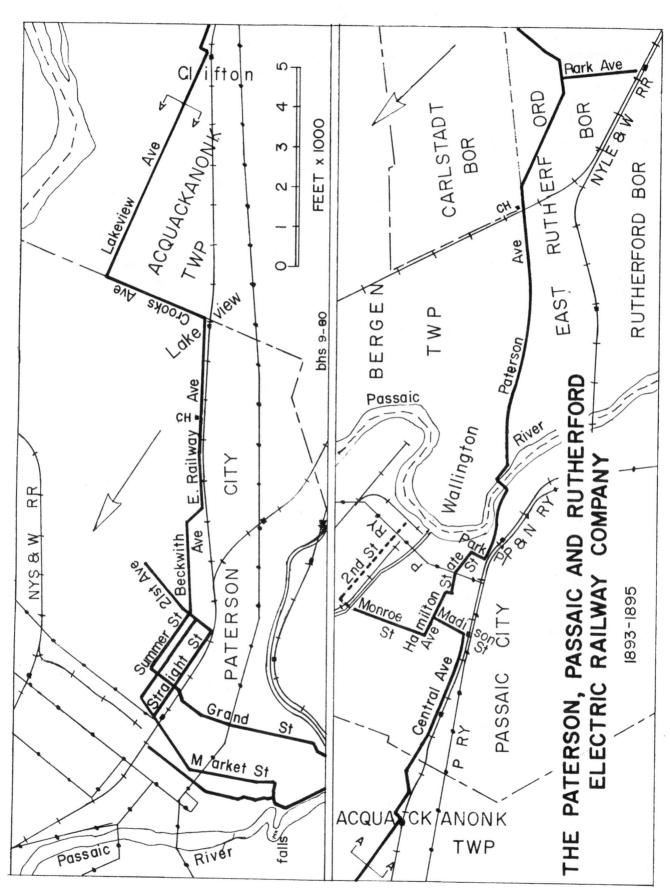

THE PATERSON, PASSAIC AND RUTHERFORD
ELECTRIC RAILWAY COMPANY

1893-1895

152

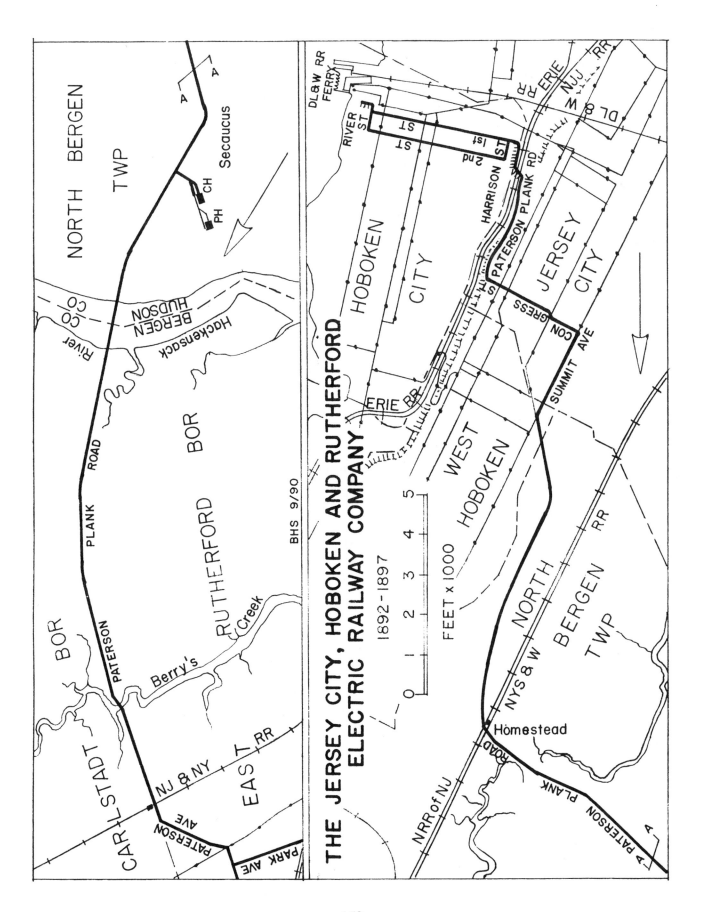

THE JERSEY CITY, HOBOKEN AND RUTHERFORD ELECTRIC RAILWAY COMPANY

1892 - 1897

FEET x 1000

0 1 2 3 4 5

NORTH BERGEN TWP

NORTH BERGEN
TWP

BERGEN CO
HUDSON CO

Hackensack River

PATERSON PLANK ROAD

CARLSTADT BOR

RUTHERFORD BOR

Berry's Creek

NJ & NY RR

EAST RR

PARK AVE

PATERSON AVE

BHS 9/90

Secaucus

CH
PH

A
A

DL&W RR

FERRY

RIVER ST

2nd ST

1st ST

1st ST

2nd ST

HARRISON ST

PATERSON PLANK RD

CONGRESS ST

SUMMIT AVE

ERIE RR

ERIE RR

NJJ RR

DL&W RR

HOBOKEN

JERSEY CITY

WEST HOBOKEN

NORTH BERGEN TWP

Homestead

NRR of NJ

NYS&W RR

PATERSON PLANK ROAD

153

The Bergen County Freeholders granted approval on 20 February 1893 for The JCH&R to occupy the Paterson Plank road from the Hackensack River drawbridge to Park Avenue or Franklin Street in Boiling Springs Township. It was stipulated that construction must commence no later than 1 April 1893. Actual construction commenced during the latter part of July 1893 in Carlstadt and was completed in April 1894. The line was double-track with one track on each side of the roadway. A single-track was constructed across the Berrys Creek and Hackensack River drawbridges.

The JCH&R built a brick car house and a power house in the Secaucus area of North Bergen Township which were completed in 1895. The car house was 80 feet by 260 feet , contained seven storage tracks and had a capacity of 32 cars. It was called Secaucus Car House even though Secaucus Borough was not formed until 12 March 1900. The building was set back from the curb line of Paterson Plank Road approximately 950 feet. The company's name was spelled out in the bricks above the front doors. The steel-truss roof was covered with corrugated steel. The power house was situated 560 feet west of the car house.

In early 1895, The JCH&R received fourteen double-truck closed cars from the St. Louis Car Company. The cars were painted white similar to the The PP&R cars. Later in 1895 The JCH&R received twelve single-truck 10-bench open cars made by American Car Co.

The Jersey City, Hoboken and Rutherford opened its line on 2 June 1895 between Congress Street, Jersey City and Park Avenue, East Rutherford. The New Jersey Electric Railway, which had leased the PP&R in May 1895, commenced service to Park Ave. on 3 July 1894. The NJER ran through cars between Singac and Jersey City — a distance of 21.62 miles — on Sundays beginning in September 1895 and ending on 6 October. Through cars also ran daily for two weeks during December. The service was not successful and the operation of two divisions was resumed, connecting at Park Avenue, East Rutherford.

In 1895, the JCH&R had completed its track only as far the municipal boundary where the Erie and New Jersey Junction railroads cross the Paterson Plank Road. The JCH&R operated shuttle cars between the grade crossing and the top of the palisade hill.

The JCH&R proposed to reach the Hoboken Ferry by a line beginning at the old Duke's House on a private avenue owned by the Hoboken Land and Improvement Co. one block north of the DL&W ferry terminal. It would operate by double track on River St. and single track eastbound over First St. and westbound via Second, Harrison and First to the Erie and New Jersey Junction railroads' grade crossing. Here the JCH&R would eventually construct a single-track wooden trestle ascending to a double-track steel truss bridge spanning the two railroads to connect with the double-track on Paterson Plank Road to Jersey City.

The Secaucus car barn and power house were built in a comparatively desolate part of the Meadowlands. The car house and yard would later be used for storing and burning abandoned cars.

Some First Street property owners opposed the line until 2 July 1896 when the New Jersey Supreme Court ruled in the company's favor. Construction then proceeded quickly despite the opposition and the White Line opened to Hoboken Ferry on 9 August.

New Jersey Electric Ry. Co.

James A. Morrisse, citing the financial necessity to consolidate the traction lines that made up the White Line system, organized the New Jersey Electric Railway Co. on 14 September 1894. The NJER leased The PP&R on 15 May 1895 and the JCH&R on 7 June 1897. The NJER owned 7359 shares of PP&R stock, 4500 of the JCH&R, and 615 of the Paterson Central. This gave the NJER control of a system extending from Singac to Paterson, Passaic, East Rutherford, Jersey City and Hoboken.

On 9 July 1898, the NJER established a new White Line schedule whereby cars left Hoboken and Paterson at 4 a.m., running every half hour until 6 a.m., then every ten minutes until 11 p.m., and every half hour until 2 a.m. The purchase of fifteen new 10-bench open cars from Brill enabled the company to run the increased schedule.

154

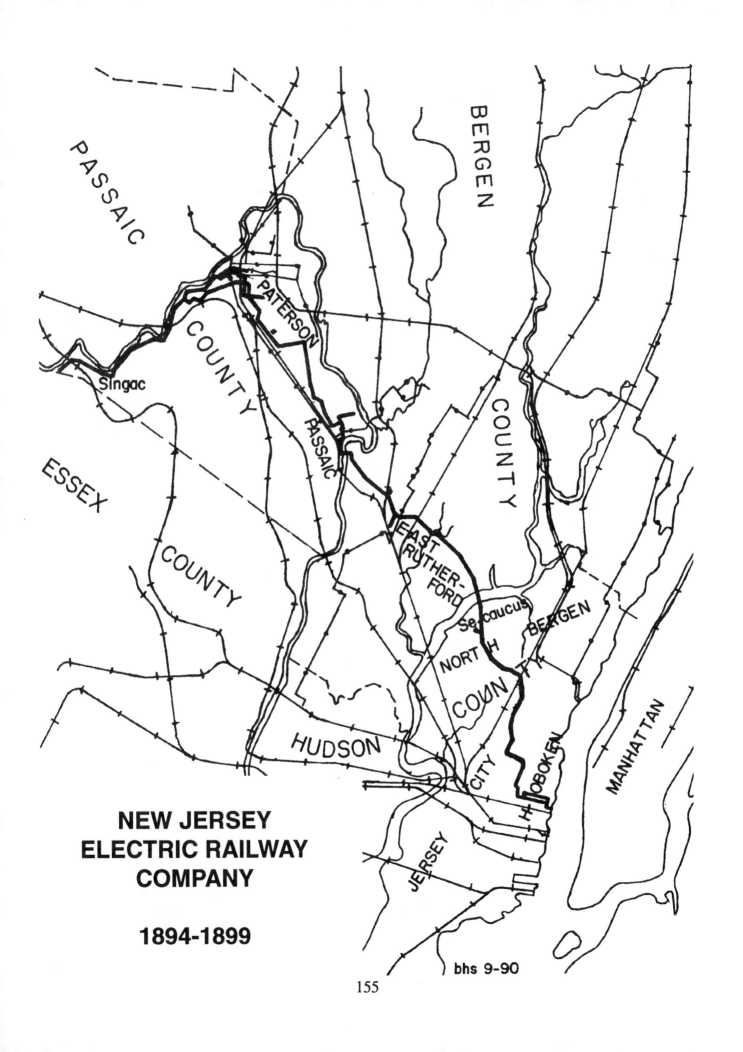

PASSAIC

BERGEN

COUNTY

ESSEX

COUNTY

Singac

PATERSON

PASSAIC

COUNTY

EAST RUTHER- FORD

Secaucus

BERGEN

NORTH

COUNTY

HUDSON

JERSEY CITY

HOBOKEN

MANHATTAN

**NEW JERSEY
ELECTRIC RAILWAY
COMPANY**

1894-1899

bhs 9-90

155

While car 56, a 20-foot Brill built in 1896, is optimistically signed for Hoboken, it is was used on the western end of the White Line, a transfer being required at East Rutherford for passengers to reach the Hoboken Ferry.

NJER employees struck on 19 April 1899 to protest the lengthening of their work day from 12 to 14 hours. By 4 p.m. the strike was over and many employees never returned to work. The 14-hour day was retained and wages remained at $2.12 a day.

The NJER never achieved financial stability. The Hoboken-East Rutherford division was never profitable and profits of the western division were insufficient to cover the losses. The NJER declared bankruptcy on 12 December 1897. The U. S. Circuit Court appointed John L. Heins, President of the NJER, as receiver. David Young replaced Heins in April 1899. A Master of Chancery sale of the New Jersey Electric Railway Company took place at the Secaucus car house on 10 June 1899 at the request of the Mercantile Trust Company.

White Line Traction Company

The White Line Traction Co. was incorporated on 9 June 1899 and on 30 June, by indenture of sale (foreclosure), acquired the property and franchises of the NJER and its leased lines for $1.5 million. The principal officers were F.W. Egner, President; Edward A. Pruden, Secretary; and J. Bayard Kirkpatrick. White Line Traction was authorized to sell $4 million in stock subscriptions and had $25,000 on hand in cash. The new company appears to have been a stop-gap corporate measure pending consolidation of area lines.

Jersey City, Hoboken and Paterson St. Ry. Co. Agreement and Consolidation

Much has been said in preceding chapters about formation of the Jersey City, Hoboken and Paterson. As was cited,

B.M. Shanley was the commanding figure in street railway development and mergers in northern New Jersey. After forming the North Jersey Street Railway in 1898, Shanley turned to the consolidation of the remaining systems in northern Hudson and Passaic counties. On 23 October 1899, an agreement of consolidation was concluded between the Paterson Central Elec. Ry.; Saddle River Traction; The Palisades Railroad; White Line Traction; The Paterson, Passaic and Rutherford Elec. Ry.; The Jersey City, Hoboken and Rutherford Elec. Ry.; and The Paterson Horse Railroad. The resulting company was named the Jersey City, Hoboken and Paterson Street Railway.

The first officers were David Young, President; John F. Shanley, Vice President; George W. Roe, Treasurer; and William C. Doubleday, Secretary. The principal office was at 21 Hudson Place, Hoboken. The certificate of incorporation was issued on 1 November 1899. The corporate existence was made perpetual on 3 February 1903, but reduced to 975 years on 24 July 1907 dated from 23 October 1899.

The JCH&P converted 35,032 shares of stock with a total par value of $3,278,200 from the seven traction companies into 200,000 shares of JCH&P stock. The JCH&P obtained a 4 percent first mortgage from the New Jersey Title Guarantee and Trust Co., on 1 November 1899. The mortgage amounted to $20 million, equal to the authorized amount of capital stock.

The JCH&P acquired additional lines between 1899 and 1903. The Bergen Turnpike Company was acquired through purchase of its capital stock in May 1900. and a new Board of Directors installed on 11 June.

The JCH&P was initially unable to acquire the North Hudson County Railway and Paterson Railway companies. A sufficient quantity of stock was held by local men not associated with the clique of lawyers, bankers and businessmen who formed the JCH&P. Edward F.C. Young of Jersey City was a large stockholder of the two holdout companies and offered in writing to sell a majority of the stock for $4.5 million. The outstanding shares were purchased on 23 July 1901 and the two companies merged into JCH&P on 2 August. At the time North Hudson County Railway had outstanding mortgages of $5.6 million and Paterson Railway had outstanding mortgages of $1.55 million.

The Hudson and Bergen Traction Co., incorporated on 22 March 1893, was merged into JCH&P on 4 November 1901. This company should not be confused with the Hudson and Bergen Street Railway which consolidated on 23 June 1890 into the Newark Passenger Railway Co.

The Weehawken wagon elevator, Peoples' Elevator Company, incorporated on 31 May 1899, was acquired by JCH&P on 12 March 1903.

The last company merged into JCH&P was the Paterson and State Line Traction Company on 21 April 1903. The Paterson and State Line was incorporated on 15 November 1901. This brought the total number of companies merged to thirteen.

Hackensack and Passaic River Bridges

The Bergen and Hudson County freeholders contracted for a new Paterson Plank road bridge across the Hackensack River in late 1900. On 15 November the JCH&P agreed to pay $20,000 to each county towards construction. The contract was awarded to F.R. Long & Co. and

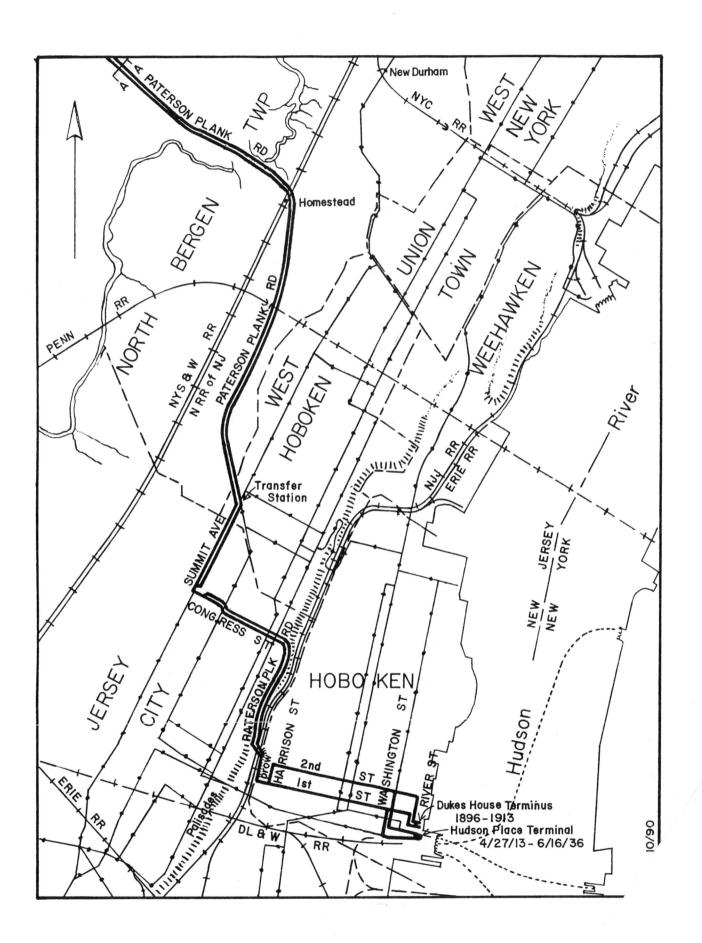

New Durham

WEST NEW YORK

PATERSON PLANK RD

TWP

NYC RR

Homestead

NORTH BERGEN

UNION

TOWN

WEEHAWKEN

PENN RR

NYS & W RR

N RR of NJ

PATERSON PLANK RD

WEST HOBOKEN

River

NJ & RR

ERIE RR

NEW JERSEY NEW YORK

Transfer Station

SUMMIT AVE

CONGRESS ST

PATERSON PLK RD

JERSEY CITY

HOBOKEN

Hudson

HARRISON ST

WASHINGTON ST

RIVER ST

2nd

Dukes House Terminus
1896-1913
Hudson Place Terminal
4/27/13 - 6/16/36

ERIE RR

Palisade

1st

ST

ST

DL & W RR

10/90

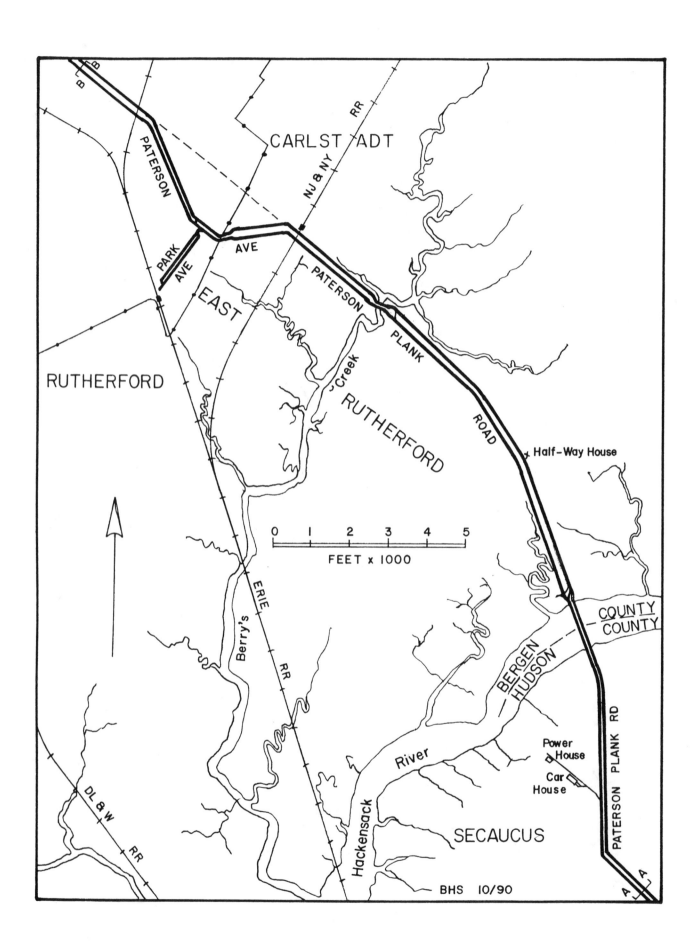

CARLSTADT

RR

NJ & NY

PATERSON

PARK AVE

AVE

PATERSON

PLANK

EAST

Creek

ROAD

× Half-Way House

RUTHERFORD

RUTHERFORD

0   1   2   3   4   5

FEET x 1000

ERIE

Berry's

RR

COUNTY
COUNTY

BERGEN

HUDSON

Power
House

River

Car
House

Hackensack

DL & W

SECAUCUS

PATERSON PLANK RD

RR

BHS 10/90

B
B

A
A

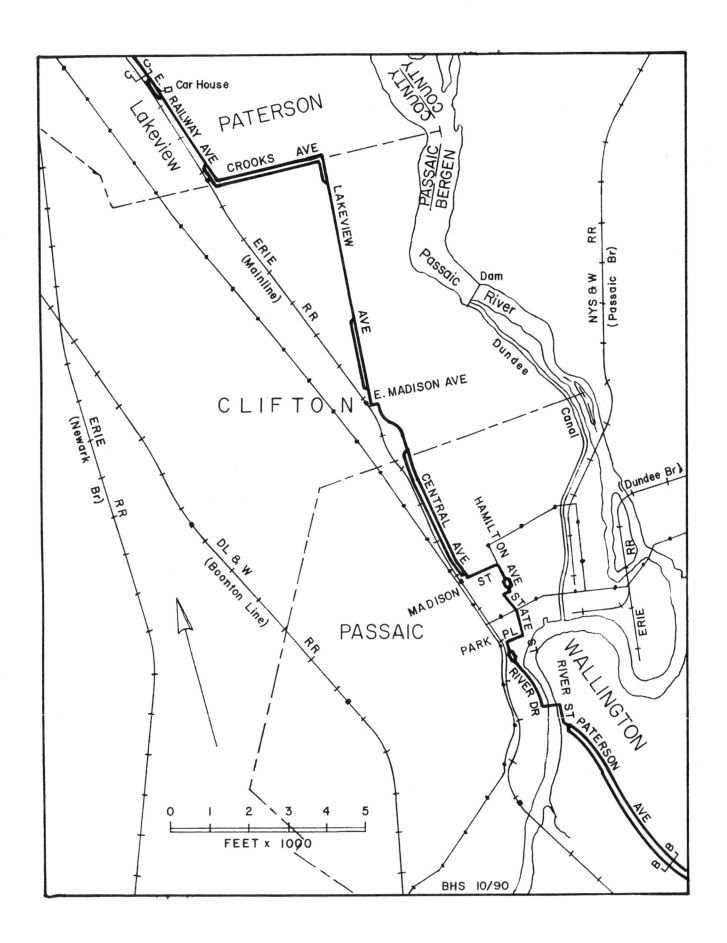

PATERSON

Car House

C. E. & RAILWAY AVE

Lakeview

CROOKS AVE

C.

LAKEVIEW AVE

COUNTY

PASSAIC
BERGEN

COUNTY

Passaic River

Dam

Dundee

NYS & W RR

(Passaic Br)

ERIE
(Mainline)
RR

E. MADISON AVE

C L I F T O N

Canal

Dundee Br

ERIE
(Newark
Br)
RR

CENTRAL AVE

HAMILTON AVE

RR

DL & W
(Boonton Line)
RR

ST

STATE

ERIE

MADISON

PASSAIC

PARK PL

ST

WALLINGTON

RIVER ST

RIVER DR

RIVER ST PATERSON AVE

B.

B.

0   1   2   3   4   5

FEET x 1000

BHS 10/90

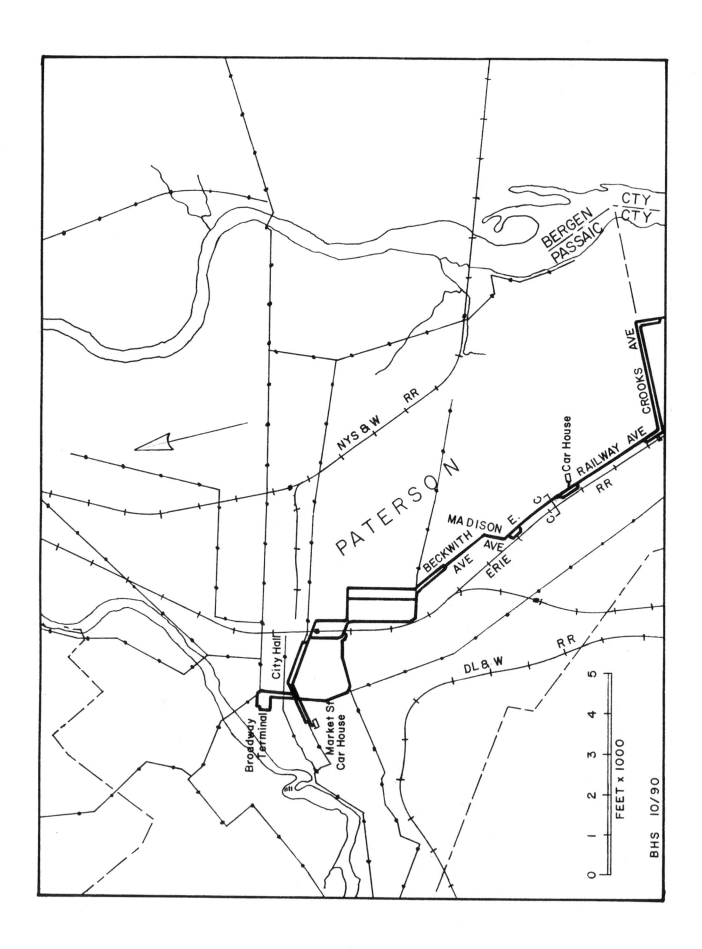

PATERSON

BERGEN
PASSAIC
CTY
CTY

CROOKS AVE

Car House
RAILWAY AVE
RR

MADISON E.
BECKWITH AVE
AVE
ERIE

NYS & W RR

City Hall
Broadway Terminal
Market St
Car House

DL & W RR

0   1   2   3   4   5

FEET x 1000

BHS 10/90

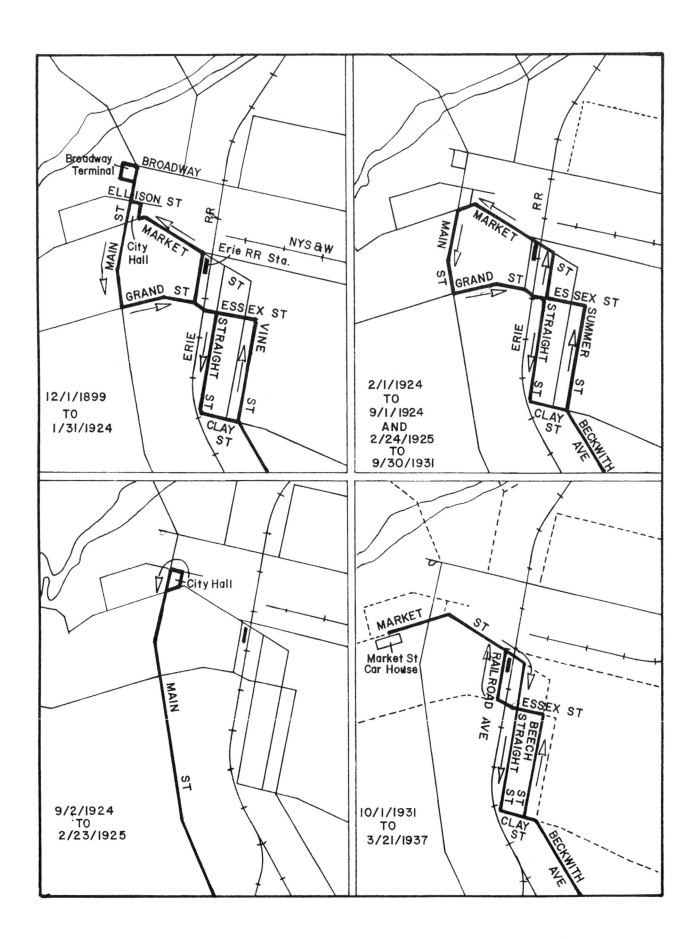

12/1/1899 TO 1/31/1924

Broadway Terminal · BROADWAY · ELLISON ST · MAIN ST · MARKET ST · City Hall · Erie RR Sta. · RR · NYS&W · GRAND ST · ESSEX ST · VINE ST · ERIE · STRAIGHT ST · CLAY ST

2/1/1924 TO 9/1/1924 AND 2/24/1925 TO 9/30/1931

MAIN ST · MARKET ST · RR · GRAND ST · ESSEX ST · ERIE · STRAIGHT ST · SUMMER ST · CLAY ST · BECKWITH AVE

9/2/1924 TO 2/23/1925

City Hall · MAIN ST

10/1/1931 TO 3/21/1937

MARKET ST · Market St Car House · RAILROAD AVE · ESSEX ST · BEECH ST · STRAIGHT ST · CLAY ST · BECKWITH AVE

Passaic Line car 3587 was inbound for the Hoboken Ferry on the trestle used between the Paterson Plank Road and 1st Street, Hoboken. By the time this picture was taken on 28 February 1936, the Passaic Line had been broken at the Hackensack River and was being operated in two divisions.

Berlin Iron Bridge Co. for $234,000, half of which is paid by each county, on 19 November 1900. The Bergen County Freeholders also determined it was necessary to raise the Paterson Plank Road for 2,500 feet north of the bridge so that the road would not be submerged at the average high tide of the river. The JCH&P pledged an additional $15,000 to raise the road and to secure permission to double-track the Berry's Creek Bridge.

After more than a year of discussion, the Bergen and Passaic County freeholders approved measures to strengthen the Passaic River bridge to support the weight of street cars. During the rebuilding, JCH&P provided a steam launch beginning in March, 1902 to ferry White Line passengers across the river. The launch sailed from the dock in front of Mary Maron's Hotel in Wallington to the old Mansion House dock on the Passaic side.

White Line Accidents

On 4 November 1900 Hoboken-bound White Line car 54 was stuck on the Homestead grade crossing after being derailed by some small stones placed on the rails and lost its rear platform to a speeding NYS&W RR train.

At the NJ&NY grade crossing in Carlstadt, a White Line car was demolished by a steam train late in the evening of 7 April 1902. The train departed Jersey City at 10:15 p.m. and was due at Carlstadt station at 10:35 p.m. When White Line car 502, heading westbound for Paterson, crossed the railroad, the

trolley pole slipped from the overhead wire causing the car to stall on the tracks. Before the pole could be replaced, the locomotive struck the car in the middle tearing the body from its trucks and knocking it 25 feet north into the Carlstadt depot. Seven passengers were injured but none seriously. It was reported that JCH&P suspended its trolley wire 18 feet above the street, but at the grade crossing the wire was raised to 21 feet. This may have contributed to the trolley pole leaving the wire. The car was not rebuilt.

White Line car 608, carrying 100 passengers, derailed in Jersey City on 19 January 1903. It was descending the Paterson Plank Road hill to Hoboken when it hit a closed switch about 200 feet north of Bowers Street. The car crashed into the retaining wall which prevented it from falling over the palisade cliff. Twenty passengers were injured seriously.

The rural character of Bergen County has long since disappeared, but in 1903 Wallington, with a population of 2400 persons, had sufficient open space to provide pasture for cattle. On the night of 17 January 1903 White Line car 70 collided with a herd in Wallington, killing one of the animals. A second car crashed into the rear of 70, smashing the windows in both cars. Some JCH&P cars had city-type headlamps, others required mounting a headlamp for night time travel. To improve nighttime visibility on the rural routes, JCH&P equipped the White Line cars with new incandescent head lamps on 23 January.

Public Service Corporation of New Jersey

As noted in chapter 6, Public Service Corporation of New Jersey was incorporated on 6 May 1903 to acquire and lease gas, electric and street railway properties in New Jersey. Public Service certificates at $35 par value were offered for each share of JCH&P stock redeemed by 27 April 1903, but not later than 1 July.

JCH&P President David Young sold his controlling interest in the railway and its subsidiaries on 16 May 1903. The financial condition of JCH&P was tenuous as reported in the annual report for the year ending December, 1902:

Gross earnings	$1,975,525.03
Operating expenses	1,120,631.67
Net earnings	854,893.36
Interest and Taxes	849,297.42
Net profit	5,595.94

Such small profits had left little capital for improving the railway. Borrowing funds increased the company's funded debt. Public Service Corporation determined that $615,921.30 was needed to meet the JCH&P's immediate requirements. The total debt of the JCH&P and its subsidiaries assumed by the Corporation amounted to $21.175 million of which $1.498 million was held by the Corporation and $19.677 million was in the hands of banks and trust companies.

The Passaic car line was plagued by competition from independent bus operators. Here Passaic Line car 1623 poses at the Broadway Terminal while a competitive bus waits on the street.

Passaic River Drawbridge Problems

On 10 October 1903 a devastating flood washed out the Passaic River drawbridge. Public Service reinstituted the steam launch to ferry White Line passengers across the river. A new temporary bridge was constructed in 40 days in early 1904 and White Line cars were permitted to cross on a single-track. The new bridge consisted of a 350-foot long trestle and a unique powered jack-knife span that could be opened for the passage of boats. When the draw was opened on 6 September 1905, the bridge sank one foot and prevented the closing of the draw. White Line trolley service was once more interrupted and passengers were required to walk across the bridge to the connecting car on the other side. Jacking, shimming and shoring of the bridge enabled restoration of through trolley service.

Through cars were suspended once again on 23 March 1906. The Bergen and Passaic County freeholders had let a contract to replace the bridge in 1906. The jack-knife draw had opened towards the Bergen County end which brought the draw almost to the center of the river. It was reversed so that it met the bank on the Bergen County end and opened towards the Passaic County end. This allowed construction of a new larger draw without interference with navigation. While bridge alterations were underway, White Line passengers were transferred across the Passaic River in a steam motor boat.

Public Service Corporation and the two county freeholder boards renegotiated the White Line's franchise during 1906 and 1907 to use the new drawbridge. The bridge opened on 29 March 1907. Public Service Corporation and the freeholder boards came to an agreement on 2 April 1907 that required the Corporation to pay an annual fee of $750 to each county. In return the Corporation was permitted to construct a single-track railway on the new drawbridge.

Public Service Railway Co.

Public Service Corporation, taking advantage of a newly enacted public utilities law, reorganized its Railway Department into a new corporation in 1907. This effectively removed the books of the Corporation, as a holding company, from public audit.

By a consolidation agreement of North Jersey Street Railway Company, Jersey City, Hoboken and Paterson Street Railway Company and United Street Railway Company of Central Jersey, the Public Service Railway Co. was created on 30 July 1907 . The corporate existence was limited to 970 years from 20 August, the date on which the certificate of incorporation was issued. Public Service Corporation owned 98.64 per cent of the $38 million outstanding stock of Public Service Railway. The $20 million in outstanding shares of JCH&P stock were converted to 200,000 shares of Public Service Ry. stock. The NJ Public Utilities Commission issued a Certificate of

Entry upon the railway and appurtenances of Jersey City, Hoboken and Paterson Street Railway on 18 October 1907.

A new $250,000 two-level trolley terminal opened on 22 May 1910 at Hudson Place, Hoboken, adjacent to the DL&W Railroad ferry and railroad terminal. The Hoboken Terminal was considered to be the best-equipped street railway terminal in the country in 1910. Both levels were used for the arrival and departure of cars. The White Line's original 1897 terminal one block north of Hudson Place was abandoned after the White Line was rerouted to the street level of the Hudson Place terminal on 27 April 1913. White Line cars used Washington Street between the new terminal and its tracks on First and Second streets.

On 14 January 1914 the White Line was renamed as the Passaic line. No white cars had run on the White Line since 1899 when JCH&P repainted the cars carmine red. All Passaic line operations were consolidated at the Secaucus car house on 2 April 1917. Cars operating from the West Hoboken and Paterson car houses were transferred to Secaucus.

Rutherford "Y" Line

The Rutherford "Y" line ran on Park Ave., East Rutherford, and was 1895 feet long. It was built by the JCH&R in 1893 and opened in 1895. In 1897, when through cars were instituted between Hoboken and Paterson, it became a shuttle between the Erie Railroad's Rutherford depot and the White Line at Paterson

Passaic Line car 3589 bound for East Rutherford crosses the Passaic River Bridge into Bergen County on 17 May 1936. By then the cars ran only during rush hours.

Ave. The line was discontinued on 10 July 1920 according to Public Service although newspapers reported that the event occurred on 17 June 1920.

Perhaps the most exciting event in the line's history took place on 23 December 1903. The shuttle car overshot its stopping place near the Erie Railroad, ran off the end of the track and bumped along the pavement to the Erie rails where the car halted with a sudden jolt!

Jitneys and Independent Buses

"Jitney" vehicles appeared in Jersey City, Hoboken and Newark in 1915, and in Paterson and Passaic during 1916. The jitneys competed with the street cars on the more profitable routes and cut deeply into railway company revenues. Jitneys were unregulated and were not required to provide the service on unprofitable lines required of the railway company.

By 1920 jitneys posed a serious threat to the survival of Public Service Railway. The Passaic car line started "short line" service on 8 October 1920 between Paterson and Passaic to cope with the competition. Public Service Railway placed 200 Birney single-truck one-man closed cars into service during 1920 on car lines in the Passaic, Central and Hudson divisions. These cars allowed light-traffic inner-city lines to provide short headways at lower cost. Paterson's local car lines were equipped with Birneys beginning 5 September 1920. The Paterson-Passaic "short line" was discontinued on 20 January 1921.

In April, 1921 the State Legislature enacted a law declaring jitney buses whose routes were located in whole or in part on streets through which street cars operated, to be public utilities, requiring approval of the Board of Public Utility Commissioners to operate. Buses in operation before 15 March 1921 were exempted from the requirement. The exemption permitted transfer of licenses. Many were transferred from small to large buses, further increasing competition with the railway.

In 1923 Public Service Railway, because of jitney competition, was unable to meet employee demands for wage increases and the employees struck. The court-approved settlement provided for both trolley and bus operation under Public Service management. The railway was permitted to purchase competing buses, employ competent bus operators, grant a twenty percent wage increase, establish a seven-cent universal fare with transfers between trolleys and buses, and permit expanded one-man operation of cars. With the strike settled, Public Service Railway resumed operations on 21 September 1923.

Public Service Transportation Company

On 15 May 1923, Public Service renamed its moribund bus subsidiary, New Jersey Transportation Co., as Public Service Transportation Co.

Virtually every street car line in Paterson and Passaic was duplicated by an independent bus operator in 1922. All local car lines in Passaic were abandoned as soon as Public Service purchased the competing bus permits. The Main-Lodi car line to Lodi and Hackensack quit on 31 August 1924. The local Monroe car line was converted to buses on 26 July 1924, which were discontinued in 1925.

The Passaic line's Paterson terminal was changed from Broadway Terminal to Main and Market streets on 1 February 1924. After Public Service discontinued the Main-Lodi line, it changed the route of the Passaic line from its original line through Passaic, Clifton and Paterson to run over the discontinued Main-Lodi line's route from Passaic Street in Passaic to Paterson via Main Avenue. The former Passaic line route via Lakeview was covered by the Lakeview line. Service was initiated on Sundays only on 31 August 1924 and daily on 2 September 1924. The Passaic line was restored to its original route on 24 February 1925.

One-man operation of Passaic line cars commenced on 13 January 1925. The Passaic line operations from the Secaucus car house were relocated to the West Hoboken (Union City) car house on 4 February 1927 except for sixteen runs assigned to the Market Street car house in Paterson. Secaucus car house became a storage facility for cars that were out of service more or less permanently.

Passaic Line car 2310 at the Lakeview car house in Paterson on 19 March 1937. Service on the Passaic Division was replaced by all-service vehicles three days later.

Public Service Coordinated Transport Company

Public Service Railway and Public Service Transportation were merged on 10 January 1928 to form Public Service Coordinated Transport Co. This consolidated the operation of both trolley cars and buses, with the exception of Public Service Interstate Transportation Co. The Passaic Division of Public Service became the first division in the system to convert all local car lines to buses which was accomplished on 1 October 1928.

The Hudson Division operations of the Passaic car line were transferred on 16 May 1930 from the Union City car house to the Hoboken car house and most Passaic line cars laid over at Hudson Place terminal all night.

Bus Expansion

As the Great Depression continued through the 1930s, PSCT and its Interstate Transportation affiliate introduced new bus lines. On 12 May 1929 Public Service started bus line 164—Paterson-New York which had been purchased from Arrow Bus Lines. The 164 line was sold to Inter-City Transportation Company, an affiliate of New Jersey-New York Transit Company, on 6 October 1935. The new line deprived the Passaic car line of through passengers.

An independent carrier, DeLuxe Coach Lines, opened in 1926 between Rochelle Park and Journal Square in Jersey City. It paralleled the Passaic trolley between East Rutherford and Hudson County Boulevard and diverted passengers to Journal Square for access to the Hudson and Manhattan tube trains.

Another independent carrier, Comfort Bus Lines of Wallington, N. J., operated a circuitous route through Passaic, Wallington and East Rutherford that avoided running on the same streets as the Passaic trolleys. Comfort operated a fleet of maroon White Model 50-A buses.

Public Service purchased independent buses in 1925 named "Passaic-East Rutherford" and "Paterson-Clifton-Passaic." The two franchises were put together end-to-end to form Public Service bus line 16 Paterson-Passaic-East Rutherford. This bus route paralleled the Passaic car line, but in some areas travelled a more direct route. This bus line rendered the "western division" redundant by 1932.

Demise of the Passaic Car Line

Because parallel bus lines diverted passengers from the Passaic trolleys, service was reduced. Beginning 7 August 1933, cars operated only six through trips between Hoboken and Paterson. The other Hudson Division cars terminated at the Hackensack River bridge in Secaucus. On 14 November 1933 through trips were reduced to four and on 8 March 1934 were discontinued. The Passaic Division was reduced to rush hours only on a 30-minute headway on 8 March 1934 between Paterson and the Hamilton Avenue turnout at Passaic. On 19 March, service was resumed to the Hackensack River bridge in East Rutherford.

A new NJ State Highway No. 3 bridge across the Hackensack River between East Rutherford and Secaucus was opened in 1935. The Paterson Plank Road drawbridge was closed and dismantled, permanently severing the Passaic line at the Hackensack River. The bascule span of the new bridge had double-track trolley tracks laid in the deck, but no one believed there was ever any intention to operate trolleys over the new bridge.

The Passaic Division of the Passaic line was revised several times during 1936 thusly:

5 May 1936 - Paterson to Park Avenue, East Rutherford in a.m. and p.m. rush hours only.

21 May 1936 - A.M. rush hour trips were cut back at the Erie Railroad's Bergen County line in East Rutherford.

25 May 1936 - The a.m. and p.m. rush hour trips were cut back to Carlton Avenue, East Rutherford.

27 May 1936 - A.m. and p.m. rush hour trips were cut back to Spears Switch, Passaic.

11 June 1936 - Rush hour headway was reduced from 30 minutes to 20 minutes between cars.

PSCT replaced Passaic line trolleys with all service vehicles between the Hackensack River bridge at Secaucus and Hudson Place Terminal, on 16 June 1936. On the Passaic Division portion of the line, Public Service replaced the cars with all service vehicles (trolley buses) on 22 March 1937. Wires for the trolley buses had been strung from Paterson over

P P & R ROLLING STOCK

Numbers	Builder	Year	Type
44-58 even	J. G. Brill	1896	20-foot closed
60-66 even	J. G. Brill	1894	20-foot closed
68, 70	Laconia	1894	20-foot closed
72	St. Louis	1894	20-foot closed
74-78 even *	J. G. Brill	1893	18-foot closed
80-84 even @	J. G. Brill	1893	18-foot closed
86-88 even @	J. G. Brill	1893	23-foot closed
90*	J. G. Brill	1893	18-foot combine
57-79 odd	St. Louis	1894	10-bench open
81-85 odd *	J. G. Brill	1893	9-bench open
82-88 even *	J. G. Brill	1893	7-bench open trail

* From Paterson & Little Falls, 82-88 renumbered
@ From Passaic, Rutherford & Carlstadt

the Passaic line route to the intersection of Paterson Plank Road and State Highway 3. It was not confirmed, but the all service vehicles may have operated over the Passaic line route between Paterson and Park Place and McLean Street at Passaic. As late as 1947 a No. 15 Passaic bus line gas-electric bus from the low 2900-series (Yellow Coach Model Z-BP-620) could be seen on the line in rush hours.

During 1927 Public Service assigned route numbers to its trolley lines and the Passaic line became route 15—Passaic. Bus substitutions retained the same route numbers. The Passaic Division No. 15 Passaic bus gradually faded away without record, having been largely replaced by the No. 16 Paterson-Passaic-East Rutherford bus line.

From 23 October 1940 until sometime during 1942, Public Service operated one all service vehicle through from Hoboken to Paterson via the new NJ Highway 3 bridge once a day.

Equipment Notes

The Paterson, Passaic and Rutherford Electric Railway Company

The PP&R inherited 12 passenger cars from the Paterson & Little Falls and five from the Passaic, Rutherford & Carlstadt. It purchased an additional 27 cars as shown in the table. All are believed to have had closed vestibules. PP&R passenger cars were painted white with carmine red dashes. Letters and numbers were gold and striping was maroon. "Paterson, Passaic & Rutherford" was lettered on the lower side panels. Along the top of the roof eaves Signs lettered "Barclay & Christopher Street, Hoboken Ferries" were located along the side letterboards and on the dash around the headlight.

The Jersey City, Hoboken and Rutherford Electric Railway Company

The JCH&R acquired fifteen double-truck closed cars, numbered 102 to 130 even, were built by St. Louis Car Co. in 1894 and delivered in 1895. They had 28-foot bodies, steam-coach roofs and enclosed vestibules. They were 40-feet long overall and had ten windows on each side. The cars were painted white with carmine red dash boards. Letters and numbers were gold and striping was maroon. "Jersey City, Hoboken & Rutherford" was lettered on the lower side panels. On the dashes "Jersey City, Hoboken & Rutherford" was lettered in an arch above the headlight and "Electric Railway" was lettered horizontally beneath the headlight. The car's number was placed in the center of the dashboard where the headlight is mounted during night travel.

New Jersey Electric Railway

All of the PP&R and JCH&R cars were acquired by the NJE and retained their white color scheme and original numbers. NJE purchased twelve ten-bench open cars (#33 to 55 odd) from American Car Co. of St. Louis and 25 from St. Louis Car Co. (#101-149 odd) in 1895. Cars 107 and 117 were wrecked during shipment and not replaced. Another fifteen were built by Brill in 1897

(#3 to 31 odd). It purchased no new closed cars but acquired fourteen sets of Brill trucks to replace St. Louis trucks used by the 28-foot closed cars.

White Line Traction Company

The White Line acquired the cars of NJE in a foreclosure sale on 10 June 1899. White Line Traction was a caretaker owner until the formation of JCH&P in October 1899 and purchased no new cars.

Jersey City, Hoboken and Paterson Street Railway Company

The JCH&P acquired all of the cars of the traction companies over which it gained control. White Line single-truck closed cars were renumbered from 170 up in no particular order, the surviving open cars from 1521 to 1580 and 1741 to 1761, and the surviving 28-foot cars (102 had been wrecked) from 501 to 514. They were repainted carmine red with gold letters and numbers. Most of the former North Hudson County and Paterson Railway cars were also renumbered.

JCH&P purchased new passenger cars that were larger, more modern and more powerful than the decrepit cars it inherited. During 1899 it took delivery of twelve double-truck closed cars from Laclede Car Company numbered 160-171. The cars were 46 feet 1 inch long overall and had 32-foot bodies. An additional four cars, purchased in 1900 by the North Jersey Street Railway (746-749) were transferred to the JCH&P in 1902 and renumbered 800-803.

During 1901 JCH&P purchased 25 Laclede double-truck closed cars numbered 101-125. Fifteen of the latter, Nos. 111-125, were owned by the Bergen Turnpike and were used on the turnpike's railway route to Hackensack. Two identical cars, 126 and 127, were added in 1902. The 101-127 series of cars were 38 feet 4 inches long overall and had 25-foot bodies. All JCH&P and BTCo cars were painted carmine red with gold numbers and lettering. The new cars were deemed by the freeholders of Bergen and Passaic counties to be too heavy to travel over the Passaic River drawbridge, and were banned until 1904.

When the New Jersey and Hudson River Railway and Ferry Company (Hudson River Line) built westward into

Car 913 was originally car 120 of the Bergen Pike line. It was built by Laclede in 1901. Photographed at the Market St. terminus in Paterson in 1913.

Paterson from Maywood, it used the JCH&P's tracks on Broadway to reach downtown Paterson. In conjunction with the new through service to Edgewater, JCH&P purchased four cars for Hudson River Line service. Two double-truck closed cars numbered in Hudson River Line series, Nos. 32 and 33, had 32-foot bodies, were 43 feet 6 inches long overall and were built by J. Stephenson in 1903. Two double-truck 14-bench open cars numbered in Hudson River Line series, Nos. 55 and 56, were built by J. G. Brill in 1904. These four cars were painted in Hudson River Line carmine red with "Hudson River" lettered on their sides. Lettered in small size letters at each end and side beneath the platforms was "JCH&P Str Ry Co."

Public Service Corporation of New Jersey

Public Service Corporation acquired the JCH&P in 1903, and operated it as a division of the Corporation's Railway Department until 1907. Therefore, new equipment for the old JCH&P system were charged to the JCH&P e.g. when PS Corporation purchased material car No. 0108 in 1903 it was charged to JCH&P accounts. This car resembled a box car with passenger car platforms. The plat-

form vestibules strongly resembled those used on the 1900-series semi-convertible cars purchased from J. G. Brill in 1903.

One of the first rolling stock purchases made by the Corporation was an order for fifty new semi-convertible double-truck cars from J.G. Brill in 1903. The new cars were numbered 1900-1949 and delivery took place in late 1903. The White Line was equipped with 25 of these cars and was so noted by newspapers on 1 October 1903.

Public Service repainted all of the JCH&P passenger cars from carmine red into chrome yellow with light cream trim, black numbers and maroon striping. Public Service renumbered JCH&P cars thusly:

JCH&P #	PSC #	Type Car
755	42	18-foot closed
Various	163-199	22-foot closed
1061-1064	223-226	8-bench open
Various	310-328	18-foot closed
Various	329-347	20-foot closed
172-186	510-524	25-foot closed
200	525	25-foot closed
188-199	526-537	25-foot closed
187	538	25-foot closed
725-736@	539-546	23-foot closed
1051-1060	681-690	9-bench open
101-108	792-799	25-foot closed
1521-1580	800-859	10-bench open

JCH&P #	PSC #	Type Car
1741-1761	860-880	10-bench open
109-110	900-901	25-foot closed
126-127	902-903	25-foot closed
111-125	904-918	25-foot closed
701-720 *	919-938	25-foot closed
153-159	954-960	27-foot closed
501-514	961-973 #	28-foot closed
1001-1012	1000-1011	12-bench open
1731-1740	1012-1021	12-bench open
1721-1730	1022-1031	12-bench open
55-56	1058-1059	14-bench open
160-171	1506-1517	32-foot closed
800-803	1518-1521	32-foot closed
32-33	1857-1858	32-foot closed

@   4 cars burned in 1902.
*   700s not renumbered in sequence
#   JCH&P car No. 502 was destroyed on 4-7-02.

The complete history of JCH&P rolling stock will be found in a volume on the car fleet of Public Service to be published in 1993.

Railway Generating Stations

Secaucus Generating Station

The Secaucus generating station was built in 1895 near the Hackensack River and set back about 1770 feet to the west from the Paterson Plank Road curb line. At its peak operating period in 1906 the station contained three 375 kw and two-

675 kw direct connected engine-driven generators for railway power at 500 volts d.c. One 1800-kw 25 Hertz engine-driven alternator was installed in 1904. It supplied power to substations at Passaic, New Durham, Palisade Avenue and Hackensack. Secaucus station became part of the railway power system of Public Service Corporation, which also included Coal Street station at Newark, and Marion station at Jersey City. Transmission was over open wire lines at 13,200 volts.

Secaucus station was shut down in March 1912 and held in reserve until October 1917. The station was operated from December to February during the winters of 1917-18, 1918-19, and 1919-20. The station was shut down in November 1920, and officially discontinued on 1 May 1925. The 180-foot chimney was torn down on 18 August 1938 and the

entire power house building was razed during 1938.

Motor coal car No. 0-100 was assigned to the station to move coal from a coal yard on the Erie R.R. The car was assigned Public Service No. 5659 but was never renumbered. When scrapped in 1924 it was Public Service Electric Company property.

Passaic Generating Station

The Passaic generating station, located at Harrison St. and the Erie R.R., was built by the Passaic Electric Light Company organized in 1885. The station generated power for street railways and commercial customers. The railway generators were belt driven and consisted of two-100 kw, one-200 kw, and one-300 kw generators producing 700 kw at 500 volts D.C. The station operated until July 1910, and then shut down with boilers

This photograph of the Secaucus power house was taken on 10 February 1916 as part of an appraisal to determine the value of Public Service Railway property.

cold. It was discontinued on 9 March 1915. Railway power had been supplied since 1910 by the Passaic substation.

Paterson Generating Station

The Paterson Generating Station was the second station built by Edison Electric Illuminating Company of Paterson. It was built in 1895-96 and when completed was one of the largest power stations in the country. The railway generators first supplied power on 1 February 1896. The Edison Company was merged into the Paterson and Passaic Gas and Electric Company on 28 February 1899, This company was leased to Public Service Corporation on 1 June 1903.

During 1905 and 1906 additional railway generators were installed. On 21 January 1910 an explosion of a boiler economizer wrecked about 50 per cent of the boiler room. The station operated at reduced capacity for two weeks until repairs were completed. In 1910 the early rope-driven generators on lighting circuits were removed and the building space used for two modern turbine-generators for lighting and commercial power. The railway generators included two-100 kw, 8-225 kw, and 4-500 kw, 500 volt d.c. generators totalling 3000 kw. and were direct-connected to steam engines. Some engines were a vertical marine type with a generator at each end of a crank shaft.

The Paterson station operated continuously from 1896 until 1 November 1927, when it was shut down. The station was discontinued on 1 September 1928. Later the station was converted into the headquarters of the Passaic Distribution Division of Public Service Electric and Gas Co.

Rotary Converters

A rotary converter is a synchronous motor and d.c. generator contained in a single machine designed to take a.c. power from transmission lines and produce 600 volt d.c. power for the railways. In 1903-04 Public Service Corporation installed engine driven 25-Hertz alternators in Coal Street and Secaucus generating stations. Marion generating station at Jersey City was built in 1904-05 as the first station in the system designed for steam turbines. The first units were two-5000 kw General Electric vertical turbine-generator units at 25-Hertz which went into service during the winter of 1905-06. Transmission lines at 13,200 volts extended from Newark via Jersey City and Secaucus, to Passaic and Hackensack where substations were built to supply railway power.

Public Service Electric Co.

From 1903 until 1910 the electric business of Public Service Corporation was carried on by its electric department. On 13 June 1910, Public Service Electric Company was formed and all leases of the electric properties held by the Corporation were assigned to the new company. The electric stations and substations of Public Service Railway were also leased to it so that the entire electric

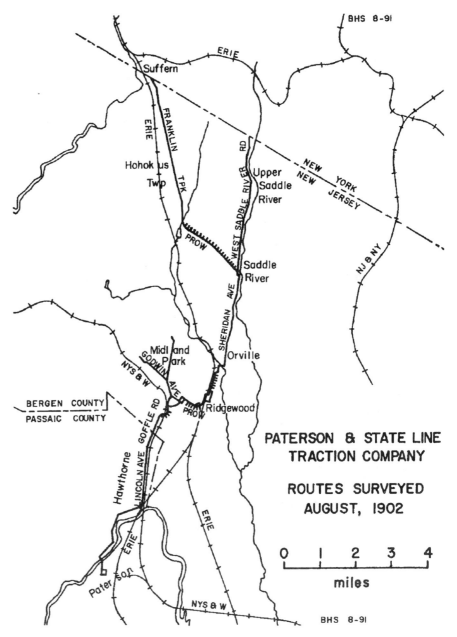

PATERSON & STATE LINE
TRACTION COMPANY

ROUTES SURVEYED
AUGUST, 1902

business including generation, distribution, and sale of power was carried on by Public Service Electric. Secaucus generating station, solely generating railway power, was leased to Public Service Electric Co. on 1 July 1910. In 1924 the gas and electric companies were merged to form Public Service Electric and Gas Company.

Paterson & State Line Traction Company — The Hawthorne Line

A company originally proposed to connect Paterson with sections of Bergen County near the Franklin Turnpike, the Paterson & State Line Traction Co., was

incorporated on 15 November 1901 for a term of 100 years. Its principal office was at 152 Market St., Paterson. The original stockholders were Thomas A. McIntyre of Manhattan (500 shares), Preston Stevenson of Franklin Township, Bergen County (50 shares), and Frank Frost of Paterson (10 shares).

The proposed route was shown on maps filed with the state in 1902 running from Paterson through Prospect Park, Hawthorne, Ridgewood and north through Hohokus and Saddle River boroughs via Sheridan Ave. and West Saddle River Road. Beginning in Saddle River, the maps showed two routes to the New York state line. One continued north along West Saddle River Road to the state line at Upper Saddle River Borough. The second diverged near Allendale Ave. and crossed private lands northwest to Franklin Turnpike in Ramsey Borough, then followed the turnpike to the state line at Mahwah Borough.

The P&SL made arrangements with the JCH&P to connect with the North Main St. track of the Lakeview line. However, it had difficulties in securing franchises, consents from abutting property owners, and rights-of-way across private lands during 1902 and 1903.

The Hawthorne Borough Council granted a franchise on 6 February 1903 to lay tracks the entire length of the borough. Borough citizens strongly supported the line and asked no special privileges other than a 5-cent fare to any point in Passaic County. Plans called for a connection with the North Main St. line and use of the Arch St. bridge to enter central Paterson. At the time no JCH&P cars were running on the line as the Arch St. bridge spanning the Passaic River required reinforcement to support their weight.

The Jersey City, Hoboken & Paterson purchased all outstanding P&SL stock on 21 April 1903 as part of the consolidation of the area lines into one company under the control of the new Public Service Corporation. The new management was no more successful than the old in getting the necessary rights of way, nor did the transfer of the rights of the P&SL to the Public Service Railway in 1907 expedite the process. The official position of the company was that construction would not start until all obstacles had been cleared and that prospect seemed increasingly remote.

By 1910, there had still been no progress, although Public Service said that it still planned to extend the Lakeview line from North Main St. to the center of Ridgewood. The North Jersey Rapid Transit opened its line from East Paterson to Hohokus Borough, several miles east of Hawthorne, on 22 June 1910. The Hawthorne Borough Council was stirred into action and passed a resolution on 6 October 1910, directing Public Service to begin construction within sixty days and to complete the line as nearly as possible within sixty days. Failure to do so would result in revocation of the 1903 franchise.

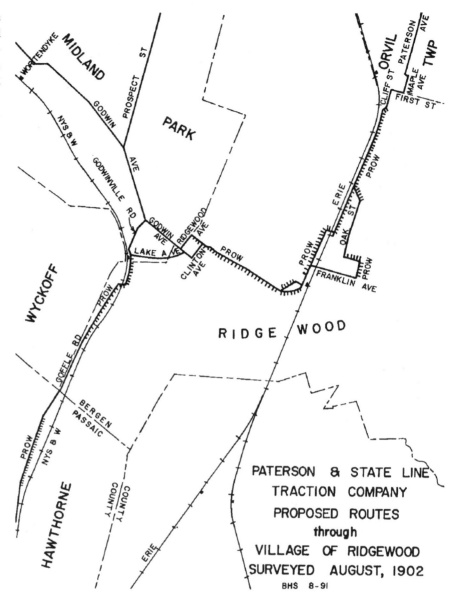

PATERSON & STATE LINE
TRACTION COMPANY
PROPOSED ROUTES
through
VILLAGE OF RIDGEWOOD
SURVEYED AUGUST, 1902
BHS 8-91

Public Service Railway finally began construction on 1 November 1910 at the Paterson City Line on East Main St. where it enters Prospect Park, then proceeded north on Goffle Road, Wagaraw Road and private right of way into Hawthorne. On 10 June 1911 the P&SL opened as an extension of the Lakeview car line, operating from the NYS&W's Hawthorne depot to a crossover on Main St. near Crooks Ave., near the boundary between Paterson and Acquackanonk (now Clifton) Township.

The P&SL was extended north through Hawthorne and by 21 August 1911 was opened over 4th St. to the NYS&W's North Hawthorne depot where the steam railroad had built repair shop

facilities. Lakeview cars began running to the Passaic-Bergen county line on 29 March 1912.

Public Service renamed the line as the Hawthorne line on 1 March 1913 and rerouted cars from Crooks Ave. to the City Hall loop in Paterson.

At long last, on 1 March 1913, construction began on the extension of the P&SL into Bergen County. on a private right-of-way between the NYS&W RR and Goffle Road in Ridgewood. The railroad refused a grade crossing and a double-track underpass was built.

The proposed route through Ridgewood was mostly private right-of-way except for short stretches on Clinton Ave. and Washington Place. The Ridgewood

Car 7034 was one of 200 Birney one-man safety cars acquired by Public Service in 1920 for use on light traffic lines. Cars of this type provided the last service on the Hawthorne line.

Commission granted a franchise on 27 January 1914 giving the right to cross Monroe St. and Godwin Ave. Fare between Ridgewood and Paterson was set at ten cents.

The line was extended to Ridgewood on 1 July 1914 with a half-hour headway. There were two fare zones, the county line being the boundary. Running time from City Hall to Ridgewood was 36 minutes.

The Bergen County portion of the Hawthorne line was never prosperous and matters were not improved by the appearance of independent bus operators in 1923. Two bus routes were permitted to operate from Paterson into Hawthorne: one via North Main, East Main St., and Goffle Road, the other via Madison Ave. through Paterson thence into Hawthorne.

In keeping with its policy of buying up independent bus operator permits and abandoning unprofitable trolley lines, Public Service Ry. announced on 7 July 1925 that it wished to terminate cars at the county line. It claimed that its revenue

during the previous year had been $7,437.50 while maintenance and operating expenses were $26,092.74. The Ridgewood Commission adopted a resolution on 6 October supporting abandonment. At the municipal meeting few persons supported the trolley and their support was unenthusiastic. Most speakers described the trolley as a noisy nuisance at night, and spoke of the danger of derailments and poor road conditions because of ill-kept track. The PUC approved abandonment on 5 November 1925 and the cars began turning back at the county line on 16 November.

No direct replacement service was provided by Public Service. Faster, more comfortable service was provided by Arrow Bus Lines between Ridgewood and Paterson. This was acquired by Public Service Transportation in 1926 and designated as Route 70 — Paterson-Suffern.

Public Service purchased nine Madison Ave. route permits from independent operators in 1925, using them to establish the 8–Hawthorne via Madison Ave. bus.

The remnants of the trolley service were gradually cut back. On 31 January 1926, Sunday service was reduced to operate only between 1 pm and 1:30 am. By 23 April, weekday service was operated only during rush hours. Public Service purchased seven independent bus operator permits for the North Main and Goffle Road route and on 11 August established the 22–Hawthorne bus route,

ending trolley service. White Model 50-A and Mack AB gas-electric buses were assigned to the new line.

The Paterson & State Line Traction Co. outlasted its purpose. The company's entire stock was owned by the Jersey City Hoboken & Paterson which, in turn, was owned by Public Service Corporation. The P&SL remained as a paper company until 6 July 1937 when it was merged into Public Service Coordinated Transport as part of a program to simplify the corporate structure of the Public Service utilities system.

On 17 April 1930, Public Service President Thomas N. McCarter gave testimony to the NJPUC explaining why lines such as the Hawthorne line were discontinued. "There is another economic factor in connection with the operating of this property [Public Service Railway] which have made it essential, or will make it essential, to write off a large amount of abandoned property. This has been done because of changed conditions, where manifestly on certain lines it has been wise to withdraw car operation and substitute therefor bus operation. I refer particularly to a place like Paterson, where the streets are narrow and where the old transportation was single-tracked with turnouts. It didn't meet the needs of today, as compared with a bus that didn't have to wait on any turnout to go up and down the street and local lines in a city the size of Paterson can be well handled by the bus traffic."

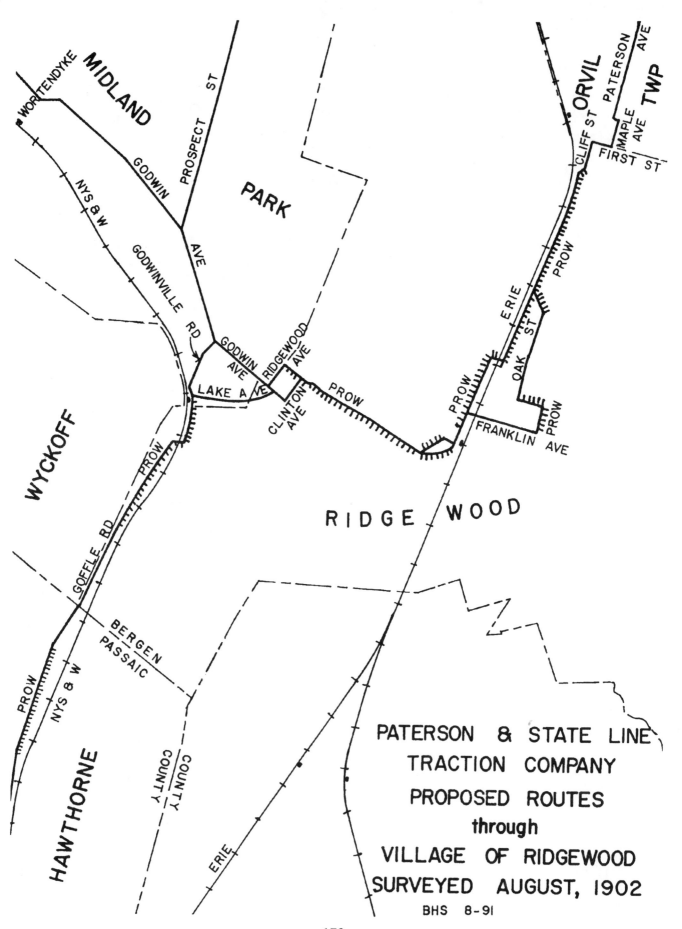

MIDLAND

WORTENDYKE

PROSPECT ST

GODWIN AVE

NYS & W

GODWINVILLE RD

PARK

ORVIL

PATERSON AVE

CLIFF ST

MAPLE AVE

FIRST ST

TWP

ERIE PROW

OAK ST

PROW

GODWIN AVE

RIDGEWOOD AVE

LAKE A VE

CLINTON AVE

PROW

PROW

PROW

FRANKLIN AVE

WYCKOFF

GOFFLE RD

PROW

RIDGEWOOD

BERGEN

PASSAIC

COUNTY

COUNTY

NYS & W

PROW

HAWTHORNE

ERIE

PATERSON & STATE LINE
TRACTION COMPANY
PROPOSED ROUTES
through
VILLAGE OF RIDGEWOOD
SURVEYED AUGUST, 1902
BHS 8-91

Hawthorne Car Line Rolling Stock							
Numbers	Body	Overall	Trucks	Motors	Controls	Windows	Builder, Date
1848, 1851	29' 5"	40' 9"	2–Standard C50P	4–GE 67	2–K35	10	American, 1900
1863	28'	37' 5"	2–FBD MCB	4–GE 57	2–K35	10	J. G. Brill, 1904
1878	34' 10"	29' 5"	2–Standard C50P	4–Wh 307C	2–K35	10	Niles, 1902
1879-1882	34' 10"	29' 5"	2–Standard C50P	4–Wh 307C	2–K35	12	Niles, 1902
7000-7199		27' 9 1/2"	1–O-B 25-96	2–Wh 508 or 2–GE 264	2–K63B	8	Osgood Bradley, 1920

Equipment Notes

From 1911 to 1916, Public Service Ry. assigned approximately 60 closed cars of a wide variety of types to the Passaic division. These were operated from a common pool with smaller cars being used on the narrow single-track local lines and double-truck cars, such as the 900s on Hawthorne and other long local lines.

It was not until August 1916 that the Hawthorne line got its own cars. Eight cars, 1878-1882, 1848, 1851 and 1863, were transferred from the Bergen Division. The first five were originally built by Niles for the Trenton & New Brunswick RR in 1902 and were among the largest cars on the Public Service system. Car 1878 was a passenger and baggage combine which had the baggage compartment removed in October 1917. The remaining three were smaller cars originally owned by the New Jersey & Hudson River Ry. and Ferry Co. The cars were returned to the Bergen Division by September 1921.

During September 1920, many light traffic lines were equipped with Birney single-truck safety cars numbered 7000 to 7199. Fifty-nine were assigned to Paterson, of which only 39 were required to handle local lines. Five of these were used on the Hawthorne line.

Motor Bus Notes

The following bus permits were purchased by Public Service Transportation Co. for the bus route duplicating the Hawthorne bus line:

Operator	Permit	Size and Model	PST No.	Purchased
Rosewall Transp. Co.	27	25-pass. 1923 White	1535	1925
Ballone Transp. Co.	23	25-pass. 1924 Mack AB	1577	1925
A. & R. Barsky	97	25-pass. 1925 Mack AB	1578	1925
Hamilton Transp. Co.	98	25-pass. 1922 White	1579	1925
H. Rothman	95	25-pass. 1922 White	1580	1925
Hawthorne Bus Owners Ascn.	-	? 1923 White	1595	1925
Hawthorne Transit Corp.	37	25-pass. 1925 White	1826	1926
Hawthorne Transit Corp.	X571	? 1920 White	1827	1926

The independent operators on the Madison Ave. route who sold permits to Public Service were:

Operator	Permit	Size and Model	PST No.	Purchased
Meola Transp. Co.	234	30-pass. 1924 Mack AB	1539	1925
Meola Transp. Co.	235	28-pass. 1925 Federal	1540	1925
Meola Transp. Co.	242	30-pass. 1925 Federal	1541	1925
G. B. Transp. Co.	230	28-pass. 1924 Federal	1542	1925
G. B. Transp. Co.	231	28-pass. 1924 Mack AB	1543	1925
G. B. Transp. Co.	232	28-pass. 1924 Mack AB	1544	1925
G. B. Transp. Co.	233	28-pass. 1924 Mack AB	1545	1925
G. B. Transp. Co.	243	23-pass. 1924 Reo	1546	1925
G. B. Transp. Co.	-	? ? Commerce	1547	1925

The old buses acquired from independent operators were replaced by new buses purchased by Public Service Transportation Co. as follows:

P. S. Numbers	
638-640, 644, 646, 651-653 (8 buses)	1925 White 50A
672	1925 Reo
4500-4536 (37 buses)	1927 Mack AL gas-electric

10

NORTH JERSEY RAPID TRANSIT CO.

In this review of Bergen County trolley lines it was not intended to overlook the North Jersey Rapid Transit Co. The history of the NJRT was covered by Cdr. E. J. Quinby in his book *Interurban Interlude,* published by Model Craftsman Publishing Co. in 1969. Therefore, a very brief account is presented here.

The NJRT ran entirely in Bergen County except for 0.67 mile of track in Suffern, New York, which was owned by the Suffern Railway Co., a subsidiary. The distance from Ridgewood Junction to the State Line was 14.523 miles. At Ridgewood Junction, NJRT passengers could transfer to Hudson River line cars of Public Service Railway to reach Paterson, Hackensack or the Edgewater Ferry.

The NJRT was incorporated on 1 September 1908. The main office was on the fourth floor of the Colt Building in Paterson. Construction commenced on 29 September 1908 at Ridgewood Junction in East Paterson (Elmwood Park). The line opened from Ridgewood Junction to Hohokus on 25 June 1910 and was extended as follows:

To Waldwick	8 October 1910
To Allendale	7 February 1911
To Ramsey	15 April 1911
To Mahwah	21 May 1911
To Suffern	5 September 1911

It was reported on July 1910 that Public Service and NJRT representatives had met to discuss a purchase. Public Service considered the price too hgh and discussions were terminated.

Aside from its Pullman-green Jewett interurban cars, the NJRT is probably best remembered for the 21 July 1911 headon collision in Ridgewood. An unscheduled car, 12, in charge of 41-year-old Superintendent Francis J. Pilgrim, was southbound through Ridgewood to reach the new turnout on the Prospect St. curve. William Hutchinson was motorman of northbound scheduled car 20 with a passenger load including a Sunday School picnic group. About 2:42 p.m. the cars collided at full speed. Pilgrim and Hutchinson died that evening at the Paterson General Hospital. A trackman, John Frotaillo, who was on car 12, died on the way to the hospital. There were injuries, but no fatalities, among the passengers on car 20. The NJRT promptly settled with all parties in the crash.

Everything was settled amicably without recourse to law. However, the settlement exhausted NJRT's resources. The company even sold its terminal site in Paterson. The company defaulted on the bond interest due on 1 November 1911. Upon application of William B. Gourley, representing the Hamilton Trust Co. of Paterson and trustee for the bondholders, the Court of Chancery appointed Henry H. Parmalee as receiver on 12 April 1912. He would remain in charge of the company's finances for more than 14 years.

Construction Engineer George Jackson, Jr., later mayor of Hohokus, replaced Pilgrim as Superintendent. In 1912, Gilbert D. Bogart, former mayor of Garfield and former President of Saddle River Traction, was elected President.

In 1925, NJRT and Public Service agreed to operation of NJRT cars into downtown Paterson via Broadway. Track gangs were put to work on 30 December installing a connecting switch at Ridgewood Junction in East Paterson and a new terminal track at the Broadway terminal for the NJRT cars. Service by NJRT cars into downtown Paterson began on Sunday, 28 February 1926.

The cars operated hourly, leaving the Broadway bridge for the trip into Paterson at 22 minutes past the hour and leaving the Broadway terminal for Suffern at 15 minutes past the hour between 7:15 a.m. and 11:15 p.m. The last car, leaving the Broadway terminal at 12:15 a.m., ran only to the Hohokus car house. It was rumored that the NJRT cars, being more than a foot wider than the Hudson River line 3500s, would be unable pass each other on the Public Service double-tracks on Broadway, Paterson. However, the schedule indicated that two NJRT cars passed each other on Broadway in the vicinity of Carroll St.

Passengers were allowed to board NJRT cars at the Broadway terminal in advance of the departure time since the schedule provided a 45-minute layover. The cars were permitted to carry local passengers on Broadway within Paterson, supplementing Public Service's Hudson River and Broadway car lines. The Broadway car line was replaced by the 20—Broadway bus on 3 August 1926.

Public Service Corporation acquired the long-bankrupt NJRT on 17 November 1926 for $200,000. On 16 December 1926, it formed the Public Service Rapid Transit Co. to operate the property. The 0.67 mile section of NJRT track in Suffern, NY continued operating as the Suffern Ry. Co. This corporation was dissolved on 9 December 1931.

At this time private automobiles and motor buses were making competition for passengers critical for the PSRT. As had been the pattern on its rural and semi-rural lines, Public Service had extended bus service into the area even before the NJRT had been acquired. Public Service purchased Stoddard's Arrow Bus Lines in 1926 and on 3 May inaugurated the Route 70 — Paterson-Suffern bus. Service was more convenient than on the cars since the buses ran through the center of the towns whereas the interurban cars ran through the undeveloped outskirts.

North Jersey Rapid Transit cars 10 and 12 on a Sunday school excursion at Glen Rock in 1911

With buses draining business away, the first major cutback occurred on 21 August 1927 when PSRT cars discontinued service between downtown Paterson and Ridgewood Junction. PSRT petitioned the NJPUC on 28 November 1928 for permission to abandon the line. The petition was approved on 27 December.

At the stroke of midnight on 2 January 1929, Superintendent Jackson opened the circuit breaker at the Hohokus substation shutting off power for the railway. Power was restored shortly thereafter to allow Public Service crane car 5671 to remove the rails, a task which took well into February. One reporter stated the rails were still in good condition and were sent to the USSR where they were used on the Trans-Siberian Railroad.

The Route 70 interstate bus line was renumbered as Route 170 on 7 January 1929. For operating purposes, the line was known as Route 70/170. On 15 December 1938, service was cut back to the state line at Mahwah and in September 1940 terminated in Ramsey. On 30 September 1954, the 70-170 and 71-72 routes were combined for operating reasons. Sunday service was discontinued on 13 June 1965.

Equipment Notes

North Jersey Rapid Transit owned eight passenger cars and one line car. Public Service scrapped all of the NJRT cars except one passenger car which survived until about 1950 as an office in the Passaic Wharf Yard at Newark.

Motor Bus Notes

In 1922 Arrow Bus Line was operating two lines out of Paterson: Paterson-Newark and Paterson-Glen Rock. Arrow operated twelve 30-passenger, Packard Chassis buses with Remmele & Maier (Newark, N. J.) bodies.

In 1926, Arrow operated three routes: Paterson-Suffern using 12 buses, Paterson-Midland Park using six buses, and Paterson-Newark using 24 buses. Arrow Bus Lines, Inc. was not incorporated until 5 March 1926.

Arrow competed with NJRT between Paterson and Suffern. The bus line provided convenient downtown service into Paterson and direct service to the municipalities along the Franklin Turnpike.

When Arrow was acquired by Public Service in 1926, it transferred ownership of 50 buses which Public Service numbered 1645 to 1694.

Public Service designated the line as Route 70. During the summer of 1926, Public Service placed eleven new deluxe buses (5500-5510) on the line, replacing the old Arrow buses. The 5500s were equipped with sprung leather cross seats and were painted duco red. They were a success with the public and stimulated a network of "super service" bus routes.

NORTH JERSEY RAPID TRANSIT - ROSTER

Even numbers only

Numbers	Builder	Year	Length	Trucks	Motors	Controls	Windows
8	McGuire Cum.	1910	48' 0"	2-?	4-GE?	2-?	-
10-20	Jewett	1910	47' 6"	2-MCB	4-W306	2-HL	11
22, 24	Jewett	1911	47' 6"	2-MCB	4-W306	2-HL	11

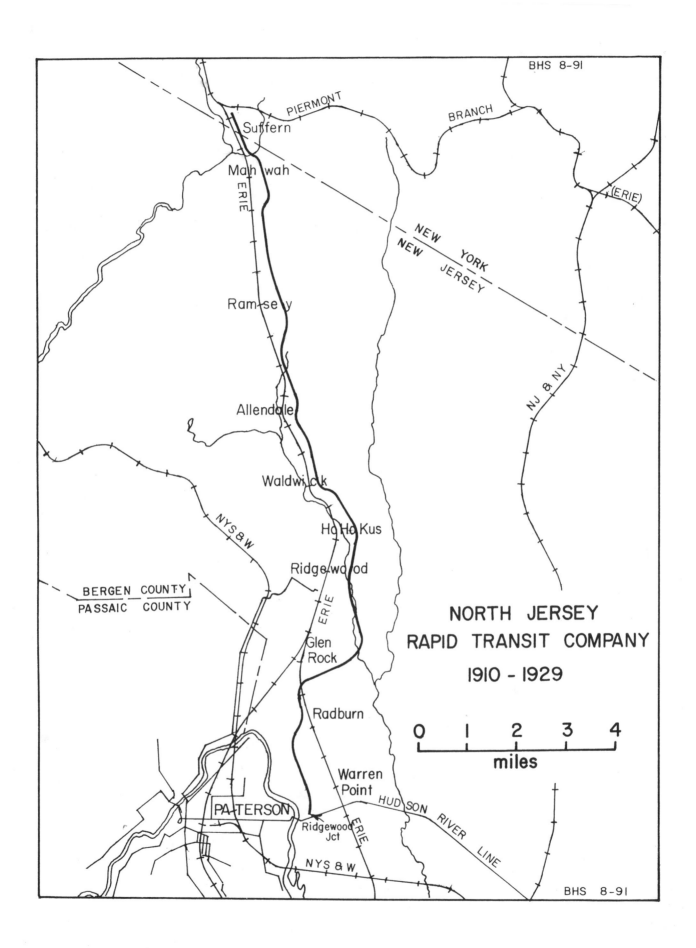

BHS 8-91

PIERMONT   BRANCH

Suffern

Mah wah

ERIE

(ERIE)

NEW YORK
NEW JERSEY

Ram se y

NJ & NY

Allendale

Waldwick

NYS&W

Ho Ho Kus

Ridgewood

BERGEN COUNTY
PASSAIC COUNTY

ERIE

Glen
Rock

NORTH JERSEY
RAPID TRANSIT COMPANY

1910 - 1929

Radburn

0   1   2   3   4
miles

Warren
Point

PATERSON

HUDSON RIVER LINE

ERIE

Ridgewood
Jct

NYS & W

BHS 8-91